BEREA'S FIRST 125 YEARS
1855-1980

BEREA's
FIRST 125 YEARS
1855-1980

Elisabeth S. Peck

With a final chapter by
Emily Ann Smith

THE UNIVERSITY PRESS OF KENTUCKY

Library of Congress Cataloging in Publication Data

Peck, Elisabeth Sinclair, 1883-
    Berea's first 125 years, 1855-1980.

    "A reissue of Berea's first century together with
a new concluding chapter"—Pref. to the new ed.
    Bibliography: p.
    Includes index.
    1. Berea College—History. I. Smith, Emily Ann,
1904-   II. Peck, Elisabeth Sinclair, 1883-
Berea's first century, 1855-1955. III. Title.
LD393.P39   378.769'53   82-6955
ISBN 0-8131-1466-7   AACR2

CONTENTS

THE GREAT COMMITMENTS
OF BEREA COLLEGE

To PROVIDE an educational opportunity primarily for students from Appalachia who have high ability but limited economic resources.

To PROVIDE an education of high quality with a liberal arts foundation and outlook.

To STIMULATE understanding of the Christian faith and to emphasize the Christian ethic and the motive of service to mankind.

To DEMONSTRATE through the student labor program that labor, mental and manual, has dignity as well as utility.

To PROMOTE the ideals of brotherhood, equality and democracy, with particular emphasis on interracial education.

To MAINTAIN on our campus and to encourage in our students a way of life characterized by plain living, pride in labor well done, zest for learning, high personal standards, and concern for the welfare of others.

To SERVE the Appalachian region primarily through education but also by other appropriate services.

PREFACE

BEREA'S FAY FOREST may well stand as a symbol of the College, for out in the hills regardless of winter's cold hand on oaks and anemones alike the forest continues to live because of its underground roots in the soil. In the Berea story, buildings, equipment, courses of study, labor adjuncts, and even instruction itself depend for their value upon the underlying intellectual and spiritual roots.

The Berea story is the narrative of a college that for a century has striven to meet social and individual needs. After the Civil War the newly emancipated Negroes needed teachers, and Berea trained them. When the mountain people needed fundamental skills, the College reshaped its organization to meet this need. When trained specialists were needed in agriculture, Berea prepared to give them the best possible training. Because mountain problems are largely those of a rural society, Berea has invited its students to add to their preparation the study of rural sociology, recreation, and health. To fortify its graduates with nourishment for future living, Berea for a century has encouraged participation in humane studies so that their lives might not become culturally undernourished.

This book has been written to call attention at this centennial date to the imperishable elements underlying the educational forest called Berea College. The reader may find more enjoyment in the book if he understands its plan beforehand. The first two chapters study the founders during the five years preceding the Civil War and the twenty-five years after the war, thus forming an introduction to the Berea story. Each of the six remaining chapters takes some one concern of the College and traces it through the century. The six subjects studied in this way are: (a) Berea's experience in interracial education; (b) growth of the idea of a geographical area—the southern Appalachian mountains—as a field of special interest; (c) a century's development in an adapted educational program; (d) growth of Berea's work program for education as well as for self-support; (e) Berea's experience in financing this private Christian college; and (f) long-continued sharing of its opportunities through extension service. By the time the reader has traversed the century in these six different ways, he cannot fail to recognize the underground roots that supply Berea's vital strength.

Berea has had great presidents, well-trained and devoted teachers, and invaluable trustees and donors. These have become greater, more deeply devoted, and more valuable through the intellectual ideas and the spiritual strength characteristic of Berea College in its first century.

So many people have helped in the making of this book that to enumerate them would weary the reader, but to select a few for special appreciation would be ungracious to the others. To an unusual degree this book is *our* book rather than *my* book.

ELISABETH S. PECK

PREFACE TO THE NEW EDITION

IN 1955 BEREA COLLEGE celebrated its one hundredth anniversary. There were many parts to that important occasion—fine speakers, fine music, an outdoor drama performed in a forest theatre, which was built especially for the centennial. To be sure that there would be a permanent account of how Berea College began, grew, suffered, prospered, and achieved, there was Elisabeth Peck's history, *Berea's First Century 1855–1955*. Mrs. Peck's history deals not only with Berea events and Berea people in the first hundred years but also with the directing philosophy of the College and with the special purposes of the institution. It was Berea's birthday present to itself.

In 1980 Berea celebrated, less elaborately but no less proudly, its 125th anniversary. To recognize the added quarter century of struggle and accomplishment, the College is sponsoring the publication of this new book comprising a reissue of *Berea's First Century*, together with a new concluding chapter. This chapter treats briefly some of the long-time effects of World War II on Berea College and gives an account of what has happened in and to Berea during the twenty-five years between 1955 and 1980.

EMILY ANN SMITH

CHAPTER 1: Early
Founders

BEREA COLLEGE is located on a narrow ridge that seems to rise like a rocky island seventy feet above the surrounding plain. This ridge, which is about two miles long, lies in eastern Kentucky 130 miles south of Cincinnati, Ohio, and 40 miles southeast of Lexington. The foothills of the Cumberland Plateau are not more than three miles distant on the east and south. They are sometimes hazy blue in the distance, sometimes lost in low-hanging clouds; and sometimes after a snowfall they are covered with a muster of tree trunks that stand black and stark against the white slope. West and northwest of the Berea Ridge there is not a hill in sight, only Bluegrass farmland for unending miles. At the foot of the Ridge on the north lies an uncommonly flat stretch of land called the Glade.

Cassius M. Clay, an influential landowner who lived in the Bluegrass section of Madison County, Kentucky, owned six hundred acres of land in the southern end of the county on and around the Ridge. In the early 1850's he sold off much of this land at an exceptionally low price because he wished to develop there a thriving community that would demonstrate the advantages of life without slavery and might even increase his political strength in the state.

He encouraged a young rural pastor, the Reverend John G. Fee, to move from northern Kentucky to southern Madison County and gave him a homestead of ten acres on the Ridge; for Fee, like Clay, was a strong antislavery man and an ardent believer in the value of freedom of speech as a means of solving social problems. In 1855 Fee and some neighbors built a one-room district school on the Ridge. In 1858 when John A. R. Rogers came to Berea, as the community on the Ridge had been named by Fee, to join him in his country preaching, Fee advised Rogers to set up a subscription term in the one-room school, for Rogers was an experienced teacher as well as a minister.

Already Clay and Fee had recognized the need for a "higher school" in this nonslaveholding community, and Rogers also brought with him the desire for such a school. In the summer of 1859, after seeing the popularity of "the good Rogers school," Fee, Rogers, and a few other men wrote the constitution for a college and arranged to buy a boundary of Ridge land that seemed suitable for a college campus. After the John Brown raid in Virginia in the fall of that year, fear sprang up in the slaveholding section of Madison County that the men of Berea might be preparing for a similar uprising. This led to the forced exile of the Berea leaders and their families in mid-winter, 1859-1860, when Clay for political reasons did not rally his friends to their support.

By the close of the Civil War, Fee had raised almost enough money among northern friends to pay for the Ridge land on which the college trustees held an option, and with the return of peace the exiles came back to their Berea work. Although this young college lacked buildings, endowment, and money for current expenses, it had no shortage of students, a considerable number of whom were newly emancipated Negroes. For whom was Berea College founded? For those who needed its service. The 1859 Constitution said nothing about a student's race or place of residence.

II

JOHN G. FEE was still a young man when he settled in Berea, having been born in 1816. He had been reared in Bracken County on the Kentucky side of the Ohio River. His father found it profitable to cultivate his farm with slave labor, but he was not a cruel master, as masters went, and he was not a great planter, for he usually farmed with about thirteen slaves. Young Fee took his diploma in the classical course at Augusta College in his home county, and entered Lane Seminary on the outskirts of Cincinnati in 1842, finishing his course there two years later. He had thought nothing about the sinfulness of slavery until he entered the seminary, where zealous students pleaded with him to take a strong stand for human freedom. At last he cried out in his solitary place of daily prayer: "Lord, if needs be, make me an abolitionist." Then and there he entered into a covenant with God that shaped the rest of his life.[1]

After returning home, he tried to persuade his father, an elder in the Presbyterian Church, to give up slaveholding, but his father replied by offering to send him to Princeton Seminary, New Jersey, to be taught sounder ideas. Young Fee refused his father's offer, and in the following year he was ordained by the Harmony Presbytery of Kentucky, and was then commissioned by the American Home Missionary Society to work with country churches along the Ohio River. When he made it plain from the pulpit that he was opposed to slavery, he met threats of violence and his audience diminished in number. Some people said that he was a dangerous man to have in the region, for Kentuckians along the river were unusually sensitive on the matter of speaking against slavery, lest slaves try to escape across the Ohio River to freedom. In 1848 he took a letter of dismissal from the Synod because he would not cease his preaching against slavery, and withdrew from the American Home Missionary Society because its funds were used to support proslavery ministers.

Because a full account of his disagreement with his Synod was published in the *New York Evangelist,* Fee was immediately offered a commission by the newly organized American Missionary Association (A.M.A.), which took a positive stand against slaveholding. Soon he was tending nine small rural churches in Ohio River counties. Sometimes rough men mobbed him, angry men cursed him, and hired men waylaid him; but by the time he had ministered to these churches for five years, men out of respect for him as a man of God seldom annoyed him.

Cassius M. Clay saw in this fearless rural pastor a fit man for the service which he projected, namely, to build up a free community having political strength in the mountainous part of the state "where there were but few slaves and the people courageous."[2] Clay had published Fee's articles in his *True American* in 1845-1846; and had been so much interested in Fee's book, *An Antislavery Manual,* published in 1848 and revised in 1851, that he had ordered a boxful of these books to be distributed in Madison County, where he had much land and great influence. He found also in Fee's words his own emphasis upon freedom of thought and liberty of expression as natural and constitutional rights.[3]

Through Clay's influence Fee was invited to hold some religious meetings in the Glade north of the Berea Ridge. At the close of these meetings thirteen people associated themselves together to form a new church that would be nondenominational and free. The following year, 1854, this little group of people asked Fee to move from the Ohio River region and become their pastor. Clay strengthened their appeal by offering Fee a ten-acre homestead, $200 to help in building a home, and a site in the Glade for a school and a church. The A.M.A. consented to this change of field, and in the fall of 1854 when the new house was ready for Mrs. Fee and their three small children, Fee moved them from Lewis County on the Ohio River to Madison County in the interior. As there was no railroad to Berea in those days, he packed the family's household goods in a two-horse wagon, seated his family in a one-horse carriage, and set out for Berea, where he arrived at the close of the third day. "Believing as we did that we were exactly where the Lord would have us, we lay down and slept calmly, sweetly."[4]

III

CASSIUS M. CLAY, who in later years found great satisfaction in the part which he played in the Berea story, was only six years older than John G. Fee. When Clay was a student at Yale, he, like Fee at Lane, had wrestled hard with his own soul. A fellow student had taken the sensitive young Clay, a slaveholder in his own right, to hear William Lloyd Garrison, who violently flayed the evils and the unreasonableness of slavery. From that day Clay was opposed to human slavery.

The two men differed in certain ways. Fee was a country minister, though no ordinary one; Clay was a landed country gentleman whose greatest interest was politics with special emphasis upon freedom of speech. When Fee spoke in public, he appealed to men's conscience by words which Clay said were full of tender passion, by his rather sad expression, and by his style, "concise, terse, and earnest."[5] Clay used the impetuous style of address common to southern orators of his day, characterized by strong words, fiery charges, and black denunciations. Fee always went unarmed, but Clay was likely to have a bowie knife stuck in his belt and at least one pistol close at hand. The two men differed also in their arguments against slavery. Fee based his antislavery talks on the idea that slavery is a sin against human brotherhood. Clay emphasized the evils arising from slavery: depression of education, manufactures, agriculture, the fine arts, and constitutional liberties, as well as the encouragement pressed upon white nonslaveholding people to emigrate from Kentucky because of the low condition of their economic life and their schools.[6] When Clay sold land near the Ridge to such a liberal as Hamilton Rawlings, when he gave a homestead to Fee, and when he let it be known that he was Fee's defender, he was laying the foundations for his democratic free community in the hill country.

In spite of their differences Fee recognized the importance of Clay to his pastoral work in the hills. There he was doing the same kind of work as he had done previously in the northern counties of the state, directing missionary colporters and calling on lonely families, giving both tracts and kindly words to people who had no church near at hand, as well as preaching in newly founded churches that met in homes or schoolhouses. People even in remote places in southern Madison County had known of Cassius M. Clay before ever they heard of John G. Fee, and they were inclined to regard Clay as the young preacher's protector. In his first year of residence in Berea, Fee wrote to the A.M.A. in New York that Clay had been the chief means by which this field had been opened to him.[7]

IV

A ONE-ROOM SCHOOL was built in 1855 on a lot contributed by a local man, William B. Wright. This lot was located on the Berea Ridge near the Fee homestead, not on the low Glade lot which Clay had given to the new community for a school. The teacher of this school in its first two terms was William E. Lincoln, an Oberlin student paid by the A.M.A. to use his long vacations in helping Fee with his mountain work. In later reminiscences Lincoln wrote: "Brother Fee came to me one day . . . and said, 'Mr. Burnam . . . has offered to build us a preaching place and a schoolhouse, if you will teach for six months without pay.' I eagerly agreed, for it was also promised that all we preached should be allowed."[8] Some men, even Fee himself, furnished labor, and so the community on and around the Ridge soon had a schoolhouse, where the followers of Fee could also hold their church service. This one-room slab school was

the beginning of Berea College. It is nothing to be ashamed
of now at the close of a century, since in spite of its cracks and
its board benches it met an urgent social need. It had begun
with the best of all aims for a college.

In this year, 1855, Fee planned a Fourth of July celebration
with Cassius M. Clay as the chief speaker. A large audience of
orderly citizens gathered, and Clay held the audience for two
hours. He showed that slavery, which had been retarding prosperity, was now taking away liberty of speech. Fee followed
with further words on slavery and freedom of expression, and
the audience was favorably impressed. On this occasion Fee
was speaking in the shadow of the great Cassius M. Clay.

On the following Fourth of July, 1856, a rally was held at
Slate Lick Springs, a few miles from the Berea Ridge. The
fact that this was a presidential election year turned the gathering from a picnic into a serious argument over political plat-
forms. To Fee, Cassius M. Clay seemed to be following the line
of expediency for the sake of helping his party to win the fall
election. Men went home in confusion of mind. Many a man
said: "Fee is religiously right; Clay is politically right."[9] After
this 1856 rally men thought that Clay had withdrawn his support from Fee and his young preachers. For many months after
this picnic Clay did not call at Fee's house as he had been accustomed to do, and some men began to be afraid to be counted
as Fee's friends.

In 1857 and 1858 the mob spirit raged in Madison and adjoining counties, and several times endangered Fee's life; but
he continued his preaching and his pastoral calls. When the
grand jury made no presentment for an unusually serious attack upon him in nearby Rockcastle County, lawless men
threatened him repeatedly, in order to force him to leave their
county, but without avail. A friend of Fee's in 1857 urged Clay
to speak some words that would calm men who took too literally
Clay's words "revolutionary" and "insurrectionary" as applied
to Fee; but within a week Clay replied: "While I denounce all
mobs, I can give him neither aid nor comfort."[10] One is bound

to ask how John G. Fee could pass through these trying experiences with so much quiet courage. He himself wrote the answer: "I had anticipated something of this when, fifteen years previously, I had entered into covenant with God to preach in my native State the gospel of love, of justice, and of liberty. I had counted the cost, and did not then, nor in the hands of any mob, have to decide what to do."[11] John G. Fee's repeated demonstration of courage in defense of his principles is a precious part of Berea's intangible endowment.

The one-room school that contained the germ of Berea College continued its sessions in spite of terrors. In two letters written by Fee concerning the school of Otis B. Waters, an Oberlin student who succeeded Lincoln in the winter of 1857-1858, these points are of special interest: Fee mentioned that six young men from outside the district had enrolled, to receive some preparation for becoming teachers; and several slaveholders had sent their children to this school taught by an antislavery man.[12]

v

BEFORE BEREA's one-room school became a genuine college, at least three men had conceived of a college in the Berea region. Clay had suggested to Fee that he "take land for a school, to be enlarged to a college hereafter."[13] Already on November 9, 1855, the year in which the Berea school opened, Fee had written to the *American Missionary* about the need for a higher school "which would be to Kentucky what Oberlin is to Ohio, antislavery, anti-caste, anti-rum, anti-sin. . . . Why can we not have such a school here?"[14] Two months later he wrote to Gerrit Smith in New York: "We have for months been talking about starting an academy, and eventually look to a college—giving an education to all colors, classes, cheap and thorough."[15] In 1858 the Reverend John A. R. Rogers came to the Ridge, aflame with the idea of establishing a college in eastern Kentucky.

Rogers was twelve years younger than Fee, had graduated from Oberlin College and Seminary, had taught in New York, and for a year had served as a pastor in Illinois. His sister was the wife of James S. Davis, Fee's successor as rural pastor in the northern Kentucky work. Many years later Rogers wrote: "I did not know Mr. Fee and had never written him a line or consulted with him in any way. I had become deeply interested in eastern Kentucky and in helping to start a college there. . . . This work was so on my spirit that when a friend went to Kentucky and then turned back, I told my wife that if she would give her consent, we would go ourselves."[16]

This young minister, his eighteen-year-old wife, and their baby spent the winter of 1857-1858 at Cabin Creek in northern Kentucky with the Davis family, and Rogers at this time secured a commission from the A.M.A. to be, like Davis and Fee, a rural minister of the Association. Alone he walked more than a hundred miles to Berea and talked long with Fee, who had recently been mobbed near the Kentucky River. Fee was vague about where Rogers might work, and Rogers returned to his family rather discouraged at the prospects; but before many weeks he received a letter from Fee saying that he wanted Rogers to work at Berea.

If Fee had had only a college in his mind, he probably would not have hesitated in his talks with Rogers, for already he saw that the young man was the very person he needed for taking the next step with his school. Fee, however, like Clay, had in his mind the idea of setting up a kind of colony, an industrious, nonslaveholding community, as a protest against the sluggishness of a slaveholding society.[17] Because of the poor soil in the Berea region he was uncertain as to whether a colony could prosper there. William E. Lincoln wrote: "I went with Brother Fee to examine sites on which a school, to grow, should be founded; and one place in Rockcastle where a man offered land and where there was a waterfall was seriously considered by Brother Fee and myself. . . . The land was level and rich, underlaid by limestone, and not slate, as in Berea."[18]

But there were lawless men in that county who had burned
down the church-schoolhouse where Waters had taught and
preached one vacation, and had threatened the Reverend
George Candee, and even Fee himself. In Fee's mind there was
a controversy between water and limestone on the one hand
and such good men as Hamilton Rawlings, John Burnam,
Squire William Stapp, and Thomas Jefferson Renfro on the
other hand; and in time the good men won in his mind over
water and soil.

After receiving Fee's letter of welcome, Rogers and his little
family traveled from Cabin Creek to Berea by steamboat, train,
stagecoach, and livery carriage. The driver took them to Fee's
house: "What an oasis it was in the wilderness," Mrs. Rogers
wrote, "and what sweet music was the sound of Mr. Fee's voice
welcoming us! . . . We found Mr. Fee most cheery. His Scotch
Irish ancestry was always most evident. Sandy complexioned,
kindly in heart, it were as well to try to move the mountains
about Berea, as Mr. Fee when he felt he was in the right."[19]
As there was no vacant house for the Rogers family to rent,
they lodged with a local family for some time.

On the Monday morning following their arrival J. A. R.
Rogers and his wife began teaching an extra term of school, a
"pay school," though no one was turned away who could not
pay. They taught in the same one-room schoolhouse where
Waters had taught the regular winter term before returning
to his seminary work in Oberlin. The school started with fifteen
children, three of these being little Fees. Mrs. Rogers left her
baby at the Wrights' home across from the school, and did most
of the teaching at first, while her husband called widely in the
neighborhood. Soon fifty names were on the roll, and Professor Rogers taught the older pupils while his wife cared for the
younger pupils. By the end of the term in June almost a hundred pupils, including slaveholders' children, were enrolled.

The schoolhouse was poorly built and shabby, but the
school had some features that made it attractive. It was a
happy school with much singing. Later Mrs. Rogers wrote:

"I think our little songbook, *The Oriole,* was splendidly adapted to our needs. Those songs set the countryside afire. They were something new and different from anything they had ever known, and they sang them . . . on the hillsides and in the valleys. They entered every home."[20] To add to the school's enjoyment Professor Rogers and the boys cleared a playground in the adjoining woods, and there both boys and girls enjoyed many sports and games. To relieve the long day, five-minute rests were frequently called. But this was more than a happy school. Professor Rogers was a well-educated man who brought new ideas into the crowded room when he taught geography with plenty of astronomy in it and performed experiments in chemistry and physics before their eyes. Every Friday afternoon the school gave an entertainment, which parents were invited to attend.

At the end of the term in June, 1858, the school gave a closing exhibition in an improvised arbor under the tall oaks. A large platform had been built to seat all the pupils. On the program there were recitations, dialogs, orations, and choruses. When the young valedictorian reviewed the term and gave his words of farewell, the audience was brought to the brink of tears. This was Berea's first Commencement. After a basket dinner on the grounds and encouraging words from out-of-town speakers, including the county judge, a subscription was easily raised to add another room to the schoolhouse. The kindliness of Mrs. Rogers, the resourceful scholarship of her husband, and the pupils' joy in music and in play have remained a part of the Berea tradition for a century. Of course, no college association in the entire country, had there been such in 1858, would have recognized this live, progressive school as a college, except in its hope for the future.

When the second term opened in September, this school had all the students that the building could hold even with its additional rooms divided into sections by partitions of sheeting. There was a new teacher added to the staff, John Gregg Hanson from Bracken County, a cousin of Fee's, an interesting inventor, expert in surveying, and with plans to set up a sawmill and a planing mill. A program of the exhibition at the close of the second term, December 1, 1858, still remains, and it shows that already the school had become something of a "higher school" in spite of the elementary children who shared in the exercises. The program opened with a student's salutatory address and closed with a valedictory and a benediction. There were many recitations, declamations, and essays, but only two orations, one on the subject of "Modern Society," and the other on "The Scholar's Mission." Between every four spoken numbers there was music by the school, making a total of sixteen songs. In the middle of the program there was a discussion by the Dialectic Club on the subject: "Should Caesar be called Great?" The last number before the valedictory certainly had the flavor of a higher school. It was a drama: "Catiline: Scene I, Cicero addresses the Senate against Catiline. Scene II, Banishment of Catiline and his Reply."

The school ran successfully for two terms in the following year, though there was some unrest among the parents because of the antislavery views of the school trustees. When a spirited school election in the summer returned a candidate of Fee's preference, the majority's choice was quietly accepted for trustee.

V I

In September, 1858, Fee and Rogers invited a number of men to meet with them to talk over the matter of setting up a constitution and securing a charter for a college in Berea. These men met many times during the ensuing year, and completed their draft on July 14, 1859. The articles of agreement were proposed in the names of John G. Fee, J. A. R. Rogers, and John G. Hanson; three substantial farmers of the community: William Stapp, John Smith, and Thomas Jefferson Renfro; and three rural ministers: George Candee, Jacob Emerick, and J. S. Davis.

The fundamentals of the first Constitution remain, for the most part, the essentials of Berea College today. The opening words remain, "In order to promote the cause of Christ." The name of the institution was "Berea College." The aim of the College was clearly stated in the first bylaw: "The purpose of the College shall be to furnish the facilities for a thorough education to all persons of good moral character, at the least possible expense, and all the inducements and facilities for manual labor which can reasonably be supplied by the Board of Trustees shall be offered." The second bylaw shows distinctly the historical background of the founders: "This College shall be under an influence strictly Christian, and as such opposed to sectarianism, slaveholding, caste, and every other wrong institution or practice." There was no statement made in this document as to any specific area or group of people that this institution was to serve. The expression as to labor did not provide that the College would set up organized industries or farm tasks to furnish labor for the students. Although this Constitution empowered the trustees to appoint a president for the College, they did not do this until the institution had been several years in operation. Instead, they immediately appointed a Prudential Committee for administration, and instructed it to buy land for the new College. The first Prudential Committee included Fee, Rogers, Hanson, and Renfro. These men arranged for the purchase of a beautiful wooded boundary of land owned by John G. Woolwine. This tract of some 110 acres on the Ridge they bought for $1,750 and accrued interest, "for the purpose of erecting the college buildings upon it, and for a town plot." The College had no money yet, but these four trustees assumed responsibility for payment of the debt.

It is hard to realize now that when this Constitution was drafted, application made for a charter, and arrangements made for buying the Woolwine land, hardly five years had passed since the Fees set up housekeeping on the Berea Ridge. It was providential that the trustees made these definite arrangements for the future, to give a certain concreteness to their hopes. It seems now as though they were battening down their hatches before the storm should break upon them in the following December, 1859.

VII

IN THE WINTER of 1858-1859 the young men of the Dialectic Society had discussed long and earnestly the question of whether Negroes should be admitted to the school, if any applied. This question was soon discussed throughout the neighborhood. The view of the teachers and of John G. Fee was that certainly they should be admitted, if the school was to be truly "anti-caste."

There were other causes of unrest, however, besides the hypothetical question of admitting Negroes. A political campaign was approaching, and Republicans were deep in the discussion of their party's stand on slavery. Such men as Fee and his co-workers in Berea were opposed to this "weak" position and to any candidate who did not take a stand against slavery altogether.

In spite of noisy unrest and talk of a possible mob coming to their homes, men like Fee, Rogers, and Hanson would carry no weapons; but Mrs. Rogers revealed her fear when she laid beside her bed some sticks and a syringe filled with a stinging chemical from her husband's school cupboard. Then as though with a laugh she wrote: "I have a feeling that the mob, if they had ever come, would have gone away unmolested."[21]

The general unrest was heightened by news of John Brown's raid at Harpers Ferry in October, 1859. Men in the Bluegrass end of Madison County where there were many slaves pointed to the Berea Ridge as a strategic place from which a similar raid might be launched, which in this case might be successful. Kentucky newspapers added to the common fear by reporting falsely that boxes of Sharpe's rifles had been seized on the way to Berea. When men searched the household goods of a man who was moving to Berea and discovered in one of the boxes a dangerous-looking machine, the "infernal" thing they found turned out to be nothing more deadly than a set of candle molds.

Then on a Sunday evening, November 13, 1859, in an address at Henry Ward Beecher's church in Brooklyn, John G. Fee, who had gone East to raise money for the new school, unintentionally raised the fears of Madison County proslavery men to a climax. In his appeal for men and money with which to spread the gospel of impartial love in Kentucky, he said that there was need for more John Browns—not in the manner of his action but in the spirit of consecration, not with carnal weapons but with the word of the spirit—men who would appeal in love to both slaveholders and nonslaveholders.[22]

Soon Kentucky newspapers were flaming with an incomplete fragment from Fee's address, "We want more John Browns," and the report spread that he was in New York raising money to finance an uprising in the hills back of Berea. Numerous public meetings were held in the Madison County courthouse, and at length a committee was appointed to remove the Berea leaders from the state, Fee and Rogers being especially mentioned by name.[23] Both of these men wrote letters to Kentucky papers explaining how completely Fee's words had been misinterpreted; and from Pittsburgh, Fee sent out a printed circular far and wide to correct the error. But these efforts failed to quiet the storm that had been raised.

Mrs. Rogers gives a picture of these days of terror:

"Meetings were held at the county seat to consider the best means of disposing of us. Oh, those days grew darker and darker. . . . Our closer friends, the planters, had little to say. While they, with their Richmond neighbors, disliked Berea's sentiments, they loved *us*. But they were too greatly cowed to speak for us if they had wished; . . .

"I think Uncle Ham Rawlings was our true friend, our traveling newspaper, bringing us news that we could not get

outside. . . . The coming of our brother, Mr. Davis, escaping
in danger from Cabin Creek, did not add particularly to our
feeling of safety. Still, we hoped to stay. We had had our fall
butchering. I had made lard and put away hams and pork for
winter's use.

"Mrs. Fee, left alone with her little children, rose to the
occasion . . . and I do not know but she with her brave spirit
was my husband's greatest help. Her knowledge of Kentuckians, of former mistreatment no doubt often gave her more
insight into conditions than could have been possible to those
of later date. . . .

"Daily we watched for what was to come, and we grew to
fear the worst. The tension was terrible, and I believe I grew
to wish that the mob would come, do their worst, and have it
over. . . . Yet all those days we never locked a door nor owned
the simplest piece of firearms. We were a feeble few, entirely
at the mercy of the mob when it should come."[24]

Then at last the men came. The time was near noon two
days before Christmas (December 23, 1859) and Fee had been
detained in Cincinnati. The men who came on this December
day were not rowdies in a mob. They were "organized gentlemen," sixty-two of them, mounted and fully armed, men of
standing and substance from the northern part of the county.
They rode into the Rogers' yard in wedge-shaped formation,
their captain riding a white horse. Mrs. Rogers wrote: "As they
surrounded our little cottage, they looked like a regiment. Mr.
Rogers stepped quickly to the door, I following with our little
first-born clinging to my skirts. The captain, handing my husband a document, asked him for an answer."

Mr. Rogers read the printed paper, and replied that he was
a quiet, law-abiding citizen who had broken no law and had
done nothing to disturb the peace of the commonwealth. He
refused to give up his work in Berea. "I cannot promise to go.
I have only one Master to serve, and I must do his bidding."
The men moved nearer as if for attack, but the captain, wheel-
ing before them, cried out, "Not today, boys. If he is not gone

in ten days, come back." They rode away in the snow to deliver the same message to Mrs. Fee, to Hanson, and to eight others on their list, and then rode off.[25]

That evening the Bereans under ban of exile met in the district schoolhouse, which was also the church, to counsel together. Hanson read aloud the thirty-seventh Psalm, which seemed like the voice of God speaking words of courage to them: "Fret not thyself because of evil-doers." Some wished to stay, defying fear; others advised that they leave, to avoid bloodshed in the peaceful community. Next day they decided to petition the governor for protection. Two of the banned men took the petition to Frankfort in person. This paper stated clearly their innocence and their danger, and was signed by eleven men. Governor Beriah Magoffin received them courteously, but refused the Bereans protection because of the excitement of the public mind. If they would leave at once, he would assure them of protection during departure.[26] Upon receipt of this message the Bereans decided to leave as soon as possible.

They did not sell their homes nor their chattels, because they had complete confidence that they would return. They could take only the most necessary possessions, because transportation from the village was difficult, especially in midwinter. Before they left, Mr. and Mrs. Wright, old residents on the Ridge, made a feast and invited the banned families to enjoy it.

The exodus began on the seventh day after the warning. The day was Thursday, December 29, the weather cold and rainy. The exiled families gathered under the trees in front of the Rogers' unfinished cottage, with many neighbors and friends to see them off. The Reverend George Candee had ridden in from Jackson County to be with them in their trouble, and as they stood with bowed heads, he prayed for God's guidance upon those who were about to leave their dear homes. Later Mrs. Rogers described the first part of their journey:

"A drizzling rain was falling, the snow had melted, and everything was dreary without as our hearts within. One old man sat in an open wagon with his arm around his aged wife as if to shield her from every storm. Mrs. Fee with her carriage full of little children, a bride and a groom in another carriage, and these, with a few men on horseback and Mr. Davis and his family, and a great white covered wagon which carried our trunks, a lady or two, and waiting for me to climb into it with our babies, formed the crowd that was 'a menace to Kentucky's best interests.' . . . I took my place under the rude shelter of the wagon, and the word came to move on.

"At Silver Creek we had to face another trial, and it did look as though the elements were against us. . . . Heavy rains and melting snows had conspired to make the stream most dangerous. A sudden halt in consultation, then the horseback riders rode into the stream. Our great wagon being the heaviest, we were chosen to cross first. Where we went it was safe to follow. It certainly was like the Children of Israel passing over the Red Sea, and like them we were carried safely through the depths to dry land."[27]

They spent the night in Richmond, the county seat where the plans for their exile had been laid; but since the exiles were ahead of time in their exit, they were well treated. Next morning the Berea group left by stage for Lexington, where they took the train for Cincinnati.

Cassius M. Clay had much to say about the Berea case. He and Fee had fought for freedom of speech since the old days of the *True American*. Their co-operation (but not their mutual respect) had suffered a serious break in 1856 when a political issue was at stake; but they still agreed that free speech was a much better means of solving problems than the use or threat of force. Less than two weeks after the Bereans left Kentucky, Cassius M. Clay on January 10, 1860, delivered a long campaign speech from the steps of the State Capitol in Frankfort. Before he had gone far in his address, he spoke about the expulsion of Fee and his companions from the state, saying that in the matter of expulsion he, Clay, had taken a position of strict neutrality, though a citizen of Madison County. He regretted that many respectable Kentuckians had been misled into an attack upon so worthy a community, for no better people lived than those around Berea. Then he reverted to his earlier idea of the importance of a good community on the edge of the mountains, and said that John G. Fee had nothing to lose from this exile, but that the losers were the sons and daughters of the people for whom Fee and his friends had been preparing so good an education.[28]

After reaching Cincinnati the exiles scattered. Before long Professor Rogers became the pastor of a church in Decatur, Ohio. Fee, Hanson, and Davis soon returned to their old homes in Bracken and Lewis counties; but within a month of the time when the mounted gentlemen had called in Berea to order the eleven families to leave, a Bracken County meeting approved the Madison County action, and ordered the Bereans and some others to leave because they were dangerous citizens. Fee settled his family on the north side of the Ohio River, close to Cincinnati.

John G. Hanson's experience was quite different. About March 1, 1860, he and a companion returned to Berea to saw three hundred logs left at the mill and possibly to sell his sawmill unless there seemed a good chance for him to move back to Berea soon. Rough men who heard of his return threatened to take vengeance upon him if he could be taken, and so Hanson hid in the nearby hills. A month passed, Hanson keeping well to the woods. One Sunday at the end of March, Clay was in Berea, and Hanson had a long talk with him. After this Hanson knew that he would receive no protection from Clay. The following day the mob returned, fortified with whiskey, to search for Hanson and hang him. Again he fled to the Jackson County hills, while the unruly mob abused men who were thought to be Hanson supporters. They sent to Lexington for cannon and raised more volunteers. When they could not find Hanson, they completely wrecked his mill. John G. Hanson walked safely through the state and again crossed into Ohio. Then he wrote, like the good Christian that he was: "When I reflect what I had at heart and wished to do for my countrymen in Kentucky, and think of what I have received at their hands, it makes me weep and love them more, as they show by their madness that they know not what they do."[29]

But it was not only Hanson who suffered loss from the roistering rabble. Before finally leaving Berea they had warned fifteen more families that they must be gone in ten days. Clay's list gives the number in each family forced away from home, making a total of ninety-four.

VIII

FEE AND ROGERS were so eager to return to their work in the Berea neighborhood that each year they made one or more ventures into Kentucky to learn whether they would have freedom to preach a whole gospel there. They were anxious also that the young community should not be demoralized or scattered from discouragement. They soon heard the good news that "Ham" Rawlings' daughter was teaching the district school in Berea. Then Fee heard from Renfro, the one remaining school trustee, that he was having difficulty in collecting school money: "Bro. Fee, . . . You understand how it is with me as a trustee. The subscribers many of them had to leave, so I am left minus."[30]

Fee, reminding himself that reactions generally follow gross outrages, wrote several articles and a new tract in the first year after his expulsion, and preached in Ohio and Indiana; but his heart cried out within him for Kentucky, his chosen field of labor. He set about raising the money due for the Woolwine tract in Berea, and by the close of 1860 had paid off $1,460 of the $1,750 due for the land, though he was in exile. In the early summer of 1862 he and Mrs. Fee prospected safely in Madison and neighboring counties. He preached two Sundays in Berea to a larger congregation than had ever been known there before, and on July 4 between these two Sabbaths he and George Candee gave addresses on the nature of liberty to an orderly, interested audience.[31] After this experience the Fees decided that they were warranted in bringing their children to Berea.

About the same time Rogers visited Berea, looked over the cottage that he had left unfinished, and concluded that he could soon reopen the school. Though he returned to Ohio for the summer, he came again to Berea on August 27, 1862, and found Union troops along the road from Richmond to Berea. This highway running north from Tennessee through the Cumberland Gap to the Ohio River was so close to Berea that sometimes the village people heard the Civil War knocking at their east door. Rogers learned that the way was clear and so passed through tented fields homeward to Berea.

About the same time Mrs. Fee drove home to Berea with her two older children in her buggy. She had been stopped along the way, but her quiet explanations and the Union flag painted on her carriage enabled her to pass through the lines. She arrived in Berea on the eve of battle, but she did not find Fee there as she had expected. On Saturday, August 30, the battle of Richmond was fought on the Richmond Pike between Big Hill (southeast of Berea) and Richmond. By the close of day the Union troops had been defeated and much of eastern Kentucky, including Berea, was left under the sway of the Confederate army. Rogers wrote: "The booming of the cannon during Saturday's fight, which we could hear with great distinctness at Berea, was a doleful sound to our ears."[32]

Fee on the day of the battle was trying to ride from Richmond to Berea. With his eleven-year-old son he had taken the boat for Cincinnati at the same time that Mrs. Fee set out for Madison County. When he had finished a matter of printing business, he took the train and stage for Richmond. There he hired a horse to complete his journey. Father and son rode halfway to Berea, but meeting the Union forces in retreat at Kingston, they turned back to Richmond. Fee speedily took his son to safety in Bracken County, intending to go south again for his wife; but while waiting for the boat at Augusta, a mob took him by force to the Ohio side of the river under threat that if he returned again, they would certainly hang him. Their only charge against him was that of being an abolitionist. When he returned to Bracken County, he was again treated roughly and put across the river with fierce threats. Communications with the interior had been cut, and he was in great anxiety lest Mrs. Fee suffer from shortage of money. His best friends insisted that she was safer behind the Confederate lines without him than with him, and so ten weeks dragged by from the time when the Fees had set out for Berea by different routes.[33]

Mrs. Fee was undaunted by the succession of events. Strange what one remembers about a day that turns out to be very different from other days! She remembered that on the day of the battle she was mending a bedstead, and Rogers down Chestnut Street remembered that he was working on his roof that day. Presently she hid her horse and buggy in the woods so that they would not be stolen. She wrapped her silver spoons in a flag and hid the bundle under the eaves. Soldiers and officers passing along Chestnut Street stopped to look at her roses and to speak a word with her over the fence.[34] After the battle of Perryville elsewhere in the state in October, the troops of occupation gradually withdrew. Late in the fall Mrs. Fee's mother drove from Bracken County in her carriage and took the little Berea family back to Fee.[35] After this harassing experience he settled his wife and children in New Richmond, Ohio, with his friends the Parkers, who conducted an academy there, thus giving his children a chance for a good schooling during the next two years.

Rogers stayed in Berea about six weeks this autumn. There were persistent rumors that some day the Confederates would hang him, and so he had better keep in hiding out in the hills; but in time all anxiety dropped from him, and he said that these weeks were among the most pleasant of his life. He rode a circuit of about a hundred miles in the hill country to visit the rural churches whose antislavery pastors had been driven out. When he was in Berea, he worked on his new house, preached, studied, and visited much from house to house. In mid October while Kentucky was still swarming with Confederate troops and Union Home Guards, he rode his horse Rosa four days "through highways and byways, woods and fields" to reach the Ohio, and swam her across the river to safety, having on the way "many adventures and apparently narrow escapes."[36]

The early winter of 1863 saw Fee preaching again in Berea and the adjacent mountain communities, to strengthen them by his words and his presence. In February, 1864, the people of the Berea community on and around the Ridge held an all-day meeting with "a most bountiful basket dinner" between Fee's morning and afternoon addresses. All were invited to eat at a common table, and "past discussions and persecutions were forgotten in the greetings of the assembled crowd." A few slaveholders were present, and parts of two families of slaves. In the morning Fee spoke on the duty of sustaining governments, and in the afternoon on immediate emancipation.[37]

Two months later Fee moved his family, including a new baby, back to Berea again, although there was still some raiding in the region. The following September, 1864, before the three-months district school began, he opened the subscription school, the "good Rogers school," with seventy-three pupils, most of them children, but some ten or twelve young men and women. Rogers had not yet returned. The teaching was done by an old man hired by the day, Fee and his daughter Laura, and Mrs. Fee, who helped with the very little ones. This was Berea College again, welcomed back by the people in their need.

Soon after returning in the spring of 1864, Fee took up a new interest. One day he and his oldest son Burritt rode horseback to Camp Nelson, thirty-five miles to the northwest, because he had heard that Negro troops there were being organized into regiments. The next Sunday he went among these soldiers and in the evening preached to several thousand of them. It was his first experience in preaching to a large assembly of Negro people, a moving occasion to him. It was as though freedom that night had actually come, though the war was not yet over. Before this time his messages on slavery had been messages to white men, with occasionally a few Negroes present, usually slaves. Now there flooded over him a sense of duty to provide pastors and teachers for the new freedmen.

He did not wait until a future time of nationwide emancipation, but began his work there among the free troops at Camp Nelson. He asked the quartermaster at the camp to let him have a place for regular preaching, and the officer added that the men needed teaching too. Before long Fee secured the gift of a bell, and mounted it on a derrick in camp, to call the Negro soldiers to class and to worship. "This was a time of thrilling interest to me," he wrote. "I had long been shunned . . . by those who had a secret sympathy with me, and had long been hated and persecuted by others."[38] In his inner heart he had paid a price for his uncompromising stand on slavery. When Rogers visited Kentucky in the late summer of this year (1864), he found Fee and another minister along with thirteen volunteer teachers hard at work teaching Negro troops.

After the coming of peace three Berea trustees, Fee, Rogers, and Hanson, met in April, 1865, to make Berea College more than a phantom college. Their first business was to pass a resolution of thanks to God for carrying them safely through the years of violence. They then agreed to open the College early in the coming year, and to seek money with which to erect a suitable building.[39]

Although the trustees had drawn up a Constitution that was accepted in July, 1859, before the exodus, the College had not yet been incorporated because of certain legal delays, chief of which was an insufficient number of trustees. Now at the end of the war only three of the original trustees were left, and so seven new trustees were selected. They completed the incorporation of Berea College on April 5, 1866. Then on May 23, 1866, since the College was now able to hold land, they secured a deed for the Woolwine tract.

According to its first catalog (1866-1867), the "Berea Literary Institute," as the catalog called it, had a total attendance of 187, of whom 96 were Negroes and 91 whites. Emancipation had changed the constituency of the Berea institution while it was still in its swaddling clothes.

CHAPTER 2: Founders during Reconstruction

IN FINANCIAL matters the best friend of the youthful Berea College after the Civil War was the American Missionary Association (A.M.A.). The second publicity pamphlet of the new school (1867) made acknowledgment of the school's debt of gratitude to this Association, "without whose fostering care it never could have existed."[1] Sometimes members of the Association spoke of the A.M.A. as the founder of Berea College, as in a resolution of 1869 which referred to Berea as the "first of the institutions founded by the Association in the South to enter a regular college class."[2]

The A.M.A. did not make the plan to found a higher school on the Ridge, nor take a conscious part in shaping its Constitution, nor in selecting its teachers; the Association did not give Berea College money for buildings, land, or scholarships; but it did render certain services, especially in the first decade of the College's corporate life, that entitle it to recognition as one of the founders of the College. J. A. R. Rogers wrote in 1882: "The friends of the American Missionary Association have made the College largely what it is, and it certainly would not be right to pay no attention to their wisdom and work."[3]

The fostering care of the A.M.A. took three forms: (1) providing small basic salaries in the early years; (2) furnishing access to benevolent people through a widely read magazine, the *American Missionary*, and social contacts at the Association's annual meeting; (3) recommending Berea College to donors as a wise investment in Christian education. Berea College did not begin its career with a large endowment, nor with any college building, nor with a farm for a manual labor program; but it did begin with certain ideas expressed in the Constitution and with a character that had been tested by persecution.

On its fiftieth anniversary in 1896 the A.M.A. sent a greeting to Berea as "the earliest college founded by its missionaries."[4] John G. Fee had been commissioned as a rural minister in 1848 when the A.M.A. was very young, and he had remained on its payroll of commissioned ministers for the following thirty-four years. When he came to serve as a minister in the vicinity of the Ridge, he received from the A.M.A. $400 a year, and when J. A. R. Rogers joined Fee in the Berea work in 1858, he too received $400 a year as a rural minister, for the A.M.A. was then engaged in religious, not in educational work. After the war when there was a pressing need in the South for educational as well as religious work, the Association frequently rendered help in the form of salaries to schools that were doing a much-needed service. In the annual report of the A.M.A., 1869, three men and six women in Berea College were listed as receiving part of their salary from the A.M.A.[5] Secretary J. E. Roy of the A.M.A. in an obituary of John G. Fee in 1901 summed up the situation when he wrote: "The Association never made any appropriation toward the support of the College directly; it was furnishing stipends to the missionaries who with Mr. Fee were becoming its founders."[6]

The Association's *American Missionary* welcomed the letters of Fee, Rogers, and E. Henry Fairchild, the first president of the College, which were sure to give a lively picture of recent events not only in Berea but in the outlying work. Hundreds of people gave money year after year simply because in the *American Missionary* they had read articles written by Berea workers. Such letters would end with the simplest of appeals: "Will friends help? I will acknowledge the receipt of every dollar through the *American Missionary*," or "I pray this may attract the attention of some of God's stewards."

The annual meeting of the A.M.A. was usually attended by John G. Fee, J. A. R. Rogers, or President Fairchild. The delegate from Berea usually served on some committee and might even be invited to give an address. The meeting would be followed by invitations to fill several pulpits after the three-day convention had closed; and thus through the living word of a Fee, a Rogers, or a Fairchild further chances were given to present Berea's cause to prospective donors. It was through the fellowship of the annual meeting that Rogers and Fee became acquainted with General O. O. Howard, long an active member of the A.M.A., who as commissioner of the Freedmen's Bureau had it in his power to give Berea its first college building and money for freedmen's scholarships.

It meant a great deal in those early days to be recommended by the A.M.A. In a publicity pamphlet of 1866 bearing the headline "Commendations," there were two pages of recommendations of the Berea undertaking, including along with the good words of the chief justice of the United States Supreme Court, the governor of Ohio, and the president of Yale University, the commendatory words of the president of the A.M.A. and four of its lesser officials.

There were men of substance who would hesitate to turn over money directly to Berea College, a young institution far away in a small Kentucky village where there was neither a railroad nor a bank; but they would deposit a considerable donation with the A.M.A. at its New York office. The Hammond and Dike scholarship funds were built up by deposits of $5,000 at a time until $30,000 was reached, and the care of this money rested for many years with the A.M.A. The Beers gift consisted of railroad bonds which were deposited with the

A.M.A., and the Tuthill King fund was handled in the same manner.

In 1868 on the suggestion of the A.M.A. a district secretary, the Reverend E. M. Cravath, was added to the Berea Board of Trustees, which up to this time had consisted largely of local men. The A.M.A. secretary in asking for this change wrote to John G. Fee, chairman of the Berea Board, saying that the officers of the Association felt to a certain extent responsible for its correct management and the wise administration of its trusts.[7]

It was because of these relations that Secretary J. E. Roy wrote with a clear understanding of the situation in the earlier decades: "The A.M.A. by its publications and its limited aid was serving the part of foster parent, and so in this way Mr. Fee and the College were receiving much of support from the Association, and the Association became indebted to them as standard-bearers of its cause of impartial education in the South."[8]

II

BEREA'S FIRST president, the Reverend E. Henry Fairchild (1869-1889) certainly should be named among the founders. He was fifty-four years of age when he came to Berea, a year older than Fee and thirteen years older than Professor Rogers. He had had experience as a pastor, a teacher, and a successful financial agent; but it was his experience as an executive that most directly prepared him for the Berea work. For sixteen years this wise and gifted man as principal of Oberlin's preparatory department had studied over practical problems of human management at a time when this branch of Oberlin College numbered more than five hundred students. Moreover, his long-continued relations with Oberlin had given him an understanding of principles also fundamental to Berea.

This Henry Fairchild, whose father, like J. A. R. Rogers' father, had moved long since from New England to northern

Ohio, had had his youthful antislavery concern intensified by
certain college experiences. He was a twenty-year-old freshman of Oberlin College when the "Lane rebels" came to
Oberlin to enter the Seminary, because they had been ordered
by the trustees of Lane Theological Seminary to cease their
disturbing antislavery discussions. Henry Fairchild was present on that day in 1835 when these students were welcomed to
Oberlin.[9]

Before the end of the fall term Theodore D. Weld, the
leader of the Lane rebels in Cincinnati, came to visit them. He
delivered a series of more than twenty lectures on slavery, and
both Henry Fairchild and his brother James were profoundly
influenced by these talks; "lectures of marvellous power," wrote
James Fairchild, "all charged with facts, with logic, and with
fervid eloquence. To listen to such an exhibition of the system
of slavery, was an experience to be remembered for a lifetime.
. . . From first to last, through the evenings of three full weeks,
the whole body of citizens and students hung upon his lips. . . .
Oberlin was abolitionized in every thought and feeling and
purpose."[10]

Under the influence of Weld, Henry Fairchild became one
of the "Seventy," commissioned while still a college student to
spread the emancipation ideas of the American Antislavery
Society into the Middle West. This work he carried on during his long winter and summer vacations, teaching refugee
Negroes in Cincinnati and giving addresses in Pennsylvania
and Ohio even though his meetings were frequently disturbed.
While the abuse that he encountered was mild compared with
that which Fee suffered for many years in Kentucky, yet in
retrospect it made a bond of understanding between the two
men. In essence the bond that united John G. Fee, J. A. R.
Rogers, Henry Fairchild, and the members of the A.M.A. was
the moral ferment in which these men had spent their youth,
a ferment which was the social cause of the founding of Berea
College, a ferment which in these devoted men showed itself
before the Civil War in antislavery ardor and after emancipa-

tion in the will to bring education to the disadvantaged, whether born free or in bondage.

When Henry Fairchild came to Berea as president, he found the College already provided with a satisfactory constitution and a legal charter. Soon after obtaining this charter in 1866, the College had received an endowment of $10,000. The enrollment consisted of about three hundred students, two-thirds of whom were below the rank of the Academy and slightly more than half of whom were Negro. The first college class was registered in the September following President Fairchild's arrival in Berea in the spring of 1869.

Fairchild soon perceived that the material needs of the infant institution were permanent buildings, increased endowment, scholarships, and more income for current expenses. Without these things the College would die almost before it was born. In the twenty years of his administration he had unusual success in providing these necessities.

When he took up his duties in 1869, he found that the school had moved from the district school neighborhood to the Woolwine purchase. The classrooms were in and around the Chapel, which was located south of the present Tabernacle. It was a rough frame building, whitewashed inside and outside. In front it had a lean-to for the use of the janitor and the bell ringer. On the roof of the shed was an open belfry. This Chapel was divided into classrooms by movable partitions which could be swung so as to unite the schoolrooms into an auditorium for service. Clustered around this building were several frame classrooms and two small houses for boys' dormitories. Where Fairchild Hall is now located, there was a two-story frame house to serve as a rooming house for girls and as a boarding hall. Many students lived with town families.

This was not all, however, that the new president saw on the "college green." Near the makeshift Chapel a new building was being erected, a three-story hall for men, a dignified frame dormitory which the catalogs for many years called "commodious" and which President Fairchild in his inaugural address referred to as "the noble one." Small wonder, I would say, considering the other structures around, for this hall would accommodate eighty-two "young gentlemen" and cost $18,000, the gift of the Freedmen's Bureau upon the recommendation of General O. O. Howard. It was the first campus structure in Berea that looked like a college hall, even though it was not built of stone or brick.

III

PRESIDENT FAIRCHILD saw clearly that a proper dormitory was urgently needed for the young ladies, and four years after his arrival he dedicated a beautiful brick building that was much more "commodious" and "noble" than Howard Hall. This large dormitory, which cost $50,000, towered above the village as though it were a medieval cathedral looking over its little town. A tradition about Ladies' Hall related that when a railroad surveyor looking through his theodolite first saw this brick building towering above the forest, he dropped his notebook and exclaimed, "Whoever put up that building in this wilderness must have had faith!"[11] The faith was that of the new president, supported by Fee, Rogers, Hanson, and two eastern businessmen, R. R. Graves and his brother E. A. Graves, who saw the dawning in the South.

It was easy enough for the trustee committee in March, 1870, to accept President Fairchild's suggestion that the plan of the new dormitory "be essentially the same as that of the Ladies' Hall at Oberlin,"[12] but they had no mind to build ahead of their funds. In the fall of 1870 they were able to let the contract for moving an old building off the chosen site. Presently they were driving stakes to locate this Ladies' Hall. In 1871 President Fairchild and his committee ventured to order bricks to be made in the brickyard south of the site, stone to be quarried not far from the village, and lumber to be prepared from the adjoining forests, including butternut and chestnut for the varnished wood finishings. It was not until spring, 1872, that money began to roll in from the Graves brothers, who were practical businessmen holding high positions in the A.M.A. Such progress was made in donations and construction that the building could be dedicated on September 24, 1873.[13]

The college catalog for 1873-1874 succinctly described the building: "A Ladies' Hall of brick, three stories high, containing well lighted and well ventilated rooms for ninety-six young ladies, besides parlors, assembly room, library, reading room, dining room, kitchen, laundry rooms, etc. . . . An equal number of gentleman students can be accommodated with table board at the Hall." Elegance is, of course, a relative term, and there was an unmistakable elegance about this building. Although the two upper floors were heated by small wood stoves, the first floor rooms were heated by a furnace. The only elevator in the village was in Ladies' Hall, and this elevator, worked by ropes and a wood boy, carried wood to the second and third floors for the young ladies. There were water tanks in the attic, filled from a cistern with a pump at ground level. Room rent without provision for linen and laundry cost seventy-five cents a month, and ten years later the charge was the same.

President Fairchild was too modest a man to name the building from himself, though he had taken so large a part in providing it; but in 1937, almost fifty years after his death, the College changed the name from Ladies' Hall to Fairchild Hall in his honor. The interior of the building has been modernized by the introduction of electricity and central heat, but the exterior remains much the same, even to the widow's walk on the northeast side of the roof. Instead of two hundred young men and women eating in the boarding hall of this building, eight hundred are now fed at its cafeteria.

In 1874, the year after Ladies' Hall was finished, President Fairchild wrote: "A Chapel with two or three schoolrooms, all of which could be built for $10,000, are greatly needed. With these the College would have all its essential facilities for many years."[14] No plans for such a building were made, however, until the old Chapel burned to the ground on New Year's Eve, 1878. To be more accessible, this new Chapel was built close to Chestnut Street. A frame building that would seat about five hundred people, it was in excellent style, suggestive of Gothic. It had its own kind of elegance, double lancet windows, a beautiful bell tower, a furnace, and gas lights. It looked like a Chapel, just as Howard Hall looked like a college hall of residence.

In the same week of 1879 in which the trustee committee decided upon the site for a new Chapel, they began a discussion which eventually led to the building of a beautiful recitation hall: "The question was discussed at length relative to President Fairchild going out among our friends and those of the late William Lloyd Garrison, with a view to raising funds to erect a memorial building in which to place our library, the varied belongings of the different scientific departments, and in which should be located the college offices. Much interest was shown in the discussion, but no action was taken."[15] It was six years before the money for such a building was available. In 1884 Roswell Smith, president of the Century Company and a founder of the *Century Magazine* and the *Century Dictionary,* sent $1,000 through the A.M.A. for Berea's current expenses. The following June, 1885, he attended Berea's Commencement exercises in company with his literary friend George W. Cable. Among the guests present on that notable day were also General Cassius M. Clay and Judge W. M. Beckner of Kentucky, and among the senior orators was the eloquent William E. Barton. When Roswell Smith in looking over the college plant saw the great need for classrooms, library space, and offices, he remarked that we should begin to make bricks. Reminded how hard it was to "make bricks without straw," he replied, "Put me down for five thousand for straw."[16] When the visitors left the campus after this wonderful day, President Fairchild wrote with unconcealed satisfaction: "It was a new thing in our experience that a prominent business man from New York should, without solicitation, and contrary to programme, call for the 'hat' and put down himself $5000 for a new 'Recitation Hall,' which he saw to be a great want of the College. . . . But $5000 will only begin it, and the College must not contract a debt."[17]

The building, when completed, cost $32,000, almost all of which was given by the donor of the first "straw." It contained eighteen rooms. The first floor rooms were used for classrooms and offices, the second floor for the library and more classrooms, and the third floor for laboratories, museum, and society rooms. When the donor was asked to name the beautiful building, he wished it named not from himself but from Abraham Lincoln; and after the dedication of Lincoln Hall at Commencement, 1887, he sent for the building a choice bas-relief of Lincoln done in bronze by J. S. Hartley. Roswell Smith put into this structure more than money. He was a cultivated city man who wished the new hall to be well designed and beautified by structural refinements. He provided the architect and wrote many letters regarding details of the building. It is now more than two-thirds of a century since Lincoln Hall was constructed, yet it seems today neither old-fashioned nor outworn.

During the Fairchild administration of twenty years, the college endowment increased from $10,000 to slightly more than $100,000. By the time of President Fairchild's death, the annual income from invested endowment funds amounted to almost $5,000, but the cost of instruction was twice this amount, and the salary aid of the A.M.A. was gradually withdrawn in the early 1880's in accordance with the Association's policy of ending financial assistance as soon as a school seemed able to be self-sustaining.

In those days Berea charged a small tuition fee. Between 1872 and 1876 the Dike and Hammond funds were secured, an endowment the income of which was used to provide seventy-two scholarships for students needing help. Since Berea College was intended for students of small means, and since there was not yet a labor program sufficient to care for the students needing help, ceaseless effort had to be made to keep down the cost of board and room, and the income from the student aid funds was essential to the very existence of the institution. President Fairchild bore successfully the responsibility for meeting these problems.

IV

FROM THE BEGINNING of his term of office, President Fairchild was concerned with problems of improved public services for the community. The Ridge needed better connections with the outside world, especially with the county seat to the north and the timber lands of the mountains eastward. As Berea was not yet an incorporated village, it had neither a mayor nor a town council; so it remained for President Fairchild and his Prudential Committee to do the work of a mayor and council, and perhaps also of a Chamber of Commerce, in securing the needed civic facilities that lay within their reach. For instance, in 1872 President Fairchild and the Committee subscribed $1,000 to the Kingston and Boone's Gap turnpike, secured by ten lots along the pike, on condition that "the pike be opened to Berea passing over the Ridge."[18] After the Prudential Committee voted to donate $3,000 to secure the right of way of the proposed Kentucky Central Railroad through Berea, some trustees rebuked this Committee for pledging so large a sum when the College already had a $10,000 debt. "We see nothing in the prospective enhancement of the college property to warrant the giving away so large a sum."[19] The single-track railroad, when it was eventually approved, did not go more than thirty miles south of Berea, to be sure; but on the north it made connections with Cincinnati, and thanks to the toll roads leading out of the mountains to the new railroad station at Berea and similar villages along the railway, the lumber from the mountains—logs, staves, crossties, and tanbark —found a way to market. It mattered little that the only passenger service on this line was on a mixed freight and passenger train. Thanks to the leadership of President Fairchild, business was coming into Berea.

When President Fairchild came to Berea, Kentucky was full of violence. Some of this was the work of Ku Klux men, but much of it was organized rowdyism to avenge old grudges or to keep Negroes in a state of fear and white men in order. In both editions of President Fairchild's history there is the plain statement: "The Ku Klux never paid us a visit. Many rumors of their hostile intentions have reached us, and rumors that our college buildings and some of our private houses had been burned have been spread through the country; but from what we knew of their operations near us, we did not apprehend any disturbance from them."[20] There was a certain annoyance from intoxicated country fellows who shouted and occasionally fired their pistols recklessly as they rode through town. Once a shot passed through President Fairchild's window, but it injured no one. People said that the rowdies liked to see how near they could come to shooting the college bell as they galloped along Chestnut Street and clattered over the footbridge near the president's house, but men like Fairchild, Fee, Rogers, and Hanson did not live in fear.

The institution of an excursion to the mountains goes back to 1875, when the faculty voted that such a spring excursion might be made under the conduct of President Fairchild.[21] Year after year this college picnic was held, some years in the spring, some years in the gorgeous autumn; but the most memorable Mountain Day in the Fairchild administration was in the spring of 1886. By this time there was a college paper, the *Berea College Reporter,* and the issue of June, 1886, gave a full account of the great day. Some groups made arrangements to ride, but more than a hundred preferred to walk the three miles to the Pinnacle. The brass band went early to West Pinnacle and "was discoursing sweet music" as the rest of the students climbed the steep incline. The food wagons took their baskets of food to a spring halfway between the valley and East Pinnacle. The picnickers inspected the Rockhouse, squeezed through Fat Man's Misery, risked the Devil's Slide, and wandered around Indian Fort. At East Pinnacle they sat on the rocks, telling stories, singing songs, and wishing that they could climb Pilot Knob far across the valley. They returned home by way of the Crater near Blue Lick. There was no hunger like Mountain Day hunger, and no memory like that of Mountain Day, or so it seemed as they dragged their tired feet homeward at the close of the day. Mountain Day left a much better flavor than pistol toting or knife swaggering.

While President Fairchild was a founder in providing a material foundation of buildings, endowment, and scholarships, improved connections with the outside world, better public utilities inside the village, and a pattern of student life that was both Christian and humane, his greatest work was probably in the field of race relations. The race situation was not like that in Oberlin, where the Negroes constituted a very small minority of the student body. On the Berea campus at least half the students were Negroes. With great wisdom and kindness President Fairchild guided hundreds of young Negroes into the fellowship of an educated Negro-white society, and hundreds of young white students into an understanding of the Negroes' problems and the Negroes' worth. That this social experiment could prove successful in a former slave state so soon after the Civil War and legal emancipation adds interest to the study of Berea's century of interrace relations.

When President Fairchild died, the college paper wrote that the way to build him a more enduring monument than the hills that watched his grave would be to confirm and extend his Christian principles of liberty and impartiality.[22]

3: A Century of
Interrace Education

BEREA COLLEGE from 1866 to 1904 educated both Negro and white students. During this time the College relieved some pressing social needs and learned important lessons in social adjustment, though it cannot be said to have solved the hardest problems of Negro-white education.

When compelled by the passage of a state law to forego interracial education, the College chose to continue in Kentucky as a white school. However, it provided for a well-endowed Negro school in the Bluegrass area of Kentucky, where the Negro people were especially numerous. In the years that followed, Berea College repeatedly showed its concern over Negro education, and in 1950 when it could once more admit Negroes legally under certain conditions, it again registered Negroes in its classes, though they were few in number.

II

ALREADY IN 1859 feeling was running high as to whether Professor Rogers should be allowed to use the district school building for his subscription school if Negroes were admitted. In

March of that year John G. Fee wrote to Gerrit Smith: "The opposition party called a meeting to vote him out of the schoolhouse. They could not get the people to vote against the school when they were convened. We have now quite a large majority in favor of the school."[1] The question of admitting Negroes to a private school did not face the patrons as a practical matter, however, till after the Civil War.

Before the war there were plenty of men in Kentucky who were opposed to the institution of slavery, but were "castemen" instead of what Fee called "anti-caste," that is, they were not yet reconciled to the idea that freedmen might ride in a white coach, partake of communion along with white church members, and attend school with whites. When slavery came to an end at the close of the war, Berea had to struggle with the problem of the Negroes' social privileges; and Berea College, for which a constitution had been made and land bought to serve as a campus, lost some of its students and even some of its trustees on the issue of the admission of Negro students to the Rogers-Fee school.

The problem of Negro attendance was faced in the first term after the war. By a compromise the first two months of this term were to be considered as part of the district school, and therefore Negroes would not be admitted until March 1, "so that none might make charge of usurping privileges in using the district house." At the same time John G. Hanson "as architect and builder for the College" was directed to build before September two new cottages where classes might be held without offense to any patrons of the district.[2]

Early in March, 1866, the first Negro pupils were admitted. W. W. Wheeler, assistant to Professor Rogers, reported later that the attendance for the term was low "on account of absence of 27 members who unceremoniously and in a disgraceful manner left the school at the end of two months on account of the presence of colored children who had been admitted to equal privileges with others."[3] Across the road from the schoolhouse the wives of the two teachers sat at a window of Berea's first boarding hall, which was managed by Wheeler and his wife.

Since it was against the law to enroll Negroes in the district school, Mrs. Wheeler had been teaching several Negro children in her own quarters. On this March day they could enroll in the private Rogers-Wheeler school, which met by agreement in the district schoolhouse since the new buildings were unfinished. Mrs. Wheeler later wrote: "From the front window Mrs. Rogers and I watched the little black children enter on that memorable day, and watched until we saw the flight of the white boys and girls."

In April of this year, 1866, several adult Negroes registered in the school, one of whom was Angus A. Burleigh, a sergeant who had met Fee at Camp Nelson. Someone had told the sergeant that a man wanted to see him at the chaplain's office. "There was a small man, grey of hair and with kindly face," wrote Burleigh in later years. "He arose as I entered, and took me by the hand. 'I am Mr. Fee,' he said, 'John G. Fee.' " Fee had asked Sergeant Burleigh what he intended to do when war ended. When the sergeant had replied that he meant to get an education, Fee had said that he was looking for young men to go to Berea for schooling and that everyone would have a chance to work his way through school. "He took out of his pocket a small notebook. . . . 'I have here forty-one names, and yours will make the forty-second. Will you come?' " When Angus Burleigh had said that he would come as soon as he was mustered out, Fee had told him to take the stage to Lexington and change for Richmond. From Richmond, he had said, it was only a fourteen-mile walk to Berea. When the sergeant arrived in Berea, he found a welcome. "Mrs. Fee met me at the door with the same gentle smile she always had. Next morning bright and early I was in the school embarked on an education." He was assigned to Professor Rogers' room. Before long he was converted and was baptized in Brushy Fork. Nine years later he graduated from Berea College with a B.A. degree.[5]

THERE CAME A TIME in Berea's history, especially before and after the passage of the Day law (1904), when many people, both white and Negro, believed that Berea College was founded for the Negro people; and in the decades since 1911 even more people have believed that it was founded specifically for the people of the southern Appalachian mountains.

From the first Constitution, approved in 1859, until a revision made in 1911 the purpose of the College was stated to be the promotion of the cause of Christ by offering a thorough education to all persons of good moral character. No special preference was given in this statement to any one group of people.[6] From other sources than the Constitution itself it is clear that from the earliest days of the school the founders intended it to be for all people regardless of race. Already in 1855 John G. Fee had spoken of the school as an anticaste institution;[7] and in 1858 Professor Rogers declared that he would not teach the Berea school unless it was open to all.[8] In the first catalog (1866-1867) appeared two paragraphs under the title "The school is greatly needed." The first paragraph spoke of the need of the Negro people for a higher school in the state; and the second spoke of the educational need of the white people of the mountains of Kentucky and adjoining states.

After the Civil War the freedmen poured into Berea to secure the magic of education. The catalog of 1866-1867 listed 187 pupils, of whom 96 were Negro, 91 white. In 1875-1876 there were 237 enrolled, of whom 143 were Negro, 94 white. In the total enrollment of 369 in 1880-1881, 249 were Negro, 120 white. In the last year of President Fairchild's administration, 177 were Negro, 157 white. In one year only between 1866 and 1894, namely 1877-1878, did the record show more whites than Negroes, 144 to 129.

In 1869 the first freshman class of the College Department was enrolled, and in 1873 the first degrees were bestowed upon graduates who had completed an exacting four-year course. During the sixteen years between 1873 and the close of the Fairchild administration, 1889, forty-three four-year degrees were awarded, thirty of them to white students, thirteen to Negroes. Although in the lower departments the Negroes almost always outnumbered the whites, the Negroes were less numerous than the whites in the College Department because: (1) the Negroes had to start lower in Berea's school system because of previous lack of preparation; (2) they were more likely to stay out of school for an occasional term to work; (3) they were more needed as teachers, especially after 1874, when the first public schools for Negroes were set up by law in Kentucky.

Even though Negro graduates were few in this period, they became outstanding leaders, especially in education. Eleven of the thirteen Negro graduates became teachers, one a lawyer, and one a minister. Only two were women, both of whom became teachers. The men teachers taught in Louisville, Lexington, Danville, Covington, Princeton, Somerset, and Maysville. One of them, John H. Jackson, became the first principal of the present State College for Negroes in Kentucky, and served for fourteen years. Another, James S. Hathaway, was its principal for nine years. It is noteworthy that most of these graduates came from Kentucky cities, where educational opportunities for Negroes were better than in the country. Of the eight from Kentucky, three were from Louisville, three from Lexington, one from Danville, and one from Mount Sterling.

Possibly the Negro teachers who left the Preparatory or the College Department before graduation were even more important than the graduates, because they were so much more numerous. When an Ohio man wrote in 1878 asking President Fairchild what he could say about Berea College, the president replied: "Not less than 100 Negro schools were taught last year by colored teachers educated at Berea."[9] Kentucky did not at this time have a state normal school for training Negro teachers.

PRESIDENT FAIRCHILD in an A.M.A. conference at Nashville in 1881 expressed clearly the reason why he wanted to provide a college education for as many promising young Negroes as possible. While his sympathy was with the slow of wit, his hopes for the advancement of the American Negro lay with those who were able to do college work. "They must be as well prepared as white people in every way, in order to secure the respect of the white people and maintain their own respect."[10]

In his baccalaureate sermon of the same year Fairchild developed this idea in greater detail: "They need to be scientific farmers and skilled mechanics, artists and architects and contractors, as well as common farmers. They need to be qualified for magistrates, jurors, lawyers, and judges; for teachers, preachers, editors, physicians; for professors and presidents of colleges; for legislators and congressmen; for consuls, ambassadors; in short, for every position which citizens are expected to occupy." Later in the same address he said: "Not only must common school education become general and of a high order; many thousands of colored men and women must become highly educated—graduates of colleges and seminaries; of theological, medical, and law schools; of musical conservatories and schools of art. . . . Thorough education, high culture, exalted character, sound judgment, exquisite taste, and eloquent delivery will win their way in spite of prejudice and custom."[11]

On the Berea campus there was no organization and no activity in which both Negro and white did not share. They recited in the same classes, sat in the same rows in Chapel, played on the same baseball team, sang in the same Harmonia Choral Society, debated in the same literary societies, and ate at the same boarding hall. In the first issue of the new college paper, President Fairchild said that with such arrangements as these the school moved along "in perfect harmony from year to year, all treating each other with respect."[12]

During this administration Negroes were officers as well as members of all campus organizations. Take the men's literary society, Phi Delta. There were five elective offices, and Negroes were sure to be elected to any two or three of these positions without discrimination. The minute books show that a Negro was just as likely as a white man to be elected president. The Phi Delta weekly programs give firsthand evidence of the good relations existing between the two races. This society consisted of such College and Preparatory men as cared to join, and its motto was "We love discussion." A program consisted of various literary offerings, but a meeting without a debate was rare indeed. In a debate there would be Negroes on each side, either assigned beforehand or volunteers; but these discussions were carried on with a tradition of interracial forbearance. One night in 1882 the subject for discussion was: "Resolved, that the colored people should emigrate to the mountains of Kentucky." If the debate had been carried on with mountain boys on one side and Negro boys on the other, the situation might have been unfortunate; but with an assigned Negro speaker on each side to lead the discussion, there was no trouble. Upon this occasion, a situation arose that elsewhere might have been decided by prejudice. When the treasurer (white) challenged the negative speaker's right to present his argument because he had an unpaid fine against him, the Negro's privilege of speaking to the question was upheld by a unanimous vote of the house.[13]

A white member of this literary society, and also of the brass band and the baseball team in the Fairchild administration, wrote many years later: "Were I to make a list of former students whom I would genuinely enjoy meeting again, to sit down for a chat over old times, I would find a majority of them colored."[14]

The Commencement programs show the same freedom from caste. In those days instead of an address at the graduating exercises by some out-of-town speaker, numerous orations and essays were presented by upper-class students. The ratio of

Negroes to whites on the program was about the same as their ratio in the College Department, and their subjects were usually free from racial implications; for example, "Civil Reform," "A Judicial View of the Labor Question," and "The Mountains of Kentucky."

In those times a Ladies' Board of Care assisted the "lady principal" in handling social regulations. When a resignation occurred on this Board in 1878, the Prudential Committee chose a town woman for the vacant place, "providing she is in sympathy with the work of the co-education of the white and coloured."[15] In 1872 after school closed for the year, the trustees spent two days in thoughtful study of social relations between the two races. The decisions of the trustees were in substance as follows: that persons of opposite sex and race should not be prohibited from attending each other to and from social gatherings; but if their going together would expose them to violence or to the charge of impure motives, or if they made "an offensive display of themselves," then they should not receive the lady principal's permission.[16] Under this qualified social freedom the Berea students lived without scandal or undue tension for seventeen years.

At the post-Commencement meeting of the Berea College alumni in 1889, with the presiding officer a Negro alumnus who had become important in Negro education in Kentucky, the alumni approved the principle that had been expressed in a recent baccalaureate sermon, namely, that as human beings they were all equal regardless of race. They requested that the trustees rely on the wisdom of the faculty and the good judgment of the students as to social relations,[17] and on the following day the Board of Trustees acceded to this request.[18]

There was a Negro upon the Board of Trustees before there was a Berea College graduate, Negro or white. This trustee, the Reverend Gabriel Burdett, known to Fee because of their work together at Camp Nelson late in the war, was an eloquent preacher who understood the sensitiveness of educated Negro men. After twelve years as a trustee he was succeeded in 1879 by Jordan C. Jackson, a Negro educator of Lexington, Kentucky, who served Berea for sixteen years, a wise man who was of great help to the Berea administration in its efforts to meet the Negroes' needs in education. The Negroes continued to have a Negro member on this Board until James Bond resigned in 1914.

During the Fairchild administration Berea had two Negro teachers. Miss Julia Britton taught instrumental music, 1870-1872, while she was also a student. James S. Hathaway, after graduating from the College in 1884 with a B.A. degree, was appointed instructor (tutor) in Latin and mathematics. When he did not receive a professorship, his unfulfilled ambition tended to embitter him and some other young Negro intellectuals.[19]

v

WHEN WILLIAM G. FROST, professor of Greek in Oberlin College, became the president of Berea College in the autumn of 1892, it was clear that the College was far from prosperous. President Fairchild had been in failing health during the two years before his death, and his successor, the Reverend William B. Stewart, had for two years devoted his attention to teaching rather than to raising money. President Frost, then in his thirty-eighth year, was unwilling to accept the *status quo* as inevitable.

When he looked over the enrollment figures of the preceding year, 1891-1892, President Frost saw that there had been thirty-one students in the College Department, twenty-two Negroes and nine whites. Aside from the white students whose parents lived in Berea, there were very few mountain students enrolled in the institution as a whole, though President Fairchild had taken so profound an interest in their welfare.[20] The College graduates of the preceding Commencement, five Negro men, greatly interested President Frost. Each of the two classical graduates had studied in Berea for eleven years; the three scientific graduates had been in Berea from ten to thirteen years, taking a term out now and then to earn money. One of the five had enrolled in Oberlin Theological Seminary after his graduation from Berea, and the other four had secured positions as principals of schools for Negroes in Kentucky municipalities.[21]

At the close of his first year in Berea, June, 1893, President Frost delivered to the trustees and faculty a scathing report, of which he had only the milder portions printed. He spoke of "the air of dilapidation about the place," the vacant rooms in the dormitories, and the empty seats in the classes and the Chapel.[22] In his report of June, 1894, he wrote: "Our success in breaking down caste is measured by the number of white students. . . . Our great work is to reconcile the two races, and make friends for the colored among the white. To this end it is very important that our colored students should be of a superior quality. In this we are fortunate."[23] In his 1895 report he wrote: "The people who contribute money to Berea rather than to Hampton or Atlanta are interested in it as a mixed school, and measure its success by the number of white students."[24]

President Frost increased the total enrollment by increasing the number of white students, leaving the Negro numbers about the same as before. Twelve years after his coming to Berea the total registration was 961, of whom 157 were Negro, in contrast to the total registration of 1893, which was 354, of whom 184 were Negro students. The actual number of registered Negroes had decreased only 27, but the proportion of Negroes to whites had fallen from 52 per cent to 16 per cent. As Negroes formed about one-seventh of Kentucky's population, this reduction seemed reasonable to President Frost and others. They did not take into account the fact that this change in ratio had caused the Negroes to become a minority group on the campus.

In 1902 President Frost said to the faculty and trustees: "It is no unimportant part of a white boy's education to see the

Negro treated as a man. In the final account, Berea's work for
the abolition of caste may be the brightest jewel in her
crown."[25] Because President Frost's mind was set upon increasing the number of white students, he allowed himself to
be drawn into a bitter controversy in the state press, with
angry charges and countercharges regarding the future Negro
policy of the College. These sharp words tended to weaken
his influence among some of his most capable Negro graduates
when the crisis of hostile legislation overwhelmed the institution. The interracial truce crumbled under the Negroes' fear
that they would soon be excluded from Berea, judging from
President Frost's emphasis upon the education of mountain
people, who were white, and the steadily decreasing ratio of
Negroes to whites in the College.

VI

SOON AFTER THE TURN of the century there were rumblings
that a segregation law might be passed to close Berea as a
mixed school. Already Kentucky had a segregation law applying to its public schools.[26] President Frost's anxiety on this matter led him in the fall of 1901 to correspond with several
friends in the East in regard to the danger of such legislation.
To a prominent Brooklyn minister he wrote:

"We feel that there is a conspiracy throughout the land to
defame the colored man and discourage his friends. Last year
the light of liberty went out in Tennessee when a law was
passed forbidding Maryville College to receive both white and
colored students. That college itself . . . turned over a portion
of its endowment to a neighboring colored school.

"This event happening so near us is occasioning a great
deal of 'talk' in Kentucky, and many people think a bill will be
introduced in our legislature to bring about the same result.
Now it is my judgment that we ought to fight such a law to the
very end. I do not see how we can possibly exist under it.

Berea's foundation was laid and its chief endowment given by people who understood and approved our position."[27]

In correspondence with a Chicago friend President Frost said that in case such a law were enacted and were upheld by the courts, he could see nothing for Berea to do except to retire temporarily to some point in Ohio or West Virginia and carry on its work without its Berea properties. To President Frost's suggestion that such a withdrawal would be in the line of Berea's history, his friend replied that Berea's early history afforded no parallel. "The persecuted workers withdrew, but the school was not exiled." He suggested to the troubled president that such a withdrawal might result in the loss of Berea's charter and the extinction of Berea College.[28]

The causes leading to the passage of a segregation law in Kentucky in 1904 were diverse. The act was aimed directly at Berea College, the only mixed college in the state at that time; but it was not passed because of any interracial misconduct in the College. The causes were certain regional, local, and personal factors that were distorted by a political or social bias. An anti-Negro wave of feeling that was sweeping over the South had already caused stricter registration laws and a poll-tax requirement for voting to be passed in some southern states, though not in Kentucky, and had showed itself in Kentucky by the passage of a separate coach law. There were Bourbon politicians outside the state who said that a thoroughgoing segregation law in Kentucky might help to make the South more "solid."[29]

Though very few Negroes lived in the mountain counties, enough anti-Negro feeling was in the air to lead some mountain politicians to think that a vote for a piece of anti-Negro legislation would bolster up their election record in the home precincts, and that a vote against such a law would ruin their political careers forever.[30] There were mountain families who would not send their sons and daughters to Berea because it was a mixed school. Now that Berea College had become a prosperous and well-known school, they were sorry indeed that it was spoiled for them by having Negroes among its numbers.

There was a fast-growing prosperity in the little town of Berea, and it led some of the white businessmen to regret that so many good lots on the Ridge were owned by Negro families. Business was booming in Berea with the coming of a new bank, a stave mill that worked ten men, a long-distance telephone, an oil boom, and the opening of coal mines at Big Hill. These visible marks of progress led to a hopeful feeling that with lily-whiteness on the Ridge more mountain students would come to Berea College and business might become even better than at present. A few of these men lent their support to the passage of legislation hostile to mixed education in Berea.

VII

ON JANUARY 12, 1904, Representative Carl Day (D) of Breathitt County in the heart of the Kentucky mountains introduced a segregation bill into the House of Representatives of the Kentucky General Assembly. This House bill no. 25 was sent to the Committees on Education, which held separate hearings of those favoring and those opposing the bill. Representative Day told the press that he had introduced the measure for the purpose of preventing the contamination of the white children of Kentucky.

The bill in its final form declared it "unlawful for any person, corporation, or association of persons to maintain or operate any college, school, or institution where persons of the white and Negro races are both received as pupils for instruction." No previous Kentucky law had specified penalties for non-segregation in schools, but this bill stated that the penalties for violation were to be as follows: upon the institution, $1,000; upon the teacher, $50; and upon the student, whether Negro or white, $50 for each day's violation of the law. It applied to any private school that maintained any interracial branch within a radius of twenty-five miles.[31]

Race feeling rather than party affiliation determined the vote in each house of the General Assembly, and a nasty smear of insinuations about life on the Berea campus immediately aggravated traditional attitudes and political fears. The remonstrance sent by the Berea faculty and the paper of protest signed by many townspeople against the bill were of no avail. President Frost delivered a thought-provoking address to the Senate Committee on Education, including certain words for those who based their defense of the Day bill upon their desire to preserve the white race from contamination: "We believe that today there is less race contamination in the sphere of Berea's influence than anywhere else in the State. . . . The Berea way of preventing the mingling of the races is not by repressing the Negro and calling him by humiliating names, but we put such character and self-respect into the Negro that he keeps himself in order."[32]

During this stormy session of the General Assembly, President Frost preached in Berea a noteworthy sermon which showed the meaning of the Berea spirit. His text was: "Remember them that are in bonds," Hebrews 13:3. He appealed to his white and Negro audience to remember in a spirit of love those that were in bonds put upon them long ago by slavery—Negroes with their bonds of ignorance and shiftlessness, and white men with their bond of caste prejudice. "How long must it take the white and the black to cast off the bonds which the great curse of human slavery has left upon them?"[33]

When House bill no. 25 had been passed into law on March 12, 1904, the Berea Board of Trustees voted to test the constitutionality of the law in the Kentucky courts. The College's lawyers took the stand that this state law was a violation of the Fourteenth Amendment to the United States Constitution, which prohibited any state from abridging the privileges and immunities of the citizens of the United States. The case was not a Negro case at all, according to this reasoning, but a case involving the rights of colleges and persons, regardless of race. In the Circuit Court, Judge James M. Benton's decision was that the legislature was within its powers in providing for the exercise of that police power which has always been regarded as proper when the situation demands it; and that in this case the racial situation was such that the state should prevent the coeducation of the races. The case was then taken to the Kentucky Court of Appeals, which upheld the lower court's decision for the most part, but declared the twenty-five mile clause tyrannical and void.[34]

Berea College then appealed the case to the United States Supreme Court, which rendered its decision on November 9, 1908, four and one-half years after the Day law was passed by the Kentucky legislature. It simply affirmed the previous judgment: "The right to teach white and Negro children in a private school at the same time is not a property right. Besides, appellant Berea College as a corporation created by this State had no natural right to teach at all. Its right to teach is such as the State sees fit to give it. The State may withhold it altogether or qualify it."[35]

The College did not sit with folded hands while lawyers and judges pondered over legal technicalities. It announced that it could receive no Negro students until the constitutionality of the law had been tested in the courts. The trustees, no longer a local group, realized that President Frost's impulsive wish to move temporarily to the North involved the risk of losing Berea's charter. Some trustees favored the idea of making Berea College into a Negro school, while others preferred the plan of making Berea a white institution. The donors, too, were divided on this delicate subject. As a result of conflicting views the trustees took one cautious step at a time, and their decisions were not those of any one man on the Board, not even of President Frost.

The trustees' committee issued a printed statement expressing their sympathy with the Negro students "in this hour of their trial and ours. We and they are sufferers together. . . . We will seek to help them in all legitimate ways to continue their education in the best available methods until a final decision is rendered by the highest court." To help them in this emergency, the College would provide education in other good institutions and would make up to those students the difference in their railroad fare and in living expenses, so as to relieve them from financial loss by reason of the change. In the first year of the trustees' offer, 1904-1905, fifty-two of the more advanced Negro students attended such schools as Fisk, Tuskegee, Knoxville, and Kentucky State Institute for Negroes. It was a dramatic occasion when two Negro students who had finished the scientific course at Fisk University in June, 1905, returned "home" to deliver their graduating orations in Berea's Tabernacle on Commencement Day after the white exercises were over.[36] Each year until 1911 the trustees voted this aid to their former Negro students and a few additional Negroes of special promise; and the names of those accepting the offer were listed in the Berea catalog as "Berea College Students at Other Institutions." The numerous letters received by the College from these students *in absentia* show how great was their appreciation of their Alma Mater's care for them.

VIII

AFTER THE KENTUCKY Court of Appeals in 1906 upheld the legality of the Day law, the Berea trustees planned the establishment of a new Negro school or department. To some trustees and friends this action seemed like a disloyal retreat from the principle of interracial education; to others it savored of scorn for Negro rights. The trustee committee on care of the Negro people called attention to several important factors that influenced their decision to set up a good Negro school separate from Berea College; namely, that the Negroes seemed to be impressed by the success of such segregated schools as Fisk, Hampton, and Tuskegee, and that many of them expressed themselves as preferring schools for their own race. Believing that the Negroes had an equity both in the funds of the College and in the love and care of its trustees and workers, the committee recommended that the trustees undertake to raise a fund large enough to represent the Negro people's equity in the present college holdings and commensurate with their needs.[37]

The next task of the trustee committee was to determine in dollars the amount of the special fund to be raised for the Negro institution. The money given to Berea College in the past specifically for Negro education amounted to about $28,000. It was impossible to estimate how much was meant for Negro use in grants made by friends of the Negro people without definite designation of its purpose. Some other formula must be used.

Before 1892 the Negroes had constituted about half of the enrollment. If one assumed that they were entitled to half the property of the College in 1892, they would be entitled to a credit of $100,000. In the last school year before the Day law was passed, the Negroes numbered 157 to the whites' 804. If the property acquired by the College between 1892 and 1904 were divided on the basis of this enrollment, the Negroes would be entitled to about two-elevenths of this property, that is, $100,000. President Frost insisted, however, that $200,000 was not enough for setting up a worthy school, and so another $200,000 should be added. Since he would bear the burden of raising this sum, the trustees authorized the larger amount. Berea College would sequestrate $200,000 of her fixed property for the Negro school, and this loss to the white people would be replaced by that amount from the Adjustment Fund.[38] Within a year this $200,000 for replacement came from a single source, Andrew Carnegie.

Little by little other pledges were secured. In the fall of 1908 a donor offered $50,000 on condition that the people of Kentucky give the same amount. It was decided to raise part of Kentucky's share among the Negro people of the state, since they would benefit most from the fund. Two Negro alumni, Dr. James Bond and Principal Kirke Smith, did most of the work in raising this money among the Negroes. Altogether about 4,000 Negroes made subscriptions, which ranged from fifty cents to two hundred dollars, and amounted in all to $19,000. With the raising of Kentucky's share the Adjustment Fund was completed by July 1, 1909.[39]

From the time the Day bill was introduced into the House in 1904, there had been persistent whispers that President Frost would be altogether willing that the bill should pass, thus painlessly eliminating Negroes from the Berea school and increasing the number of mountain students willing to come. The president was aware of this sinister talk and repeatedly denied that it had any foundation in fact; but still it persisted. He was cut to the quick by the insulting words of a vocal minority, both Negro and white. The good news of Carnegie's grant of $200,000 to the Fund overwhelmed the Negroes living near enough Berea to know President Frost, and they held several praise meetings in Negro churches and schools to thank Carnegie, President Frost, and Berea College for their help. Letters were read from former students, old-time hymns were sung, and soul-stirring testimonies were given, such as, "I thank God for President Frost and for all the white people, for they all help us," and "All I am and hope to be I owe to Berea College." A meeting, with supper served by the women, was held in the Berea Negro schoolhouse in March. After many short speeches were made, President Frost explained why progress had been slow and asked for the prayers of all in his hard task of keeping one college going while starting another. He closed by revealing his heart to his Negro friends, saying in broken voice that he would be glad of the Judgment Day because then his heart could be seen and would give the lie to men who said that he was unfriendly to the Negro people.[40]

It was finally decided that the new Negro school should be an independent institution, not a department of Berea College, and that it should be of the Hampton type, emphasizing normal and industrial work at first, and adding college work when the situation should so demand. It was hard to find a site for it, but at length some 450 acres of good farm land were bought about twenty-one miles east of Louisville. The new institution, incorporated in January, 1910, was called Lincoln Institute, and its large administration building, the cornerstone of which was laid in November, 1911, was called Berea Hall. Lincoln Institute had its own Board of Trustees, its own president, the Reverend A. E. Thomson, its own donors, and its own funds.[41] After its incorporation in 1910 its history ceased to be a part of Berea's history.

IX

THE SEGREGATION LAW forced upon Berea College halfway through its first century created the most severe crisis in Berea's history. Even the best friends of the College held diverse opinions as to the wisest and most honorable course to follow. To many men the crisis seemed to have passed when the Adjustment Fund was raised for Lincoln Institute; but thoughtful men would continue to question Berea's sincerity if the institution could lightly turn its back upon a half century of interracial concern. From the days of Fee and Rogers, Berea's voice had said plainly that it was good for white and Negro youth in their college years to share their problems, their hopes, and their gifts, respecting the humanity of one another. The testing of Berea continued in the forty years following the Supreme Court's decision upholding the Day law.

Berea's interracial policy in the Fairchild administration had been based upon the idea that true education lies less in indoctrination than in providing rich experiences through which students could discover challenging causes and enduring values. Although under the Day law the enriching experience of interracial classrooms was forbidden, lawful ways were soon discovered by which the College might in a certain sense live above segregation. One of these ways was to bring to the college audience outstanding Negro speakers and musicians, so that students might learn how good the Negro "best" really was. President Frost was too deeply concerned with great financial and building plans to carry out this idea in a large way, but during the administration of President William J. Hutchins (1920-1939), Berea students each year heard at least one important Negro speaker or group of musicians. In this administration, the students heard Dr. George Washington Carver, the Fisk Jubilee Singers, Professor Alain Locke, Dean Howard Thurman, Principal Wallace Battle, and other important Negro leaders of thought. Perhaps the deepest impression was made by James Weldon Johnson in the college Chapel. The house was filled with an expectant audience. Quietly in his beautiful English the poet spoke of some Negro contributions to American culture, and they listened with respect and interest. Then he began to speak in a more intimate medium, "Listen, Lord," and "Creation." The young listeners saw God there on Creation Day, God looking at his sun, his moon, and his little stars. The boys drank in his words as though they were alone with him in a mountain cove. They saw God scooping the clay from the bed of his river and toiling over man's crude form to the last amen. Then the poet held them in the hollow of his hand with "Go down, Death," and "Crucifixion," and after that they belonged to him forever. The notebooks in their hands were left blank, for that day's lesson was written upon each soul.

Since 1940 Berea College has taken another step in interracial understanding. Berea students have had the opportunity to share in interracial conferences on their own campus, meeting Negro students from other colleges in round-table discussions. Mrs. Charles S. Johnson in opening one such conference expressed in a single telling sentence the spirit of these meetings: "I assume that we meet on the ground of a common concern."[42]

In recent years Berea College has publicly honored some of its Negro alumni distinguished for outstanding public service. In 1932 the College granted the degree of Doctor of Literature to Wallace Battle, an alumnus of the class of 1901, the founder and for twenty-five years the president of Okolona Industrial College: "Educator and advocate of the colored race, leader of his people from servitude to the service which is perfect freedom." At Commencement, 1944, a citation of honor was given to John W. Bate of Danville, Kentucky. The veteran educator was presented to President Francis S. Hutchins in words that immediately captured the audience, most of whom had never before seen an ex-slave and had only the faintest idea of what a little slave boy could do with his freedom: "Born in slavery, December 22, 1854; plunged into unspeakable poverty by emancipation; member of a despised race; caught the vision of complete living and rich service through education; laid his foundations for education in mission schools of Louisville; entered Berea as a student at the age of sixteen; received from Berea the A.B. degree in 1891, and an honorary A.M. degree in 1896; studied in Germany. By his unimpeachable character, vital interest in the community, and achievement, he has won the signal honor of First Citizen of Danville, to whom the citizens affectionately refer as OUR OWN BOOKER T. WASHINGTON."[43] President Hutchins then awarded Professor Bate the citation of honor, reading these words as well as others from the citation: "For six decades the leader of a school in the city of Danville—a school which grew from one teacher to fifteen, from six students to six hundred, . . . a son who has treasured and practiced the finest teaching of this College." Professor Bate's presence and his affecting reminiscences during this visit revived the memory of Berea's heroic past, from which the Day law was powerless to segregate the Berea of 1944.

Another means through which Negroes and whites were helped into a better understanding was the Middletown Consolidated School established in 1927 about one mile north of Berea. A $12,000 brick building was erected by the county with the help of a $1,000 grant from the Julius Rosenwald Fund. Berea College gave four acres of land for this elementary school, and extended its water and electric lines out to the building. At its dedication the president of Berea College, after speaking about the ugliness of race hatred, showed how this school might become a bridge for all who came there.[44] The College, it is true, has helped this school, but the Middletown School in its turn has been of great help to Berea students. Robert Blythe, the principal of this school for twenty-eight years, has co-operated with the College in providing valuable experience in race relations to white students. The College Y.M.C.A. and Y.W.C.A. help in the school's recreation program. College classes in social case work have been able to include Negro families in their studies through Principal Blythe's aid. Students in Bible and in social problems have presented programs to the school, and student groups have been welcomed by the Negro teachers to help in preparing for the Christmas and other entertainments.

x

THE DOOR THAT HAD been closed in 1904 to Negroes wishing to study in Berea was opened again in 1950. In 1949 a federal district judge ordered the University of Kentucky to admit Negro students to its graduate schools, since segregated education was not "equal" education. Then at its next session, 1950, the legislature of Kentucky amended the Day law so as to allow the coeducation of white and Negro students in public or private schools above the high school level, "provided the governing authorities of the institution, corporation, group or body so elect, and provided that an equal, complete and accredited course is not available at the Kentucky State College for Negroes."[45]

In their April meeting, 1950, the trustees of Berea College reaffirmed Berea's dedication to the youth of the Appalachian mountain region "to which we have tried to minister for nearly a century," and after expressing Berea's "interest in the efforts of Negro youth of this region to secure an education," they empowered the administration "to admit such Negro students from within this mountain region whom it finds thoroughly qualified, coming completely within provisions of the Kentucky law, and whom in its judgment it appears we should serve."[46]

By this action Berea has remained an institution especially devoted to the mountain people. The Negro candidates for admission are expected to present the same character and scholastic qualifications as the whites. In 1950 three Negro students were admitted to the College; in 1951, eleven; in 1952 and 1953, twelve each year; and in 1954, sixteen. The small number of Negro admissions since 1950 is explained by: the small number of Negroes resident in the southern mountains; the poorer educational opportunities for Negroes in elementary and secondary work; and Berea's policy of admitting Negro applicants most likely to do college work well. Another factor that probably has helped in the new adjustment has been the presence upon the campus of an unusual number of students from the Orient who are somewhat different in complexion and features from Americans of west-European ancestry.

After Negroes had been admitted in 1950, they were welcomed into campus organizations according to their gifts and tastes. One played in the students' "royal collegians"; another sang in the varsity women's glee club. Several sang in the chapel choir. One man played on the varsity basketball team, and another was a member of the track team. Negroes also were chosen to carry responsibilities. One of the leading parts in a major spring production of the dramatic club was taken successfully by a Negro, and another Negro girl was chosen president of the women's association. In 1953 a Negro girl was selected to give the address on an all-student Thanksgiving program, and one was named for *Who's Who in American Colleges and Universities* by vote of upper-class students and faculty. In 1954 a Negro girl, admitted to Berea's School of Nursing, was awarded a four-year scholarship of $200 a year by the national board of the Daughters of the American Revolu-

tion in order that she might fulfill her desire to become a public
health nurse among her people in eastern Kentucky.[47]

Berea College in its century of interrace experience has not
disproved either the existence or the strength of race prejudice;
but it has illustrated some ways in which traditional inocula-
tion can be overcome by men and women of good will, closely
knit into an interracial college community where there is co-
ordination of study, labor, recreation, and social service, accompanied by a patient confidence that time is of the essence
in working out problems of human relations.

4: The Mountain
Field

THE FIRST Constitution of Berea College, as has been said,
stated no preference for any one race of students, nor did it
mention any region which would receive Berea's special care.
At the close of the Civil War, however, the first Berea catalog
(1867) mentioned two groups of people who were in need of
Berea's educational offerings: (1) the recently emancipated
Negroes; (2) "the white people of eastern Kentucky and similar
regions in adjoining States." The Negroes were so few in number in the mountain counties that to speak of mountain people
meant to speak of whites. The preceding chapter has considered Berea's experience in Negro education. The present
chapter will deal with the mountain area as a field of work,
the growth of interest in the mountain people's nature and
needs, the rivalry that eventually sprang up between Berea's
two fields of concern, and after Negro exclusion, the use of a
quota to protect the mountain people from other white applicants who were less in need of Berea's improved facilities
than were the people in the mountain counties, so that today
about 90 per cent of the students attending Berea College come
from 230 counties in eight states which lie in the southern
Appalachian area.

II

Cassius M. Clay, though opposed to the institution of slavery, was primarily interested in the white man's freedom, and he bestowed his favors upon the Berea community because it would strengthen the nonslaveholder's position. Later in life he frankly said that helping the Berea cause "served a great purpose" in his political career.[1]

Before the Civil War, John G. Fee as a thoroughgoing abolitionist worked against the institution of slavery, and his experience with emancipated Negroes at Camp Nelson turned his thoughts strongly toward plans for educating them after war had ended. Ultimately Negro education became almost as consuming an interest to him as the abolition of slavery had been in antebellum days. Therefore he tended to devote himself more fully to the Negro than to the mountain students.

Fee and Clay were Kentuckians, and knew much more about the mountain people than did Rogers, who had been reared in Connecticut; but Rogers was determined to become better acquainted with his new field of work. In the summer of 1858 soon after his first term of school on the Ridge had closed, he set out upon a mountain trip by horseback with Fee. Today we might say that he did not go very deeply into Kentucky's hill country, as his journey took him from Berea through Rockcastle, Pulaski, and McCreary counties, and back through Laurel and Jackson; yet it was an eye-opening experience to him, and upon his return he at once wrote four articles about what he had seen. These were published in the *Independent* (New York) in the fall of 1858.

Rogers saw things with a teacher's eye, and he wrote down his impressions so soon that they did not become colored by time's fantasy. He remarked that in mountain schools the poor equipment, "seats made of rails and slabs, few books," was less distressing to him than the poor training of the teacher, who was usually a very poor reader. He saw "many scholars who went out and came in as they pleased," and a teacher with his heels on a desk. "Before I left, he commanded his scholars to study; thereupon the members of the school set their lungs as well as their eyes to work. Spelling, which with reading and writing not unusually comprises the whole course of study, was the order for an hour. A roar ensued, not unlike that of a pack of artillery. The air seemed filled with splinters of words and syllables."[2]

In speaking of religion in the hill country he said: "Christianity has sunk to a mere formalism on the part of some, and is supposed by others to consist in ebullitions of feeling." As to homes he wrote: "Though travelling over productive lands, which in a wild state can be bought at prices varying from one to five dollars per acre, you will rarely see any other than a log house—frequently not for thirty miles. The use of glass in some localities is scarcely known. . . . Corn meal, coffee, and bacon are the universal articles of diet, and many families rarely taste anything else." As to the origin of the people his words were: "The inhabitants are the descendents of the early settlers of Virginia and North Carolina, and not a few of them are of houses of note." When he turned to the individual mountaineer he said: "One of the first mountain men I saw was in form, feature, and bearing a perfect facsimile of a Spanish cavalier of the olden time. The degree of admiration I felt for him was lessened when I visited his cheerless cabin, occupied by a numerous family, alike devoid of knowledge and comforts."[3] At Cumberland Falls he was impressed by the amount of unused water power: "There is scarcely a house within a hundred miles of the Falls in which there is not a loom; and here is a power sufficient to drive a thousand of them—but unused."[4] These articles written by Rogers in 1858 form a coherent statement of mountain life at the beginning of Berea's history.

In 1869 Rogers in speaking of mountain students who were registering in the newly opened College remarked that many of them were Union veterans "whose ideas had been enlarged and energies developed by the War," so that they were seeking an education. He remarked that some of them had had to endure great reproach from their relatives and companions because of going to an institution admitting Negroes. "Three years ago it required a degree of moral courage for a young white man to connect himself with the institution quite as great as for Luther to go to the Diet of Worms. And although three years have made astonishing changes in this respect, there are many who secretly long to be at Berea, who cannot endure the scorn that would be heaped upon them, if they should enter an institution very unpopular with many."[5]

III

THOUGH PRESIDENT Fairchild in his earlier years had been a strong worker against slavery and though as president of Berea College he gave loving care to his Negro students, he paid an increasing measure of attention to the people of the hills. In 1873 he published an article about the fine mountain families who were preparing to move to Berea to enjoy its educational advantages.[6] In his book (1875) introducing Berea College he devoted seven pages to the educational famine among the mountain people, calling attention to their high rate of illiteracy, their poor schoolhouses sometimes without floors or even a door, and their lack of schoolbooks; and said that the best means of raising the standard was "to induce many of their most promising young men and women to go to some good school and fit themselves for teachers."[7] In 1882 he issued a donors' folder containing an article on the social needs of the mountain people, "The Other Folk of Kentucky," by Dr. A. D. Mayo of Washington, D. C.

Charles G. Fairchild, professor of science in Berea College and eldest son of its president, in 1883 wrote an account of rural life in the Kentucky hills as he had seen it: "They are an agricultural people, . . . the homestead often having been handed down through two or three generations. . . . Often a family will not see $50 in cash the year round. Even the old hand looms find friendly shelter in those Rip Van Winkle hollows. A man that moved from these regions to Berea that he might give his children an education, wore upon his back his carefully preserved wedding suit, the wool for which he himself had cut from the backs of his father's sheep. . . . A little shovel, a handmade hoe, and an unkempt mule with a straw collar make up the agricultural outfit. . . . More than half of the adult white population native born, of the same stock and lineage that furnished from the more favored sections the Clays and Breckinridges, that gave to this country Abraham Lincoln —more than half of this white population cannot read or write."[8]

The most interesting expression of President Fairchild's concern over mountain backwardness was his baccalaureate sermon of 1881, where he laid before his students the improvements which he would expect them to make in the mountain communities where they would serve as district schoolteachers. This long-range plan for the betterment of superrural mountain life was in a sense an outline that forecast Berea's program for the next fifty years.

1. Improvement in housing. "The log huts without windows and with one or two rooms, must give place to neatly painted and glazed dwellings surrounded by neat fences and beautiful yards, and with fine orchards and vineyards."

2. Ceiled and painted schoolhouses provided with desks, windows, and stoves.

3. A supply of books and papers in each home and in Sunday school and district school libraries.

4. A public school fund four or five times as large as at that time.

5. "Comfortable free roads in every direction through the mountains."

6. Preaching and Sunday school every week conducted by ministers who could devote their entire time to spiritual and educational work instead of doing manual work for a living.

IV

PRESIDENT FROST's emphasis upon the mountain field grew rapidly in the early years of his administration. In July, 1892, while considering Berea's second invitation to him to accept the presidency of Berea College, he wrote from Goettingen a long letter in regard to his understanding of Berea's work: "The peculiar work of Berea for years to come, that which secures for her the support of men and the blessing of heaven, is for the colored race."[9] After his retirement from the presidency this grandson of the abolitionist William Goodell wrote that he was not sure that he would ever have come to Berea "if it had not been for my ancestral and personal interest in befriending the colored race."[10] In his inaugural address, 1893, the nearest approach he made to the mountain field was to say: "Our cities may be purified by air from these Cumberland Mountains," and about the same time in his first annual report he wrote: "So too, the mountain whites belong to Berea. We are under the impression that Berea discovered them. But it is not Berea which is educating the mountain whites today. We can hardly count up two score mountain whites in all the school."

In the summer following his inauguration (1893), President Frost spent several weeks traveling horseback in Jackson and Owsley counties with Frank Hays, a mountain veteran who had moved from Jackson County to Berea for his children's sake. Each schoolday President Frost would speak in three schoolhouses, and then at night he would speak to parents on the value of education. When the day was done, Hays would answer the president's questions and would put his finger on the president's words that might offend his audience. On Saturday and Sunday, President Frost would preach, and again his monitor would work upon him. After a few weeks of such training President Frost ceased to use the opprobrious term "mountain whites," and out of his increasing respect for the mountain people he began to show an unusual interest in mountain students and their homes.

Already before coming to Berea College as its president, he had suggested a plan for the recovery of Berea's institutional health: that the number of students should be increased and the quality of instruction improved. He suggested that if a considerable number of students from northern states were drawn to register in Berea College, an increase of "white students from the South" would soon follow. During his first year in Berea he corresponded with the Reverend William E. Barton, a Berea College alumnus of 1885 who held a pastorate in Ohio, and through Barton's help secured twenty-six northern students to enter Berea College in the fall of 1893. "A pitifully small return for all our effort," wrote Barton; but the northern students excelled in effort and ability, and their example led other Ohio students to apply for admission long after Barton had taken a Boston church.[11]

In February, 1894, President Frost wrote one of the most significant documents of his entire administration, a paper which shows how far he had traveled in a year and a half of thinking over the mountain field. He admitted that Berea had lost its white students except the children of the village, and was ready to give up its College Department and become simply a Negro school like Camp Nelson. Now he outlined to the faculty the three steps by which Berea might retrieve this defeat, steps which had been vaguely in his mind when he wrote from Goettingen and which had been clarified by his month in the mountains.

1. Berea should continue to bring in white students from the North. Barton's twenty-six good students from Ohio were already on the campus.

2. Berea should use these white students year after year as a means for recovering the white students from the mountains. In ardent words so characteristic of this sanguine leader President Frost wrote: "The presence of these northern whites will enable us to reach the mountaineers and not only save

them from the contamination that is creeping in among them, but actually bring them up as a re-enforcement to the moral force of the nation."

3. Berea College should create such enthusiasm and re-forming zeal among its students, Negro and white, as would make them forget their everyday hardships, "and fit them to become recruiting officers for the College and exponents of the Berea idea in the uttermost parts of the earth." This third step, said President Frost, remained to be taken. Improvement in scholarship and finances would be of little value until the spirit of self-improvement and helpfulness to others was infused into the hearts of Berea students.[12]

President Frost had adopted the improvement of mountain life through education as his life's cause—a cause for donors, for students, and for his faculty—as opposition to slavery had been his grandfather's cause. He showed his newborn love for the mountain people in a tangible way in this February report when he urged the faculty to use corn bread rather than white bread and to give thought to building their new homes after the mountain type "with the outside chimney, the charming rafters, and the broad porch." In his June report to the faculty in the same year (1894) he went so far as to say, "Our success in breaking down caste is measured by the number of white students." On the same page he referred to the Negroes, but in a sympathetic tone that might seem both patronizing and irritating to a young Negro about to graduate from Berea College: "Our colored students for whose sake we are undertaking the great burden of obloquy and opposition, constitute a fine body of young people."[13]

When speaking to a teachers' convention in Cincinnati, Ohio, a year after this time, he reflected the joy that he felt in his new-found cause: "I am here to announce the discovery of a new world, or at least a new grand subdivision. Have you ever heard of Appalachian America? Just as our western frontier has been lost in the Pacific Ocean, we have discovered a new pioneer region in the mountains of the central South."[14]

In the same year (1895) it became clear that he had introduced his new cause to prospective donors, for Dr. D. K. Pearsons of Chicago, in making his pledge of $50,000 for endowment provided the College would match it by raising $150,000 of new endowment funds, closed his offer with these words: "I make this gift to all humanity, and especially to the loyal people of these mountains."[15]

Before the Day law, passed in 1904, diverted his attention, President Frost aroused great interest in the mountain cause by writing a number of articles on the mountain people for outstanding magazines: *Ladies' Home Companion*, September, 1896; *Outlook*, September 3, 1898; *Atlantic Monthly*, March, 1899 (nine pages); *American Monthly Review of Reviews*, March, 1900; and *Missionary Review of the World*, January, 1901 (eleven pages). In 1895 he established the *Berea Quarterly*, which continued until 1916 and ultimately constituted a thesaurus of uncopyrighted mountain material available for public use.

President Frost also captured public attention for Berea's cause by notable meetings. The first of these was a dinner meeting at the Thorndike Hotel in Boston, November, 1894, which included among its speakers the distinguished Harvard professor Dr. N. S. Shaler, who had been born in Kentucky and had served there as state geologist from 1873 to 1880. This was followed over the years by similar dinner meetings in New York and Cincinnati as well as in Boston, each with an address by President Frost and some notable guest speaker. After the Negro exclusion issue had been adjusted, President Frost arranged a great meeting in Carnegie Hall, New York, with the former president of Columbia University, Seth Low, as chairman and with Governor Woodrow Wilson as the principal speaker. In a letter from President Taft and a telegram from Justice John M. Harlan of Kentucky that were read to the audience before the addresses, emphasis was laid upon Berea's mountain work, and Woodrow Wilson devoted his entire time to the presentation of the southern mountain area as a frontier region. In President Frost's last great meeting, held in Washington, D.C., in 1915, he spoke on "The Scotland of America" and President Wilson spoke upon the general theme of Berea's work for the mountains and thereby for the nation. These meetings built up a new group of friends who took to their hearts President Frost's cause, Appalachian America, as he called the mountain area.

In 1896 President Frost began to use in his publicity a small map which showed very distinctly by hachures the southern mountain region. Personally he had a strong antiquarian taste, and he often indulged this taste to relieve the heaviness of his serious words. He loved the quaint old English words and phrases that he heard in his frequent journeys to the mountains. Though he was not musical by nature, he grew to love the old ballads that came from the hills. He loved the mountain grease lamp as an Anglo-Saxon survival, and he drew his breath in wonder at sight of a homemade wooden lock on a mountain meathouse, the handiwork of some ingenious man working in the old way. Out of his love for the mountain people he began to call them by a phrase that came from his own fertile mind, "our contemporary ancestors."

He was soon able to inspire some of Berea's most gifted teachers with his new cause. In 1900 Silas C. Mason, professor of forestry, wrote an excellent pamphlet for mountain people on "Hints on how to get money to come to school." Miss Josephine Robinson, professor of higher mathematics, took up the task of buying and selling the mountain women's weavings, although such handwork was entirely aside from her professional work. Principal Bruce Hunting before his death in 1898, and two women who excelled in teacher training, Mrs. Daisy Carlock (a sister of Elbert Hubbard) and Mrs. Eliza Yocum, repeatedly traversed the mountain valleys to tell young teachers what Berea College offered them.

By 1902 President Frost was able to say in his annual report: "This College now stands before the public as the representative school for the mountains, as Hampton and Tuskegee stand as the representative institutions for the colored people."[16] By this time Berea College as a whole had a student registration of more than eight hundred students; but President Frost's cares extended far beyond the problem of increasing the number of mountain students. He must find more donors to finance the buildings and the salaries of such an institution, and his financing would be in vain if he did not adapt Berea's academic program to the needs of these students. He must develop such a work program as would enable students without money resources to make their way in school, and also he must adapt Berea's men and resources to the solution of problems in the mountain area of eight states.

He knew that the mountain problems were too great for one generation to solve, but he could never forget the illiteracy that made life dull, the isolation that bred feuds, the ignorance that made life harder than it need have been, and the poor teaching that handicapped every mountain child. Although he sometimes waxed sentimental over the log cabins and the spinning wheel, more often he was grim at thought of the bareness of the mountain man's inner life.

For five years after the Day law was passed, President Frost devoted most of his time to the Negroes' cause, but finally in 1909 he was able to return to his main concern, writing in his annual report of that year: "The mountain work, the field of Berea's discovery and devotion, now claims our full attention. . . . The changes of new life are knocking at every door. The mountain people will be quickly spoiled and lost if they are not befriended, guided, and saved." When he returned at last to the mountain work, he had to limit his activity to a greatly reduced time schedule. The last decade of his administration was marked by a constant struggle to surmount the nervous exhaustion resulting from his years of overwork. The wonder is that one man could have accomplished as much as President Frost did accomplish.

He learned about mountain life from scholars, from statistical tables, from faculty criticisms, from visits in the hills, and from such intimate letters as those from which the following excerpts were made in order to reveal his closeness to the human side of his "Cause."

The first was written by a mountain preacher on behalf of his nineteen-year-old son: "How much money is it necessary that he should get there with? We are very poor. I have a little circuit that pays a little less than $200 per year. So far I have received about $20 in money, and about $6 in other articles, so I had to take my two sons from school and we have all been working at the carpenters' trade. I would love so much to send both my boys to Berea to school."

The second letter was written by a mountain boy from South Carolina. He returned five dollars to President Frost, explaining: "When leaving Berea I received more money than was coming to me. Now I have decided to lead a Christian life, and I want to feel clear of everything I have done."

The third letter was written by a girl from Breathitt County in the Kentucky mountains: "Often while at work there at home a longing would come into my heart for something that I could not understand. I knew out beyond those hills was a place where I could learn what that longing in my heart meant. One day a man came to the log schoolhouse where I had gone to school. I never was the same after hearing him speak. I realized that I was meant to do something, but I didn't know what it was. I came to Berea to find my calling. That old longing comes into my heart sometimes; then for a time it's gone, but anyway it's still there."

v

PRESIDENT AND MRS. Frost had traveled together in the Kentucky mountains many a season, but in the summer of 1914 Mrs. Frost went on a five-hundred mile journey on horseback through the mountains without her husband, because by this time he was unable to bear the strain of such a trip. As they were about to enter into a campaign to raise a million dollars for Berea's expansion, she felt their need to secure fresh information about Berea's impact upon mountain life. That she was fifty-one years old meant little to her. She took along her young son Cleveland, who was eighteen and a good hand with horses. She was an ageless kind of woman, sensitive and perceptive.

Their first three weeks were spent in Owsley County, where Berea's influence had been strong for many years. They rode by way of the creeks, since the county had as yet neither a railroad nor a hard-surfaced road, and followed a penciled "creek map" which an old settler had drawn for them. They looked up some three hundred people from that county who had attended school in Berea sometime in the past twenty years, and stayed in the home of a Berea student every night during the three weeks. Mrs. Frost visited at least one country school a day, and each Saturday afternoon and Sunday attended a country church service. What she learned in a school, a church, or a home was beyond expression in figures, but it gave her and her husband much to think about in the years ahead. Owsley County's hospitality was so warm that she wrote: "I registered a vow that when any of these old students or their parents come to Berea, they shall stay at our house even if the President of the United States has to be turned away to make room for them."[17]

When she attended a teachers' institute, she was glad to hear the county superintendent, a former Berea student, give a plain talk to fifteen school trustees, warning them that they must not ask him to make it easy for their own sons to get a teaching certificate, for he would be deaf to any such request.[18]

From Owsley County Mrs. Frost rode through Clay and Leslie counties, passing through heavily wooded lands, "log cabin country," where she often found the schoolhouse shabby, sometimes without steps or a well, often equipped with crude benches and few desks; but she noticed when the floor was freshly scrubbed and the teacher alert and sympathetic. She wrote: "I left those shut-in valleys with a fresh gratitude for the public school system. With all its imperfections, what a power if we can only put a real teacher into each schoolroom!"[19]

Because she had visited mountain schools before, she was able to recognize relative progress, though she still saw too many one-room schools with a teacher who had gone no further than the eighth grade. While she was glad to see the new graded schools that were being built, she could not put out of her mind the idea that the one-room school in the secluded ravine would remain the local school for many years to come, since good roads were slow to come into the deep valleys of mountain counties. The Normal dean at Berea, Dr. C. N. McAllister, had been talking about the need for a one-room practice school attended by rural children in a rural community. Now Mrs. Frost saw as never before the need for improving the teachers who for many a year to come would go into these one-room country schools.

She gave considerable thought to the mountain church, for Berea is a Christian college which has a concern for a student's understanding and practice of Christian ideas, regardless of his religious denomination. In the back country she found, as she had expected, preachers who made their living by farming, storekeeping, or both—uneducated men who had had no chance for an education, but men to be respected because they kept alive in human hearts the love of God and respect for the Bible. She found, as she had expected, the singing man, tuning fork in hand, lining out each verse before the people sang; but then at a funeral under the trees one day she heard the singing man lead the people in a hymn which recalled the days of her own childhood in Wisconsin, and when she reflected that there were few hymnbooks available and that many persons at the funeral could not read, the old-fashioned way seemed to her an altogether natural custom.

She heard rhapsodic preaching, as had very many Berea students of those days, and she heard the congregation respond with deep sighs and amens. Then she wrote:

"The rhapsodic style of preaching has in it an element of great value. It stands in their minds for what we mean when we say of a preacher: 'He is lost in his subject.' The man is out of sight. In some way I would like to see it brought to pass that our students, when they go home, should not go to church and sit in the seat of the scornful. Let them take part in the meetings, fall in with the lining of tunes when that is the custom of the congregation. . . . I would like to see our men let themselves go, say with fervor the things they believe, and let the grammar come as it will. When they are in accord with what the preacher has said, let them express it."[20]

When a controversy was impending at a long church service, the issue being whether a man could be saved if he was not elected to be saved, Mrs. Frost arose in her place, though a stranger, and told of her own youthful doubts. She pointed to the corn growing close to the church: "Man's part and God's part are in that crop. So it is with the spirit." The women gathered around and followed her to dinner, where twenty guests ate together. She wrote to her husband: "After dinner we talked religion all afternoon. A man said, 'People here are starving for religion.' "[21]

Mrs. Frost said that the most restful part of her trip was calling on mountain mothers. Seldom in college history does a president's wife come so close to students' mothers. She was to them Berea College, and they felt free to ask her many questions as they sat talking on a summer evening. That was why she felt free to ask them why so many of their boys left Berea before the term had ended. The mothers' most frequent answer was "homesickness." A boy had been at the hospital sick with the measles, and then he was released as well; but he still felt very weak, and he thought of his mother at home. His home might be a very small cabin, but his mother lived in it, and she was the one who understood all about things, even without his telling her in words. She knew that he was sick in his heart, homesick. Sometimes he longed for the home food at breakfast instead of the boarding hall's oatmeal, longed for hot biscuit and ham gravy so much that he went home never to come back. Some people say that nowadays boys do not go home for such trifling reasons, perhaps because the world has invaded the mountains so deeply, or because today more than 70 per cent of the students are pursuing a four-year course for a college degree. The mothers admitted, too, that sometimes the boys went home because they missed the fun of getting logs off on the spring tide. Sometimes the very thought of the piggies at home was too much for them, but that only showed how much they loved the farm. Home was home, and a mother understood all about such things.

Mrs. Frost learned that mountain women had their luxuries, such as beautiful homespun, hand-woven coverlets that were perfectly matched, soft homespun blankets, pieced quilts that were like mosaics, and well-filled feather beds and pillows. There might be a beautiful bureau in a house without a single screened window or door. There might be a grandfather's clock, brought over the mountains from Virginia in pioneer days. No matter how poorly balanced the usual family diet might be, they had their food luxuries, home-cured ham, honey from the bee gums by the picket fence, goose plum preserves, and blackberry stackpies—one delicious pie upon another until the pile three or four inches in height could be cut like a layer cake.

In the mountains of Kentucky Mrs. Frost saw some large houses that were well kept, and others that were dirty or untidy, or both. The same might be said of the smaller houses and the log cabins. Berea's voice seemed to her too weak on the homemaking side. She wished to have a homemaking experience go with each diploma given to a Berea girl. The College could fit up five old dwelling houses as model farm homes with yards and chicken coops. She resolved that in the coming expansion campaign she would raise money with which to establish a country home for each department, in order to show how families could live well without even water works, electric lights, or ice. Moreover, she resolved that courses in home economics should be introduced into the College Department's curriculum. These two ideas were finally carried into execution, and in a modified form have remained a living part of Berea College.

VI

THE TRUSTEES in 1911 added to the Constitution a brief statement that recognized the southern mountain area as Berea's special field. This statement, embedded in Article II, said that Berea's aim in education was to be promoted "primarily by contributing to the spiritual and material welfare of the mountain region of the South." Nine years before this constitutional change was made, President Frost in 1902 had expressed the same idea when he spoke of "the Mountain Region, which is Berea's peculiar field,"[22] and when he said: "Berea has a mission of its own. . . . Our largest and most prominent work at present is for the great mountain region of the South."[23]

In 1915 the Prudential Committee of Berea College, with the approval of the trustees, took a step which really grew out of the 1911 addition to the Constitution. This resolution provided "that no more students from outside the mountain region as defined by the Russell Sage Foundation shall be admitted except in rare and exceptional cases by permission of the President or the Registrar." It was also voted at this meeting that waiting lists should be established when all available shelter was occupied. The reason given for this first "out-of-territory" restriction policy was that it seemed unfair to mountain students that they should be crowded out to make room for students from more favored parts of the country.[24]

Although the new regulation was stated in the 1916 catalog, no list of what were recognized as mountain counties appeared until the catalog of 1917 listed 265 counties in the eight states of Alabama, Georgia, Kentucky, North Carolina, South Carolina, Tennessee, Virginia, and West Virginia. In 1919 a further step was taken by inserting a ten-inch map showing the location of the counties specified as mountain counties. From 1920 to 1925 no list nor county map of such counties was included in the catalog; but beginning with the catalog of August, 1921, a very small map of the mountain area was printed above the interesting subscription: "The Field of Berea—The Mountains of the South." Since 1926 each catalog has carried a list of mountain counties considered at that time in Berea's field, for occasional changes are made, including dropping twenty-five West Virginia counties from the Russell Sage Foundation's map.

The Berea Way, a bulletin designed to introduce incoming freshmen to student life at Berea College, in its 1954-1955 edition gave two pages to "The Field of Berea." Since some nonmountain students were sure to be accepted, it was, of course, important that they should feel themselves an integral part of the college community and under no handicap because of being nonmountain students. The paragraph preceding the names of mountain counties speaks of the list as that "from which students are given preference," and adds the reassurance: "However, students from outside this area will be given careful consideration." On the opposite page is a map with state lines indicated and Berea's mountain field clearly shown, and the statement appended: "Over ninety per cent of Berea's students come from 230 mountain counties of Southern Appalachia."

Much thought has been given to the possible use of a quota to restrict the admission of nonmountain students. In 1922 an 8 per cent quota was applied to nonmountain students below College rank, but none to College students. By 1925 a College quota of 25 per cent had been reduced to 15 per cent, and by 1937 the quota was fixed at 10 per cent for all departments. The catalog of the year 1937 stated what has been the admission policy since that time: "Berea College exists primarily for the people of the Southern mountains. . . . In general not more than 10 per cent of the students are accepted from outside this territory."

The records of the registrar's office for 1953-1954 show 12.9 per cent nonmountain students in the total registration for that year; 10.8 per cent in 1950-1951; 16.7 per cent in 1943-1944; 7.8 per cent in 1940-1941; 9.9 per cent in 1933-1934. The highest percentage of nonmountain students was 20.5 in the troubled postwar year of 1946-1947; the lowest in the record was 6.5 in 1927-1928. Once admitted, the origin of the nonmountain student is forgotten unless he himself causes the subject to be raised.

To recognize that Berea College draws about 90 per cent of her students from this mountain area is important for the functioning of her educational program, so that remedial work may be provided early in a student's course if he needs it, that students may be guided into course work in the social, economic, and cultural problems of the mountains, and that mountain students may be given encouragement to prepare for leadership in fields that are especially in need of trained men and women, such as agriculture, home economics, medicine, and public service.

This devotion of Berea College to the welfare of the mountain people has been followed by an unusual love of the mountain people for Berea. A traveler through the mountains in 1922 wrote what has been expressed in substance many times over: "My most profound impression was the universal confidence of the people in Berea."

CHAPTER 5: Changing Patterns
of Education

THE INSTITUTION that opened its crude door in 1855 to
the children around the Berea Ridge was legally a district
school; but in the minds of a few men it was a rudimentary
college. On January 4, 1856, John G. Fee wrote to Gerrit
Smith: "We have for months been talking about starting an
academy—and eventually look to a college."[1] Two weeks after
Professor Rogers' subscription school gave its closing entertainment in June, 1858, John G. Fee wrote to a friend: "We think
the interests of truth and humanity now require a school of a
higher grade—one that shall prepare young men and young
ladies to go out as teachers; and as soon as possible, one that
shall confer degrees."[2] Moreover, the institution for which Fee,
Rogers, Hanson, and others framed a constitution in the year
following this letter was to be a college that would furnish the
facilities for a thorough education, and Berea College still
makes this promise to its students and their parents.

These three elements were a part of the original warp of
Berea College, a *college* that would confer *degrees* at the close
of a *thorough* education; but there was a fourth element in
the prewar pattern. In the first Constitution of the College
(1859) it was written that this education was to be *Christian;*

and this thread, too, has remained a part of Berea's foundation. Repeatedly Fee interpreted the meaning of the simple words, "a Christian education," as one that would teach not merely the classics and the natural sciences, but also moral science, "that science which teaches . . . the principles of love in religion, and liberty and justice in government."[3]

Berea College shows three distinct educational patterns woven upon this original warp. The first was that which was designed to meet the clamoring needs of newly emancipated freedmen for whom the state had made little educational preparation. The second pattern was that of practical education for the plain people of the mountains "from the bottom up," when President Frost turned the full energies of a revived college to work upon mountain problems. The third pattern was that which has been woven from the time of the demobilization after World War I to the present, three and a half decades in which the nation's unusual economic, social, and religious unrest has shown the need for well-trained young leaders in the mountain field, and far beyond it.

A very noticeable peculiarity of Berea College in the period between 1866 and 1892 was that the College Department was very small as compared with the rest of the institution, especially as compared with the elementary schools below the Preparatory level, that is, Primary, Intermediate, and Grammar School. The first College freshmen, five in number, were enrolled in 1869, when the total enrollment of the institution was 307; and the first College class, numbering three in a department of nineteen, was graduated in 1873, when the total enrollment of the institution was 287. In 1880 out of a total of 309 students, 26 were in the College, 53 in the Preparatory Department, and 230 in the elementary schools. In 1885 the total enrollment was 312, but only 30 of these were College students. In 1890 when the total enrollment was 355, only 28 were College students. In but one year, 1879, did the College Department number as many as 42. The pressing demand of Berea in those days was for elementary education.

While Berea College took great pains to give the rudiments of an education to those who had a poor start in life, it was careful to see that the work of College students should be mature and thorough. It is easy to understand why Angus Burleigh in 1875 brought from the hills a cypress sapling and planted it at Ladies' Hall as his graduation memorial, for he was graduating from the classical course.[4] In those days the College assumed that classical freshmen had already studied beginning courses in Latin, Greek, and mathematics. The school year was divided into three terms of twelve weeks each, and a student took three (or occasionally four) courses each term. The classical student must offer for graduation from College six terms of Latin, nine terms of Greek, five terms of higher mathematics, seven terms of science, six terms of philosophy, two terms of history, one each of political science and of English literature, and a half term of rhetoric.

In 1874-1875 a two-year literary course was added to the College offerings. It required no Greek, only three terms of Latin, three terms of beginning French or German, and fewer courses of science. This was later changed to a scientific course of two years. In 1890-1891 between the scientific and the classical course a three-year philosophical course was arranged, which added six terms of Greek and three terms of modern language to the scientific course. The catalog of 1890-1891 announced that hereafter degrees would be given to the College graduates as follows: Bachelor of Arts, Bachelor of Philosophy, and Bachelor of Science. On the same page the catalog announced that the College by special action might grant a Master's degree to certain graduates who for three or more years had engaged in work which would greatly increase proficiency in their special field.

Before the College Department was organized, the catalog bore on its outside cover the words "Berea Literary Institute," with an explanation on page 2 that this name was used "as more in consonance with the present character of the school," but an announcement was made on the title page that this was "the first catalog of Berea College." When the College Department was introduced in 1869, the term "Berea Literary Institute" ceased to be used.

As there was a great need for district schoolteachers in the early days of Berea College, a normal course for teacher training was set up in 1867 in the Preparatory Department. This course, which was intended to be rigorous and thorough, included four terms of Latin, six terms of mathematics (ending with trigonometry), five terms of science (beginning with physical geography and ending with chemistry), as well as courses in philosophy, history, English, and lectures on teaching. In 1879 a four-week course of "Practice in Teaching" was introduced, but was soon replaced by pedagogical lectures. In 1883 a complete change in policy was announced for teacher training. Students who satisfactorily completed certain courses in arithmetic, grammar, geography, physiology, English, bookkeeping, penmanship and algebra "would be given a certificate of their attainments, recommending them to employers of teachers as having completed an adequate Normal course." A course of lectures on the theory and practice of teaching was given for prospective teachers each spring; and as for observation, the catalog thereafter repeated year after year: "It is designed that the management of daily classes shall furnish examples of correct and thorough instruction."

The elementary schools offered the customary instruction in reading, spelling, writing, arithmetic, penmanship, and geography, but the catalogs show no sign of an offer to train in any industrial skills. The nearest approach to home economics was the announcement in the catalogs of 1891 and 1892 that "the young ladies received special instruction in the making and repairing of garments," but this was as a convenience, not a course.

During this period the administration was very simple. The president was assisted in business matters by the Prudential Committee. A professor acted as secretary and treasurer, besides teaching. Another professor acted as principal of the

Preparatory Department, in addition to teaching. There was no registrar, director of admissions, nor dean of labor. A professor devoted part of his time to service as librarian.

The faculty consisted of the College professors, all of whom were well-educated men with higher degrees. Sometimes they invited the lady principal to be a member of their select body. When Miss Kate Gilbert had taught French and German with great success for ten years, they invited her to sit with them, though she had no higher degree. Those who were not professors were called teachers, and they were usually women who taught in the elementary schools. They had teachers' meetings of their own, but upon special occasions this Board of Teachers was invited to sit with the faculty for at least part of an hour. The Board of Trustees, of which John G. Fee was always chairman in this period, consisted of from ten to fourteen men, most of whom were from Berea, or at least from Kentucky.

The faculty wrote annual reports to the president and the trustees, and one of their most common concerns in these reports was the small size of the College Department. In 1883 Professor W. E. C. Wright expressed the problem thus: "How to make our advanced classes larger and how to secure more students who will stay through the course."[5] President Fairchild understood the reasons for the College situation, namely, the students' lack of money and the low state of Kentucky's common school education, which left them poorly fitted for College work.[6]

In 1884 the faculty presented a petition for three more professors: a full-time professor of higher mathematics, to relieve the Greek professor of having to use part of his time in teaching mathematics; a full-time Latin professor, in order that the College Latin might not have to be taught by the principal of the Preparatory Department; and a second science professor, preferably one who was an enthusiastic collector, who would make and arrange collections in botany, zoology, mineralogy, and geology, "such as shall make Berea College, as we hope to see it, become the leading school of the region."[7] Eight years later their petition was still two-thirds unfulfilled, because the institution could not afford to employ additional professors for a College that had ceased to grow. In 1884 the College Department had thirty-seven students, in 1891 thirty-one, and in 1892 again thirty-one students.

II

PRESIDENT FROST was by nature a reformer, and his call to Berea turned his crusading zeal into a mission for bettering rural education. In a letter to Berea written at Goettingen in July, 1892, he underscored his words that Berea's moral influence upon the public depended upon the number of her students and the quality of her instruction.[8] One of the four resolutions which he presented to the Berea trustees two months later as conditions of his acceptance contained a pledge that Berea should have "courses adapted to various wants."[9] The new president began to build his program upon these two ideas, a great increase in enrollment and the adaptation of Berea's program to the students' needs.

President Frost's inaugural address at the close of his first year was an earnest call to the friends of Berea to join with him in his new plans: "We have a mission in educational reform. . . . The world still waits for some school which will fearlessly put in practice several reforms which are approved by all thoughtful educators, but as yet nowhere fully realized." He added that while Berea would furnish its share of inventors, statesmen, and preachers, it would also find satisfaction in furnishing "some corporals and privates for the army of the Lord— and good school-teachers, good local magistrates, good deacons, and good deacons' wives."[10] The following day he was more specific in his stirring report to the trustees. "Now a college can prosper without a good many things, . . . but it cannot prosper without students," he said, and he reminded them that in the past year there were fewer students enrolled than seven

years before, and that Berea as an "engine of universal civilization" must carry on many forms of education at once, teaching
the people "how to get a living and how to live."[11]

President Frost's reorganizing zeal, however, did not extend
to the College Department. When in his inaugural address he
pictured Berea College as standing with a spade and a spelling
book in one hand and a telescope and a Greek testament in the
other, he had no mind to replace the Greek book and the telescope with another spade and speller. In each catalog issued
during the twenty-eight years of his administration, he referred
to Berea's classical course as the standard course of the American college. In his annual report of 1902, written when he was
forty-eight years of age, he said that the College course was
without "fancy" electives for the training of specialists and was
"quite like the course which men now in middle life took in
Northern colleges before the elective system came in." The
other College courses offered in Berea remained much the same
as they had been before he became president. While they were
called four-year courses, the four-year period included one or
two years of Preparatory work. The catalog of 1910 showed
that another two-year College course had been added, the
pedagogical course (B. Ped.), and the 1916 catalog showed that
while the scientific course had been raised to four College years
in length, another two-year course had been added, the philosophical course (Ph. B.).

The institution's increase in numbers made it possible for
the College to offer more courses, but these were usually additions to the fields of study already offered. To be sure, when
Berea College found itself blessed with a scholar as superior as
Professor S. C. Mason on its secondary agricultural staff, it
added three College courses in forestry to be taught by Professor Mason; but as soon as he left Berea, forestry was dropped
from the catalog. The addition of a single course in the fine arts
and one in choral music was altogether in consonance with
Berea's College traditions. The addition of pedagogical courses
was justified by state requirements. It was a different matter,

however, when two courses in agriculture were introduced as College electives in 1915-1916, and when two courses in home economics were offered to College women in 1918-1919. The courses in agriculture and home economics were forerunners of a new College policy.

A thoughtful guest who in 1919 studied Berea's adaptations to needs wrote regarding Berea College: "The institution has grown out of all recognition, but the traditional college is still small, as it ought to be. Between the mountaineer and the academic curriculum is a great gulf that must be bridged."[12] It was the bridging of this gulf that became Berea's great task after President Frost's retirement. While the College Department in the twenty-eight years of the Frost administration increased from 25 in 1893 to 215 in 1920, the ratio of its attendance to the total attendance of the institution was barely as high as the ratio in the twenty years before his coming to Berea.

In President Frost's first year the Preparatory Department was divided into two administrative sections, the secondary Academy and the elementary Model Schools. The Academy remained a conservative preparatory department until 1905, its curriculum being as little disturbed by the Frost reforms as was the College for which it prepared students. Then several short courses were added to the Academy, only one of which remained in the Academy for more than a few years. This English Academy course did not prepare for College and was of slow growth as compared with the Preparatory Academy course, which showed an attendance rising in fifteen years from 168 in 1909 to 592 in 1924 under the skillful direction of Dean Francis E. Matheny, who was a master leader of high-spirited young students.

III

PRESIDENT FROST during his first year in office revived the normal course, which had been a part of the Preparatory Department before 1883. He believed that the host of teachers

who went out to teach in the rural schools would be the most
effective means of spreading Berea's invitation to learning.
Before long he wrote that "the head of the Normal Department
should also be a university lecturer, selected with special reference to his ability to reach and win the mountain people."[13]

This normal course was at first only a program of studies
which covered three years of secondary work. Then in 1896
the president brought from Illinois an experienced training
teacher, Mrs. Eliza H. Yocum, who had as high a degree as any
of the professors and upon whom he bestowed the title of dean
of the Normal Department, a woman teacher being Berea's
first dean. For some years the Normal Department borrowed
teaching time from other departments. The use of a borrowed
teacher of horticulture such as Professor Mason, a drawing
teacher such as Charles A. King, superintendent of buildings,
and a sewing teacher like Mrs. Jennie Lester Hill soon increased
interest in the fast-growing Normal Department. The vitality
of this teacher-training department was shown by its growth
in numbers from 6 in 1894 to 452 in 1920.

Dean John W. Dinsmore was especially successful in building up numbers, increasing the department from 87 in 1900 to
301 when he left in 1913. By 1907 the Normal Department had
a faculty of its own, and from this devoted Normal faculty
came four small books written especially for rural teachers:
Dinsmore's *Teaching a District School* (1908), for which President Frost wrote an introduction in which he said: "It cheers
my heart to know that this little book is to go forth as a helper
to a country school teacher of our land. . . . Professor Dinsmore
has been in a thousand school houses like yours. He knows
hundreds of trustees, parents, and pupils exactly like those in
your district";[14] John E. Calfee's *Rural Arithmetic* (1912); C. D.
Lewis' *Waterboys and Other Stories* (1913), a delightful nature
study reader; and J. F. Smith's *Reading and Composition for
Rural Schools* (1916).

Practice teaching in the Model Schools was offered in the
catalog of 1894, and in the sixty years since that time Berea

College has put special emphasis upon directed teacher instruction. In 1910 the adult elementary students of the Model Schools were separated in organization from the town children under fifteen years of age. The young adults constituted the Foundation School, and the children became the Training School. Both groups were used for practice teaching. In 1913 Knapp Hall, a new brick building planned specifically for student observation and teaching, was dedicated as Berea's Training School.

In the year 1907-1908 the Normal offerings consisted entirely of secondary work: a one-year course leading to a county certificate; a three-year course leading to a state certificate; and a four-year course, which included geometry and some Latin, leading to a state diploma. In the catalog of this year a suggestion was made that a student with teaching experience might take certain College courses and earn a Bachelor of Pedagogy degree. It was not until two years later that the College Department explained this course, admitting that although it was a four-year course, its requirements for admission were less severe than for the classical course. The first students to receive this B. Ped. degree were two young men who graduated in 1912.

Dean Cloyd N. McAllister became the Normal dean in 1913, and brought with him a keen interest in extending Berea's practical teacher training to a genuine rural situation with rural trustees, rural parents, and rural pupils. For many years the one-room school at Narrow Gap had been used for observation, but it was not well suited for such work. After a trial in a rural community west of the Ridge, a better situation was found about three miles south of the Ridge, where in January, 1917, the Scaffold Cane Community School was opened. It was organized through the co-operation of Berea College, the Madison County School Board, and thirty-nine families of the district. Berea College had the right to nominate the teacher and to use the school for observation and student teaching.[15] Here for the next ten years under Dean McAllister's guidance Berea

Normal students learned the possibilities of the one-room country school, and Berea College learned how difficult a matter it was to conduct such a school in an actual rural situation.

IV

IN THE INTRODUCTION of vocational courses President Frost made his greatest departure from conventional college policy. His interest in industrial education had a much deeper root than its possible use as a means of earning money for education. In his inaugural address he expressed in weighted words the moral purpose that shaped his later years of experience with manual education: "We have no diviner call than to gather the multitudes who will otherwise be untaught, hold them for a longer or shorter time according to their capacity, and give each youth a bent in the upward direction." Eight years later he said with his native optimism: "The Applied Science Course will be the most adapted of all our adaptations. It will make the gifts of science available in the remote cottage. . . . In the course of ten years this Department of Applied Science ought to benefit a million people who have never seen Berea."[16] In his first year he began the construction of a $500 house where cooking and sewing would be taught, and laid plans for a woodworking shop. In the midst of these early plans he said impetuously to his faculty: "Industrial education ought to have been the first department instead of the last established at Berea. . . . For a large part of our students manual training and domestic industry are more important than anything else except the Ten Commandments."[17] By the close of his administration there were 487 students attending Berea's Vocational Department, more than twice as many as were registered in the College Department.

At first the lessons in sewing were a part of the course of study for all girls in the Model Schools; and cooking (for girls) and woodworking (for boys) were added to the Grammar

School course. When Professor Mason moved to Berea, his course in elementary horticulture was added to the offerings for the older Model School boys. Beginning in 1899 a two-year course in nurses' training was offered at the newly founded College Hospital, and a diploma was given for successful completion of the course.[18] In 1900 two diploma courses were offered to those Model School students who had finished at least the fifth grade. In these two-year courses, farm economy (for boys) and home economy (for girls), the students devoted half their time to such studies as English composition, history, algebra, and physiology, and the rest of their time to their Vocational studies. By 1909 there were five of these two-year courses in the catalog, besides some shorter-term certificate courses in such skills as telegraphy and bricklaying. Up to this time the Vocational students had taken their general subjects in some other department, but in this year they began to have their own faculty for teaching general subjects. The Vocational Schools had become a department.

It is profitable to observe the courses offered to these secondary students who would probably never enter college. Consider the offerings in the two-year (secondary) Home Science School in the catalog of 1914. Besides plain sewing, dressmaking, cooking, nutrition, home nursing, house care and buying, laundry, millinery, and weaving, the student would study physiology, beginning chemistry, everyday physics, science of wealth, science of conduct, and letter writing, and also Bible and speech. Take the offerings of the Vocational School of Agriculture in the same year: soils, farm crops, vegetable gardening, rural life, feeding stock, dairying, stock judging, forestry, poultry, farm management, veterinary science, and fruit culture, as well as beginning economics, letter writing, Bible, ethics, English classics, political science, accounts, and chemistry. It was a wonderful program, but the reader questions the ability of secondary students to handle so much in two years.

There were plenty of the faculty and trustees who criticized these short courses which President Frost encouraged, but to the very close of his administration he believed that he was in the right. In his farewell report in 1920 he wrote:

"At any rate the mountains are not needing men with long drawn out education just now so much as they are needing preachers with feeling for the common folks, teachers, farm-demonstrators, nurses, surveyors. It has been a crime for the custodians of education to say, 'We will only serve it out in car-load lots. Give us four years in Preparatory and four years in College or you can have no crown and no recognition from us.'

"The State universities, more responsive than the Christian colleges to the popular needs, are offering to give out education in quantities adapted to the consumer. They have the car-load lots, but they have also retail departments, and even ten-cent counters. But without these precedents Berea was brave enough to do what as Fairchild said, 'the people really needed.' . . .

"Beyond the Foundation School . . . we offer a number of two-year courses, one for teachers, one for farmers, one for housekeepers, one for carpenters, and one in the Academy, called the English course, which is really a shortened and adapted College course. . . . We have frankly said: 'Your age, your tastes, the family condition at home, the need for your active work are such that you ought not to try to stay four years more. So we will give you the best possible selection for a two-year course. If you finish that, we will recognize you as a scholar.' "[19]

Back in 1902 President Frost, realizing that Berea College with more than eight hundred students needed improved organization, proposed in his annual report to put some one man in charge of each existing department with responsibility for both class work and discipline. Presently he assigned each teacher to one department, even though that teacher taught in several departments. By 1913 President Frost conceived of each department as having its own type of education, its own campus, dormitories, dining rooms, and even its own athletic field. Each department, College, Academy, Normal, Vocational, and Foundation, should have an enrollment of about four hundred students, half men, half women. In his 1918 report to the trustees he wrote: "The student in any one of these schools enjoys, we hope, the same intimate acquaintance and the same personal care that he could enjoy in a small institution. At the same time he has the very great economies, as well as the enthusiasms and the inspirations that are possible only when large numbers are assembled in one place." But he was wise enough to add: "Our organization and management ought to be a matter of constant study."[20]

V

IN THE DECADE following President Frost's retirement a series of important changes took place. All of these changes grew directly out of developments then evident either in American colleges or in the mountain field. They had already been considered frequently and seriously by the faculty, especially by the College professors, to some of whom they seemed long overdue; but to Emeritus President Frost they seemed like retreat from education for the common man.

One of these changes was made in 1921 by the faculty's decision that only one degree, the Bachelor of Arts degree at the close of a four-year course, should be awarded by Berea College.[21] This brought to an end the flowering of short-term degrees that had had their beginning under President Fairchild. Thereafter a College student in his junior and senior years would pursue a major to the extent of thirty-three or thirty-six hours, and this major would be named on his diploma, as for example, Major in Chemistry. In 1921 neither agriculture nor home economics was listed in the catalog among the possible major fields, but by 1923 they appeared among the majors. Then in 1926 a Bachelor of Science degree was offered to such majors as would fulfull the Smith-Hughes requirements in agriculture or in home economics in addition to the requirements for a Bachelor of Arts degree. This addition of a four-year B.S. degree based upon a fifteen-unit secondary course, in order to qualify under the federal Smith-Hughes Act of 1917, illustrates how the pressure of the times caused changes at Berea.

A somewhat similar pressure of new opportunities during and after World War I led to a change in the School of Nursing in 1920-1921. In 1920 the catalog announced that there were to be two distinct nursing courses thereafter. The shorter course would be "exactly like the course which has been given ever since the Hospital was founded." The longer course would be for three years and would prepare its graduates for the state examination "which when successfully passed gives these young women the title of Registered Nurse, and grants to them all the legal and professional privileges which go with the R. N. They are permitted to practice in other States and are admitted to Red Cross and Government Service."[22] This course included nine-months experience in the Louisville City Hospital, where the student nurses could have a broader experience than in Berea. A year later (1921) the catalog announced that the short course had been discontinued and that the only course to be offered was the standard three-year course preparing for state registration. Additional opportunities were offered for graduates of this course, such as public health, social service, and institutional positions. The short course has never been brought back. Instead, because of developments in the nursing profession a four-year degree course in nursing is now under consideration in Berea College.

In 1924 a change was made that affected four of the five existing schools. The Vocational Department was closed as a separate disciplinary and educational unit, although vocational courses continued to be given to students of the remaining departments. The segregation of students taking vocational courses had finally given way to the free choice of vocational courses by a member of any department. The action was in no sense a blow to vocational education, but a rebuff to departmental segregation.

At the same time, 1924, the first year of the Normal Department and the ninth grade of the Academy were transferred to the Foundation School in the expectation that some of the advantages claimed by the junior-high-school movement might result from this partial reorganization of the Foundation School.

The thirteen years between 1918 and 1931 show how strong was the pressure of outside forces in shaping Berea's pattern of education. They were years of struggle for the Normal Department as well as for the Normal dean, Dr. C. N. McAllister, who was one of Berea's outstanding leaders. One of his chief concerns was the one-room school in the remote valley, and his other main concern was improvement in standards of teacher training in the state, no matter what this did to his Normal Department in Berea College.

The Kentucky law of 1918 provided that a private school doing a grade of work equal to that required by the state normal schools might after proper inspection recommend certain of its students to the state superintendent of public instruction, who would issue to them normal school certificates. Berea's Normal Department was inspected immediately, and several hundred elementary and intermediate normal school certificates were issued to Berea students.

In 1922 the General Assembly raised the requirement for the advanced normal school certificate so that it could be obtained only by those who had completed the equivalent of two years of study above the high school grade. In order to meet the requirements of this 1922 law, the College dean and Dean McAllister with fine co-operation arranged so that a student seeking this advanced certificate would be enrolled in both the College and the Normal Department, and his program of studies would have to be approved by both deans. There was considerable headshaking over this arrangement, but it was regarded as a temporary thing.[23] Under the new certification law of 1926 the only terminal course of the Normal Department was a four-year (secondary) course for which a Berea diploma was awarded; and the catalog warned that those expecting a state certificate should select their courses carefully so as to conform with state requirements. The former two-year certificate course had been eliminated in the interest of higher standards.

The Certification Law of 1930 provided that no one could secure any kind of teaching certificate hereafter in Kentucky without college training. After a year of trial the Berea Normal Department came to the conclusion that it could not operate successfully without some kind of certificate to offer its students. President Hutchins in his baccalaureate address, May 21, 1931, spoke of the death of the Normal Department as a triumph rather than a defeat. "Dean McAllister has fought for better schools and better teachers for the mountains. . . . The Normal School which is to die tomorrow salutes you."

VI

WHEN WILLIAM J. HUTCHINS became president of Berea College, the attendance of the College Department was barely 9 per cent of the total attendance. When he retired in 1939, the four years of the College contained 40 per cent of the student body, and the 1,136 students attending the College Department in 1953-1954 constituted 73 per cent of the total attendance. The reasons for this change in ratio lie in the changing times, as has already been shown in the matter of teacher certification. The Kentucky law of 1914 requiring each county to provide at least one high school created a demand for more teachers with at least a four-year college education. The developments in agriculture created a pressure that the institution should provide full college preparation for agricultural and home demonstration agents and Smith-Hughes teachers. Developments in hospitals necessitated more training for more nurses and dietitians. The new Red Cross and other social service personnel required college-trained social workers. Business required men with training beyond the secondary techniques of typing, stenography, and bookkeeping. Oil companies asked for college men who had majored in geology. Law, medical, and engineering schools were no longer willing to take applicants without college work. Even hotel management sought men who had majored in college economics. All of these pressures were youth's opportunities.

Sometimes in the early years of President W. J. Hutchins' administration people who knew of Berea's very active lower schools, which then were larger in enrollment than the College, would inquire why Berea had any College Department. President Hutchins' answer was: "Our mountain students have as good a right to a higher education as anyone else, and they are fully as likely to make a worthy use of it. For the great mass of our College students it is Berea or nothing. . . . Furthermore, if our mountain students should leave the mountains for their college course, the mountains would almost certainly lose their life service."[24] Upon another occasion he wrote: "In this department we hope to train 'the leaders of the leaders' of the mountains."[25]

Dr. John C. Campbell in a study made for the Russell Sage Foundation in 1917 showed his apprehension lest with the increase of public secondary schools in the southern mountains the "mountain colleges" would lapse into the conventional type of college that was unadapted to a special work. "It is to be hoped, however, that some will resist the temptation to develop along traditional lines and be willing to evolve, through experimental stages, into higher institutions especially emphasizing a training that will meet regional needs."[26] The thirty-eight years since these words were written have been filled at Berea College with experiments in adaptations to economic, social, religious, and other cultural needs. In 1932 in the midst of this evolution Trustee Miles E. Marsh wrote a letter of passionate earnestness to his fellow trustees, reminding them that their vision would determine the outcome of Berea's efforts. He begged them not to be led astray by standards that did not take into account Berea's great aim of establishing a better way of living in the southern mountain area. He then wrote: "The need of the mountain work now is for college-trained teachers. These people will have more resources within themselves and will feel less keenly the tinsel of civilization. They will be sustained by real vision. They will be recognized as men and women fitly trained for the work they are attempting to do. Such recognition is very important. This will mean that Berea's entire attention and effort will finally be given over to the work of the College."[27]

Since 1926 the College has been a member of the Southern Association of Colleges and Secondary Schools. Early in 1906 Berea College had been refused membership because of the small enrollment of the College Department (34) and the insufficient separation of its departments.[28] In 1924 President Hutchins in opening correspondence with the Association in regard to membership wrote: "Some of our most worthy graduates . . . are having difficulty in getting recognition as principals of schools in North Carolina, for example, and as students in graduate schools."[29] Two years later (1926) Berea was able to give its students the advantages coming from the College's membership in this Association, though this recognition was conditional upon Berea's furnishing better laboratory facilities, a condition that was met in 1928 by the erection of a Science Building.

VII

THE ELIMINATION of the Vocational Department in 1924 and the Normal Department in 1931 led to the suggestion of a further reorganization that would add the tenth grade of Academy work to the Foundation School, would combine the eleventh and twelfth grades with the College freshman and sophomore years to make a Lower Division of the College, and unite the junior and senior years into an Upper Division. This plan also provided for an evaluation of the new plan after five years of trial.

The new organization was put into effect in the fall of 1938. The evaluation began in 1942, when the weakness of the four-two plan had already become clear. This organization had broken apart the four-year college, hampering the social and academic relations of student and faculty life. The four-year Lower Division was not really a four-year school at all, for the eleventh-twelfth grade section was largely a terminal group finishing what remained in their minds as a high school course without the trappings of graduation, while the freshmen were newcomers whose only ties were with the sophomores above them. The next problem was to reorganize the reorganization so as to preserve its advantages and avoid its obvious disadvantages.

After an incredible amount of study, reading, and observation on the part of faculty committees, the present organization was put into operation in the fall of 1947. The secondary grades were made happy by being united with the Foundation School. The four-year College was reunited in administration and in student and faculty life, although there were certain scholastic distinctions made between courses of the General College (freshmen and sophomores) which emphasized liberal education, and the Senior College, in which each student pursued his line of specialization, that is, his major.

A considerable number of freshmen were likely to come to college with poor preparation that betrayed the inferior teaching of small rural high schools. A plan was made to adapt Berea's college courses to such high school graduates, if they showed by testing that aside from poor educational tools they were of college calibre. Basic courses without College credit were set up, to which freshmen deficient in English, mathematics, geography, or American history were assigned. These students, however, were admitted as freshmen and might be assigned to some freshmen courses (with credit). It was also arranged that a few superior students who had not graduated from high school but had shown that they were almost ready for college might enter upon some freshman work. These ex-

perimental basic courses were given tentative approval by the
Southern Association. The success of the remedial basic plan
depends to a large extent upon the testing program. For example, before classes begin, the director of guidance and testing can discover a serious weakness in arithmetic and take steps
to remedy it so that the student's first year in college is not
wrecked by discouragement in this one line.

The liberal arts program of the General College is planned
to develop interests and vision for the rest of life. Instead of
the traditional series of courses that divide and still further
subdivide learning, this freshman-sophomore plan of study co-
ordinates thought around a few cores such as the biological sciences in one full course, the physical sciences in another course,
a survey of the social sciences in another, an eight-hour course
in the humanities as expressed in music, literature, and art, pre-
ceded by a course that introduces the history of Western civilization, and a series of two courses in Bible that introduce the
Old and the New Testament. If a student has studied a foreign
language in high school, he may fulfill his college language requirement (without college credit) by passing a proficiency
test; or he may begin the study of a foreign language in college
(for college credit) and take his proficiency test when he feels
ready for it. All in all this two-year adventure in Western
culture and scientific thought is to an unusual degree a humane
education.

The Senior College is organized for specialization. For obtaining the B.A. degree the catalog lists twenty-three subjects
from which a student may select a major of twenty-four semester hours on the senior college level. The list includes physical
education, music, art, religion, agriculture, and home economics, as well as such subjects as ancient languages, history,
and chemistry. In order to broaden the base for prospective
teachers, area majors are offered in the field of science, social
studies, and elementary education, with the requirement of
more than twenty-four hours in the area of concentration, but
less than this amount in any one subject within the area. The

degree of Bachelor of Science is offered in agriculture, in home economics, and in business administration. These areas of special preparation have been selected because of needs in the mountain field.

An upper-class student ordinarily has time for a few electives entirely outside his field of specialization. It is not uncommon for a major in some such field as physics or political science to sign up for a course in art, sociology, or music in his senior year, saying: "I've looked forward all through college to taking this course before I graduate." In this mood the reader thumbs through the Berea College catalog at this moment to find such alluring electives as: art and civilization; spring flora; consumer economics; agriculture for elementary teachers; Greek classics in translation; petroleum geology; public opinion and contemporary politics; nursery school participation; team sports; fundamentals of counseling; marriage and the family; rural social life.

The Foundation School has become a four-year high school, besides offering elementary work that is ungraded and adapted to special needs. The work of the entire Foundation School is enriched by the opportunity to take courses in the industrial arts, agriculture, home economics, and business in addition to academic subjects. In 1953-1954 the attendance of the Foundation School was 359.

VIII

THIS STUDY would be unsatisfactory indeed if it did not show some of the steps by which Berea's exceptional program in physical education passed from narrow strife into its present diversified service. In Berea College physical education and health is now a serious department of study which offers twenty-eight hours of College courses in the catalog.

Each of the important elements of today's pattern of physical education appeared long ago on the campus. In 1879 the faculty appointed President Fairchild as chairman of a committee on grounds for ball playing. In 1894 the voice teacher mentioned his four classes of gymnastic students, saying that they had taken their exercises with wooden and iron dumbbells. He also mentioned the fact that he had given physical examinations to sixty young men. In 1898 the *Workers' Manual* announced that the superintendent of the Hospital, a trained nurse, would give general instruction in hygiene to various classes of students. In the same year President Frost, realizing the close connection between baths and exercise, wrote that one of the three buildings he most needed was a bathroom and gymnasium.

In 1901 Professor H. M. Jones commented upon the value of ball playing on the Howard Hall diamond as a means of establishing good will among the young men: "It is death to provincialism. It is a liberal education. The game room, the baseball diamond, and the new bathroom are three foci of high value."[30] But there were other sports than ball playing. In 1904 the *Student Manual* said that for participation in the field day contests one requirement was that a contestant must be passing in all his work. In 1906 the new College physician was made "Superintendent of the Gymnasium, Bathrooms, and Hospital." The *Student Manual* of 1906 announced: "The Gymnasium Committee is to cultivate a variety of athletic interests, to enlist as many students as possible, and prevent undue concentration on any one line."

Unfortunately these good ideas did not become welded into a program until Berea College had experienced fifteen years of incredible bitterness over athletic events. This animosity, which affected both the intercollegiate and the intramural games between 1906 and 1921, made each athletic season seem almost like wartime. By 1910 Berea's passionate zeal for intercollegiate victories so possessed the institution that the trustees directed President Frost to "limit contests with other colleges to those in which Berea students may meet others on terms of substantial equality and at moderate expense; and to so regulate such contests as not to detract from the interest in home contests, or tempt our students to make athletics a too absorbing pursuit."[31]

Although the president eliminated all intercollegiate contests except the uncommercialized track meet, the intramural contests remained as bitter as ever. The ill feeling that lurked between rival literary societies and the jealousy existing between departments, especially between the Academy and the Normal Department, found expression in these games. At last the futility of these perennial battles became so apparent as to cause a strong reaction against them. Dean Matheny expressed the new feeling when he wrote in 1921: "Perhaps we can start on the larger program of physical education and in this way draw off the previous intensity."[32] In the same year John Miller as physical director did lead Berea men into this "larger program." By 1922 he had six hundred boys of all departments participating in many kinds of physical activities. When he left Berea in 1924, President Hutchins in speaking of his work wrote: "Mr. Miller has believed in sport for sport's sake, and has steadfastly refused to be victimized by the prevalent mania for athletic victories at any price."[33] In 1940 the men's Physical Education Department could report 10 touch-football teams on the College level, 8 speedball teams, 8 soccer teams, 40 basketball teams playing a weekly schedule on the campus, 4 intramural swimming teams, and 4 baseball teams playing a full schedule.[34]

Since 1925 the courses in physical education required of freshmen and sophomores have received college credit. Many students also take elective college work in this field. The physical education program of today emphasizes the value of learning correct body mechanics in order to keep the body in balance for doing life's work, and the satisfaction of learning certain sports selected according to each individual's taste and capacity. Such a pattern of physical education accords well with a program of liberal education. Nowadays each student is given a complete physical examination to discover defects that ought to be observed or that might be corrected. For several days each fall a score of outstanding physicians and dentists from Lexington, Cincinnati, and Cleveland give these physical examinations—for the love of youth, not for pay. Now not a few of these doctors are Berea College alumni.

The College engages with sanity in some extramural sports: basketball, cross-country running, swimming, track, tennis, and baseball, but not football. When the Berea team wins, there is a brief but audible time of rejoicing, after which the matter is forgotten; when it loses, there echoes the philosophic reassurance that Berea's athletic program, of course, is part of a course in physical education regardless of victory or defeat.

Soon after Berea College changed from athletic struggle to genuine physical education, the work of the Physical Education Department was improved by the gift of two new buildings: in 1926 the Woods-Penniman Building, of which a women's gymnasium was a part, and two years later the Charles Ward Seabury Gymnasium for men, a well-equipped physical education center with a large swimming pool. The tablet dedicating the Seabury Gymnasium to the young men of Berea speaks words of historic importance: "that they may here train their bodies to be swift and enduring servants of the good will, that they may here learn to play in generous rivalry and co-operation, to face danger without dismay, victory without conceit."

IX

SCHOLARSHIP DAY late in the spring has in recent years become a memorable occasion in Berea. On that day honor is paid to those students who have achieved more than ordinary success in scholastic work. The program in the Chapel always opens with an address upon some phase of higher education and its relation to society. This is usually followed by announcement of those upperclassmen chosen for membership in the local chapters of various national honor societies. The criteria for admission vary, of course, with the charters of these societies. Berea College has never had social fraternities and sororities in its campus life, but with the growth of the four-year college in the past thirty-five years, Berea has welcomed Greek letter honor societies as a stimulus to young scholars.

Lists of nominees prepared by the honor societies with assistance from the registrar's files are read to the assembly. The students named stand in their places to receive this recognition of their scholastic achievement. On Scholarship Day, May 18, 1954, students were welcomed into the Berea chapters of the following honor societies: Alpha Psi Omega for superior work in writing, acting, and producing plays, and in the cultivation of good dramatic taste; Beta Beta Beta for achievement in the biological sciences; Delta Phi Delta for work in the German language; Pi Gamma Mu for achievement in the social sciences; Sigma Pi Sigma for work in physics; Tau Kappa Alpha for achievement in public speaking, especially in oratory and debate. Members were also welcomed into two local honor societies that were founded to meet a local need: Tau Delta Tau for superior work in all phases of stagecraft except acting; and Pi Alpha, an honor society in the science area to recognize ability and interest in the general field of science.

There had been much talk of founding a local chapter of some national honor society which emphasized the ideals of scholarship in all fields, including agriculture and home economics. The desired emphasis was found in Phi Kappa Phi, a local chapter of which was installed in November, 1953. It presented its first list of nominees on Scholarship Day, 1954.

The serious interest of Berea seniors in their major field is attested by the large number attending graduate and professional schools after completing their undergraduate work.

Berea College was among the institutions considered in the Knapp-Greenbaum study (1952), which aimed to discover the centers of study from which the next generation of scholars was likely to come. This study, financed by the Fund for the Advancement of Education, studied the award of graduate fellowships over $400 which were made to American college and university graduates between 1946 and 1951. This study excluded those institutions which graduated fewer than four hundred students in this six-year period, those which gave incomplete information, and, for the "all-male index," the "all-women colleges," leaving 377 colleges and universities for special investigation. An all-male index of awardees in each of these 377 institutions was secured, this index showing the ratio of the number of male awardees of graduate fellowships to the total number of graduates in a given institution in this six-year period. Tables were then made of the top fifty schools among these 377 institutions classified on the basis of their index of male recipients of scholarships for advanced study. In this list of fifty, only three southern colleges were listed, the University of the South, William and Mary College, and Berea College. Tables were also made listing the top twenty schools in index of male graduate awardees in the fields of science, social science, and humanities. Berea College was the only southern college in the top twenty in science, though it was not included in the other two fields.[35]

A part of the investigation consisted in an analysis of the 138 liberal arts colleges in the survey. Among the selected liberal arts colleges in the United States as a whole, Berea ranked thirteenth in the index of male graduate awardees, while among the twenty-five selected liberal arts colleges in the South it stood second in index of male awardees, being outranked only by the University of the South. The fellowships involved were divided into three classes—those from a governmental agency, those from a foundation, and those from a university. Most of the graduate awards granted to Berea students were university fellowships. In the selected liberal arts colleges in the entire United States, Berea tied with DePauw for eleventh place in index of university fellowships, but among the twenty-five selected liberal arts colleges of the South it ranked first in index of graduate fellowships.[36]

The records in the Berea registrar's office are interesting to study in regard to the number going on to graduate study after graduation from Berea. In the ten-year period from 1941 to 1950 inclusive, the percentage of seniors going into graduate work varied from a low of 30 in 1945 to a high of 48 in 1948, that is to say, from 32 in a class of 106 in 1945 to 75 in a class of 168 in 1948. The largest number going to graduate school in any one year of this period was 106 in a class of 238 in 1949 (44.5 per cent).

Many Berea students work for a few years before they feel financially able to attend graduate school. The registrar's records for 1954 show that sixty-five graduate degrees were awarded by other institutions to Berea alumni in that year, though some of these students had been considerably retarded in their progress by lack of funds. Of these degrees 18 were Master of Arts, 17 Master of Science, 8 Doctor of Philosophy, 5 Doctor of Medicine, 2 Doctor of Dental Surgery, one Doctor of Dental Medicine, 3 Doctor of Education, one Master of Education, 2 Master of Business Administration, one Master of Social Work, 6 Bachelor of Divinity, and one Master of Theology.

Berea College attempts to do excellent undergraduate work. As a college it emphasizes among its faculty strong teaching rather than research; but where there is a combination of student ability and great teaching, a desire to do research inevitably follows. Many of Berea's majors in the field of science are important research men in the laboratories of industry. Berea attempts through the high quality of its teaching to aid students in discovering purposes for their own lives, and encourages them to proceed on paths of social usefulness and creative expression, regardless of past handicaps.

CHAPTER 6: Labor for
Education

THE FIRST Constitution of Berea College contained a statement that the institution would try to furnish some labor as an
aid to students in securing an education; and each revision to
the present day has contained a similar statement.

Berea College was founded in the ebb of a stirring but
short-lived experiment in American education, the combination of education and labor. For example, from Oneida Institute (1827) the movement had passed to Lane Seminary in
Cincinnati and then to Oberlin under the leadership of Theodore D. Weld, who was at that time America's most persuasive
spokesman for the values of manual labor in higher education.

In the manual labor schools of the 1830's and early 1840's
several hours of manual labor were required each day from the
student, and this labor was furnished and paid for by the college. Most often a large college farm provided a demand for
such labor, and frequently the students worked in college shops
at such trades as carpentry, printing, blacksmithing, and broommaking, for which they were paid a small wage. In 1831 a
National Society for Promoting Manual Labor in Literary Institutions was founded, and Theodore D. Weld was selected to
be the general agent of the organization. His one annual re-

port, published in 1833, set forth thirteen advantages of the manual labor system in higher education. The tenth point in this long list was that manual labor would greatly diminish the expense of education. First on the list of advantages was the statement that manual labor furnished exercise most natural to man, and other points brought out its value in character development and in establishing habits of industry.[1]

Educational institutions soon found their manual labor experiment facing business difficulties. Students laboring at manual work were likely to be too unskilled to be efficient, or too proud to be industrious. The importance of management and finance was not sufficiently respected by school administrations, and teachers were frequently unco-operative because they wished for a larger share of the students' effort.[2] By the time John G. Fee was a student in Lane Seminary, Weld had already left Lane and the manual labor system had passed its prime. When J. A. R. Rogers graduated from Oberlin, its manual labor program in the strict sense of the word was a thing of the past. Both Fee and Rogers in the early days of Berea looked upon labor as an excellent means of helping a young man through college, but they did not talk of its educational values, as Weld and his European predecessors Jean Jacques Rousseau and Philipp Emanuel von Fellenberg had done.

While the Berea institution was still a district school attended by children resident in the vicinity, the pupils lived at home with their parents; but already in 1856 Fee was looking ahead to a college "that will furnish the best possible facilities for those with small means who have energy of character that will lead them to work their way through this world."[3] The first Berea College catalog issued after the Civil War announced that the institution would furnish industrious young men with sufficient labor to enable them to pay a portion of their expenses; but in a historical sketch of the College (1869) J. A. R. Rogers wrote without equivocation regarding labor in Berea College: "It was not intended that the Institution should be what is technically called 'a manual labor school.' The experiments to establish such institutions elsewhere did not seem to warrant the expense of organizing a manual labor department under the management of the college, but the trustees proposed to secure labor for the students in other ways. In this respect thus far, they have been reasonably successful."[4]

II

PRESIDENT FAIRCHILD's inaugural address (July, 1869) contained a detailed statement of what he understood to be the characteristics of Berea College. Among these he counted the provisions made so that the neediest student might secure a college education, if he had the chance to work. The College, he said, took pains to keep expenses low and to furnish the means of self-support. It could furnish labor for a considerable number, and others could find work "among the inhabitants."[5]

President Fairchild, who was fifteen years older than Professor Rogers, had been a member of the first graduating class of Oberlin College and knew by experience the rigors of the manual labor system in its original form. In a baccalaureate address twelve years after his inauguration, he said, in speaking of the effort required to meet the cost of education: "I do not speak as a theorist on this subject. My first experience away at school was at sixteen with a younger brother in a little old house, boarding ourselves. If you get into a pinch, any of you, at any time, and you know not which way to turn, you know where to find a sympathizing heart."[6]

He was also well aware of the importance of supervision over young working students. Among the interesting references to his personal supervision of student labor is that of an alumnus of the Berea College class of 1881: "Though he had a sense of the dignity of his position, this did not keep him from being the most democratic of men. . . . In my day he supervised the manual labor of the young men. He indicated the particular lot of wood the student was to chop or saw, and he personally made the measurements and issued the vouchers to us."[7]

Much of the work done by students in these two decades was unskilled labor. At a conference of college executives in Nashville, 1881, President Fairchild expressed frankly his opinion of student labor: "Our students are engaged in making roads at Berea. They have never tried to run a farm. I have seen student efforts to run a farm, but they have never amounted to much. I do not think it can be made successful. I would not undertake to run a garden with students. I can make a good garden, but I have never seen a student who could do it."[8] Angus Burleigh many years after his graduation in the Berea College class of 1875 told of his labor in the construction of Ladies' Hall in 1872, when he wheeled mud to the brick mold in what is now the college garden.[9] In 1886 the *Berea Evangelist* in a column of brevities remarked that many students were making both muscle and money on the excavations under way for Lincoln Hall.[10] It was not until Phelps Stokes Chapel was built (1904-1906) that students were trained to do the highly skilled labor required for permanent construction.

It is hard nowadays to think of a time when there were no college industries to employ student labor. In 1884 Fee and two friends had set up a small printshop and brought in a student printer from Illinois to print their paper, the *Berea Evangelist*. An editorial announced distinctly that the paper was neither owned nor supported by Berea College. Before the *Evangelist* expired in 1887, a college paper, the *Berea College Reporter*, published its early numbers sporadically on this press. After the College secured ownership of this press in 1889, the *Reporter* was published regularly for ten years.

These early student printers went far beyond the mere goal of earning their college expenses. An editorial in the April, 1890, *Reporter* brimmed with pride: "All the manual labor connected with getting out this issue has been done by students.

A class has been organized from those who indicated a desire to learn the printing business, and they have carried this work in addition to their school duties. . . . In Berea there has not been much instruction in what is generally called skilled labor. It may well be that the printing of the *Reporter* is the beginning of our Industrial Department."[11] In the next issue of the *Reporter,* the statement that all the work upon this issue had been done by young men learning the printer's trade was followed by a report of the specific service performed by each of the seven apprentice printers in setting up the paper.

Soon the student press was printing college publicity in addition to the college paper. In 1895 it began to print college catalogs and the *Berea Quarterly,* besides doing considerable work for outsiders. In 1905 its name was changed from Students' Job Print to Berea College Printing Department, which was superseded in 1913 by the name Berea College Press. It is important that the first skilled industry on the campus was organized by a group of students who wanted to acquire a skill, and who took pride in the quality of their work. The Students' Job Print stands out as a landmark in Berea's labor history.

III

PROFESSOR FROST in 1892, while he was considering the trustees' invitation to accept the presidency of Berea College, made careful inquiries as to Berea's facilities for self-supporting students. "Manual labor experiments have usually failed. President Fairchild of Oberlin says they always must, but I am not sure that he is right." He inquired as to whether there was any possibility of securing water power in Berea, and suggested that more concern for self-supporting students would cause more students to come and to stay through the school year. The labor policies which Berea pursued during the next twenty years were embodied in one prescient sentence in this letter: "If students could only rely upon ten cents an hour after a term's apprenticeship, it would be worth more than a $100,000 endowment."[12] "A term's apprenticeship" suggested the means by which student labor could become skilled. When Professor Frost accepted the presidency of Berea College on the following September 8, 1892, the second of the four resolutions upon which he based his acceptance concluded with the pledge "to secure better opportunities than now exist here or elsewhere for self-supporting students to assist themselves."

On the same day President Frost persuaded the trustees to pass another resolution, one which has been of great importance to self-supporting students ever since that time: that tuition hereafter was to be free. Although a small incidental fee was retained to cover the cost of such services as heating and caring for classrooms, the charge to cover the expense of actual teaching was removed,[13] and from 1892 to the present Berea College has had no tuition fee.

In his stern annual report to the trustees and faculty at the close of his first year's administration, President Frost paid much attention to the need for "productive industry." Though he recognized the value of the young printing office, he deplored its lack of a competent superintendent. He spoke of the college farm with discouragement, saying that it was unreasonable for the College to buy vegetables in Cincinnati and yet rent out the College's two hundred acres of farm land. The problem, he explained, was to put the college land into a proper state of cultivation and find a man of high qualifications to be the farmer, preferably a man from some state agricultural college. This college farmer would teach apprentices good farming practices and at the same time enable them to earn money for schooling.[14]

It was not until five years after his coming to Berea that President Frost found a scientific agriculturalist able to handle class instruction and actual farming, Professor Silas C. Mason, from the Kansas Agricultural College. Besides teaching College courses in forestry, he also co-operated with the farm foreman in such practical work as fencing, draining, gardening, fruit raising, cleaning the forest, and making roads, thereby furnishing instruction and employment to more than one hundred young men.

IV

BEREA'S FIRESIDE Industries grew up in the 1890's, but their origin was different from that of any other industry. They were in a very literal sense fireside industries, because they were carried on in the mountain homes where mothers with skill of hand spun, wove, and quilted for the sake of their children's education.

Soon after the Frosts came to Berea to live, a woman brought in a ten-year-old hand-woven coverlet which she begged Mrs. Frost to buy for three dollars, the amount which the mother needed in order to purchase medicine for her child. Mrs. Frost bought the coverlet because of the mother's need, and then showed it to her husband. President Frost presently took this coverlet and some other fragments of hand weaving to New England that he might show the skill of Kentucky mountain women.[15] He soon learned how popular colonial pattern weaving was among women of wealth, and already in 1895 he was writing letters home urging his wife to send him still more hand-woven goods to give to certain donors.

In a summer trip on horseback to Owsley County in the Kentucky hills he stopped overnight with a family at Travelers' Rest, and in the course of the evening his host brought out several armfuls of beautiful homespun coverlets and counterpanes, saying regretfully that of course there was no market now for these old-fashioned things. When President Frost mounted his horse next morning to return home, he rode with two meal sacks slung across his saddle, and they were stuffed hard with the woven treasures that he had purchased.

President and Mrs. Frost saw that two things should be done at once: Mountain women should be encouraged to dye, spin, weave, and quilt so that their sons and daughters might have money for education, and Berea College should act as middleman to bring these products out of the hills and find markets for them among people who could afford to buy the precious wares.

In 1896 the first Homespun Fair was held in Berea, its purpose being to stimulate production. Commencement Day was the ideal time for such a fair because several thousand people would be wandering around the campus looking for interesting sights. For the next twenty years this Homespun Fair, usually held in Lincoln Hall, was a source of great encouragement to mountain weavers (and whittlers). Cash prizes were offered for home-dyed, homespun, hand-woven coverlets, for blankets and counterpanes, linen and linsey woolsey by the piece, home-made rag carpet, hand-knit socks and mitts, splint-bottomed chairs, hickory-split baskets, and handmade ax handles. The dye used had to be homemade, with the recipe for it given in writing for each color.[16]

Already in 1900 this fireside industry was considered important enough to deserve a kind of shop, as woodworking had its own shop. The following year Squire Stapp's old log house was moved from west of the ridge to a vacant lot on Jackson Street in Berea to serve as a loom house. In 1902 another log building was set up near the loom house. It was an unfinished log church which was moved log by log the fifteen miles from Jackson County in the hills, and when it had been roofed and rechinked, it was given the name "Clover Bottom Cabin." When Mrs. Jennie Lester Hill, a teacher of domestic science, was made director of Fireside Industries, although she did not know how to spin or weave, she proved to be a successful director because she was a good businesswoman, skilled in remote production and in marketing publicity.

The mountain women's production of homespuns received recognition for quality even in the early years of this unusual labor system. In 1900 their weaving received a medal from the Paris Exposition; in 1901 a second medal from the Pan-American Exposition at Buffalo, where a coverlet made by Mrs. Mary

Anderson (Jackson County) and some other Berea weavings were shown as part of the exhibit of the National Arts Club of New York; and in 1904 a third medal from the Louisiana Exposition in St. Louis. In 1907 Berea's Fireside Industry furnished all the curtains, rugs, table covers, and hangings for the Kentucky Building at the Jamestown Tercentennial Exposition.

When Mrs. Candace Wheeler, a textile expert from the East, visited Berea in 1902, she advised that Berea College find a woman with two necessary qualifications, weaving skill and business ability. Mrs. Hill saw that the time had come when some of the young women in her Domestic Science Department should be taught to weave in order that they might be prepared to take the good positions now opening to trained weaving teachers. She wrote in 1909: "I hope my successor will be a practical weaver who can teach half a dozen girls to weave. At present the older weavers are very jealous of their art."[17]

It was not until 1911, nine years after Mrs. Wheeler's advice was given, that a woman was found—Mrs. Anna Ernberg, who knew both the art of textile handicraft and how to buy and sell. Within a year of her coming she had student apprentices weaving and earning under her direction.

v

THE BRICKMAKING and tilemaking industry grew out of the needs of the farm. Professor Mason insisted that what the unpromising college land needed was drainage. In June, 1901, President Frost reported: "The cost of tile is so great that we have felt like waiting until the farm could undertake the manufacture of brick and tile for its own use." Then the gift of $500 for an engine led the administration to undertake such production at once with student labor. By autumn, 1901, a brick plant had been set up and was able to produce excellent brick; but the superintendent had found that the clay was not good for making drainage tile. The following January (1902) the col-

JOHN G. FEE
A Founder of Berea College

BEREA COLLEGE DURING THE FAIRCHILD ADMINISTRATION
Top: Ladies' (Fairchild) Hall–Gothic Chapel–Lincoln Hall
Bottom: Library, second floor of Lincoln Hall

BEREA STUDENTS IN THE 1890s
Top: Zoology Laboratory
Bottom: Homecooking Class

GOTHIC CHAPEL

Built in 1879; burned in 1902

STUDENT LABOR IN THE EARLY 1900S
Top: College Garden
Bottom: College Laundry

BEREA STUDENTS AT WORK

Top: Woodworking Shop (about 1910)
Bottom: College Bakery (in the 1920s)

BEREA'S EXTENSION SERVICE TO RURAL SCHOOLS
Top: Travelling Library
Bottom: Rural Reader

BEREA LIBRARIANS AT WORK (1949)
Courtesy of the Louisville Courier-Journal

lege Chapel burned to the ground, and in the plans which were soon made for a new Chapel, brickmaking became more important than tilemaking. By June of 1902 President Frost reported that the brick and tile plant was furnishing employment to thirty-three students. The brickmaking industry served as a student industry for about ten years. The need that labor in the brickyard should be continuous made it a difficult form of labor for students to carry except during summer vacation. Another factor that hurt the young brick industry was the high cost of freight on coal and bricks. Local coal was not then mined commercially near Berea, and the long distance of Berea from the mines in Bell and Harlan counties put Berea-made bricks at a disadvantage in competition with those made in southeastern Kentucky. "If we could secure reasonable freight rates, we could sell all we could make," the discouraged superintendent of the brickyard wrote in 1905.[18]

Soon after the Chapel burned, a foreman of stoneworking and bricklaying was employed to teach apprentices. Boys intending to pursue long college courses were encouraged to take the apprentice course so that they could earn three or four dollars a day in the summer by plying their trade out in the state. For the next fifteen years most of the bricklaying on permanent college buildings and in town was done by these students. In the summer of 1907 Berea student bricklayers and stoneworkers were employed in construction of the new State Capitol at Frankfort. When they returned to college in the autumn, they created a sensation because they were so devoted to education that they were willing to give up four dollars a day at Frankfort for the sake of returning to their books at Berea![19] After 1908 no bricklaying class was taught for several years. With a return of college building in 1915-1916 bricklaying classes were again taught in three successive winters, and that was the end of student bricklaying in Berea College.

The building of the Phelps Stokes Chapel in 1904-1906 was another landmark in Berea's labor history. Soon after the old Chapel was burned to the ground, Miss Olivia Phelps Stokes of New York offered to pay for an adequate permanent Chapel on condition that it should be constructed by students. She accompanied her offer with a check for $500 to help in building a much-needed Industrial Trades Building for the training which must precede the Chapel project.

This $40,000 Industrial Building was the first permanent building erected on the campus since Lincoln Hall was built almost twenty years before this time. The woodwork section was equipped with various new machines, thirty benches for sloyd, rooms for freehand and mechanical drawing, and an agricultural lecture room. Although it was called the Men's Industrial Building, certain women's industries—sewing, cooking, and laundry—were accommodated in the front section. A knitting mill was to have been established on the third floor, but so great was the demand for men's housing that the idea of a knitting industry was dropped and the space used for a men's dormitory.

The visitor who looks at Phelps Stokes Chapel today cannot realize the cost in effort required to construct that structure, characterized predominantly by stately simplicity. For example, as the campus had no central heating plant when the Chapel was built, a sawmill boiler had to be placed in the basement to furnish heat. Therefore the north end of the basement had to be made deep enough for this boiler, even though students must use hand drills and picks for the excavation. The boys at the brickyard required much water each day for their brick manufacture. Since the pipes for the new college waterworks were only in process of being laid to the Ridge, the brickmaking for the Chapel was done with well water that was pumped by an engine set up in the brickyard. The building, 150 feet long and 83 feet wide, required much construction material. Students cut the lumber from the college forest and set it to dry. Other students hewed stone from rocks twelve miles south of the Ridge.

The bricklaying students laid the walls in strong Flemish bond. Construction students under the eye of Superintendent

Josiah Burdette wrestled with problems of the roof, and took special pride in building the bell tower which crowned the building. The beautiful oak panels of the walls and ceiling were made in the Industrial Building and carried on young men's shoulders to the Chapel, to be put in place piece by piece. The moldings and railings, too, were made in the Industrial Building by trained student hands. That building, like the Students' Job Print, is a historic creation of the labor system.

Mrs. Elizabeth Rogers, who had seen the first board Chapel erected, laid the cornerstone of the new brick Chapel. For the day of dedication the portraits of the founding fathers were hung upon the walls, thus in a sense uniting the past with the future. The first professor, J. A. R. Rogers, made the prayer of dedication, his last public service for the college which he had helped to found before the Civil War.

While the Carnegie Library, erected in 1905-1906, was not built to any great extent by student labor, some of the beautiful oak equipment was constructed by student cabinetmakers in the woodwork shop, including oversize tables that even today do not show their age and finely finished cabinets with many drawers which after fifty years of use and weather still react to the lightest touch.

The librarian at the time when the library was moved from its old location in Lincoln Hall to the new building was an exceptionally ingenious and successful labor supervisor. Her outstanding tactical success was in moving her library from the second floor of Lincoln Hall to the new stone building two hundred feet to the west. With her Dutch ingenuity Miss Euphemia Corwin devised a neck yoke having double hooks for holding books, and had enough of these yokes made for an emergency crew of young men carriers. On the morning of moving day the students moved a library of twenty thousand books, and this valiant supervisor wrote in her report: "There was absolutely no confusion, and when the dinner bell rang, the books were on the new shelves in exactly the same order as when they stood on the old shelves at breakfast time."[20]

Before 1902 the dormitory students were expected to furnish their own sheets, bedcovers, pillow slips, and towels, but in that year the College began to furnish all bedding for the students' rooms, and included the cost of washing this college equipment in the price of room rent. For performing this service a laundry was established, at first located in the basement of Ladies' Hall, but later in the Industrial Building when that place was ready for occupancy.

It was taken as a matter of course that the home economics teachers would manage this new industry, for were not washing and ironing a woman's function? At the close of her first year's experience in laundry supervision, Mrs. Jennie Lester Hill of the Home Economics Department said in her annual report that she had undertaken this laundry work with about as much idea of the management of a steam laundry as of an armored cruiser.[21] After ten years of struggle with complicated laundry machines, the lady teachers of the home arts gladly turned the laundry over to Clare Canfield with the frank admission that its management was a man's job. Ever since that time it has been understood that the college laundry is not an adjunct of the Home Economics Department.

President Frost in his first report to the trustees and faculty (1893) had urged that the College should set up a factory to enable students to earn ten or twelve cents an hour. At the close of twenty years after this report no such factory existed in Berea as yet. Student labor was largely performed to service the College in some way—farm, garden, and forest work, janitor-monitor-porter duty, library and office work, boarding hall duties, brickmaking and bricklaying service, laundry work, nursing at the hospital, servicing the heat and power plant, and student teaching.

In the summer of 1906, the year in which the Chapel was dedicated, the catalog announced that all students must share in the necessary labor of the school, but that no student would be required to do more than seven hours of college labor a week, and that the institution could not promise even as much

as this in the winter term. It was the first time that all students
had been required to take a share in the school's labor. If
work was so scarce that labor could not be promised for the
winter term, then why did the College requisition the labor of
students who did not wish to work? Because now that Berea
was no longer biracial, its reputation as a good college where
expenses were low attracted a considerable number of students
who objected to labor. There was as yet no "out-of-territory"
policy to limit the number of students coming from outside the
mountain area. The new labor rule was intended to keep the
campus socially democratic, so that there would not be two
classes: the many who had to work in order to go to college,
and the few who had parents of means. Both the value and
the dignity of labor were sustained by this seven-hour rule.

The faculty's annual reports to the president at the end of
the first year after passage of this rule bristled with comments.
The Normal Department was especially irritated by the labor
rule because its students were older and resented compulsion.
Vocational Dean Miles E. Marsh suggested that many of the
faculty would have to be educated to the value of labor when
it is well done before good results could be obtained from the
labor rule. In 1917 the seven-hours-a-week clause was changed
to ten hours a week, and there it has remained to the present
time.

VI

CERTAIN OF THE NEW vocational courses introduced early in
President Frost's term of service, such as agriculture, carpentry,
and cooking, were taught in part by the apprenticeship method,
and others, such as printing and bricklaying, were taught
entirely by practical work without regularly scheduled classes
for study. When Professor Miles E. Marsh was made Vocational
dean in 1908, he found that part of his new work was to supervise the work of apprentices. As there was no supervision over
labor as a whole and no Labor Department, he realized that as

Vocational dean he was unofficially a dean of labor. He took his work in this capacity very seriously, and in his annual report, June, 1910, he listed some results that student labor should achieve:

1. To carry on the institution's necessary work in such a way that the College would not lose money because of inefficient labor.

2. To make labor a useful laboratory for students in their fields of greatest interest.

3. To discover through work the interests and latent abilities of the younger students barely out of elementary school.

This year, because he considered that it was inefficient for a student to work a single period, especially at such labor as milking, fencing, bricklaying, laundering, or construction, Dean Marsh secured passage of a rule that a student's schedule should be so made that he could work two consecutive hours each day.[22] Many times he expressed his preference for a half-day labor period, but this proved impossible to plan for students taking a full course of studies. The problem of avoiding the single-hour labor period has troubled labor superintendents from that day to this.

In 1914 the duties and service possibilities within the labor system became so urgent that Professor Marsh gave up the administration of the Vocational Schools and became *de jure* as well as *de facto* dean of labor, though retaining his office as registrar, which he could handle through a capable assistant registrar. The registrar's report for 1914-1915 showed that among the sixteen departments of "Productive Labor," that is to say, student labor departments, the highest seven as employers of students were: boarding hall, 263; janitor service, 92; laundry, 82; agriculture, 72; horticulture, 63; office work, 51; and woodwork, 44. The four departments employing the smallest numbers of students were wood sawing, 7 (but this department had used 27 student sawyers in the preceding fall term when preparing the wood supply for winter); weaving, 2; and Boone Tavern, and power and heat, each one. The only departments producing for outsiders were Fireside Industries and Boone Tavern. The work of 1915 was almost completely what we call today institutional labor.

In 1915 Dean Marsh thought of retiring from the Berea work and settling on a southern farm. He was a very earnest and hard-working man, stern in manner, but burning with zeal to help the ambitious student who had very little money for an education. He feared that Berea was about to close the door on the poor boy by letting student expenses for amusements and minor personal luxuries raise the cost of living needlessly. "I have no interest whatever in a school that is organized for the well-to-do and the rich, no matter how cultured and moral the atmosphere," he wrote austerely. "I have learned most fully what a man has to contend with in trying to establish an organization that is favorable and will remain favorable to poor boys and girls."[23]

Having been assured of the president's support, Dean Marsh worked three more years as dean of labor; but in each report that followed this crisis of 1915 he reiterated his fear that the faculty was out of sympathy with student labor.

The greatest service performed by this first dean of labor was to discover and state the important problems involved in student labor at that time, though he was unable to solve them. After Dean Marsh's resignation became known, one of the deans wrote in his annual report, 1918: "It is my belief that we have reached a very critical time in the development of Berea's student labor. It must either be organized on a firmer basis or degenerate into complete confusion. No other man will ever hold together the system that we are trying to operate as Dean Marsh has done."[24]

VII

THE NEXT DEAN of labor, Dr. Albert G. Weidler, was able to build an improved system that saved Berea's labor program. Dean Weidler was a kindly, scholarly man with a rare gift for organization. This brilliant young executive had earned his Ph.D. before he was thirty; and now before he was forty, he set his hand to the work to which he would devote the best years of his life. At the close of his administration as dean of labor, 1950, all Berea's labor superintendents signed an award which they had voted for him: "Albert Greer Weidler has shown good character, fidelity, and skill, and has during thirty-two school years as Dean of Labor earned the esteem of his colleagues by his resourceful leadership, his sympathetic alertness to student needs, and his promotion of labor as an essential of effective education."

In his first annual report, 1919, Dean Weidler emphasized two ideas. One was that the remaking of the tottering labor program lay in the Labor Conference which he had set up, an organization of the labor superintendents, who met once a month to study their problems and pool their ideas. These labor managers, men and women, needed a leader and a common helpmate; the dean of labor needed their support and practical wisdom. For thirty-two years his strength lay in the fact that his own creative planning was tested and sustained by these superintendents who guided the productive industry of the students. When he spoke strongly to the administration, he spoke not as a lone man. When he spoke with feeling to the teaching faculty of the College, he spoke as one of the best-educated professors on the college staff.

The second idea that he emphasized in his 1919 report was the need for more student work, so that the rule requiring labor of all students could be enforced. The poor enforcement of the required-labor rule was due in large part to the shortage of college work, especially in the winter when the attendance was greatest. When Dean Weidler came to Berea, 1918, seventeen productive industries were listed in the registrar's report, ranging from agriculture to woodwork. By the close of Dean Weidler's second year, 1920, the list of productive industries had grown to thirty. Among the new industries was a men's stabilizing industry, broomcraft, which manufactured brooms not for the institution's immediate use but for the outside market. When jobs on the campus were scarce, this industry could operate at top speed in broommaking; and when more labor was needed at the boarding hall, on the farm, or at Boone Tavern, as in time of low registration or an epidemic or war, broomcraft could go into low production, thus stabilizing supply and demand.

In the middle of the year 1919-1920, Dean Weidler was able, through the support of his young Labor Conference, to put into operation an improved system of awards. "This," he said, "has done more than any other one thing to raise the whole tone of student labor. . . . It helps the student to see the relation of his work here to his work in life. We plan to use this labor record as the testimonial of character when such is asked for." These awards were given for two or more school years of service in any one department of labor, and testified to the student's proficiency, reliability, and length of service.[25] The first grant of these awards was made on May 20, 1921, to 134 students, who sat for the occasion in the front seats of the Chapel. This was really the first Labor Day in Berea, though the name had not yet been applied to it. These 134 students constituted about 6 per cent of the total enrollment, 1920-1921, exclusive of the Summer School registration and the children of the Training School.

At the close of the third year of labor awards 207 such awards were given, and the day was distinguished by the distribution of printed programs giving the names and departments of those receiving awards. This year the recipients comprised about 9 per cent of the total enrollment. Every year since 1921 Berea College has given these papers to especially worthy students, and 449 such certificates were awarded in 1954, the number comprising 29 per cent of the total enrollment. Many students upon going into the world to seek their first employment have discovered the value of these labor awards, since they could apply as experienced workmen rather than as "green hands."

In 1935 a new type of award was given by the Labor Department in addition to the labor award for two years or more experience in the same field of work. The new vocational award was given to students doing four or more years of service with a minimum of one year in each of four related fields of work. This plan gained considerable popularity in its first years, reaching a peak in 1941 when 110 such vocational awards were given; but in the following years fewer students followed the new plan, even though it was modified so that one could receive such a certificate for work in any four departments. One reason for the decline in favor was the fact that when a student changed after a year's work from one department to another, he suffered some loss in pay rate because he began as a new hand, though scholastically he might be an upperclassman.

Since 1930 another type of award has been given, the Danforth Creative Effort prizes, given by Trustee William H. Danforth of St. Louis, to make Berea's labor more educational by challenging students to think how college work could be done more efficiently, with less danger, or with more market appeal. The prizes are in money; and when the president calls the winners to the platform to receive their prizes, there is sure to be lusty applause from the audience.

Since 1926 it has been the custom to celebrate the day of labor awards with both an address and a series of contests. The Labor Day speakers over the years have been of aid not only in giving prestige to the occasion, but also in interpreting the social and educational significance of labor in a college program. Among these speakers in the course of the years have been included two governors of Kentucky, one governor of Ohio, two managers of T.V.A., an acting secretary of the United States Department of Labor, an administrator of the National Youth Administration, a director of the Harmon Foundation, an outstanding lecturer on problems of labor and management in Harvard's Graduate School of Business Administration, three executives of great business corporations, and the president of a nationally known firm of consulting engineers in management. Occasionally several outstanding students or experienced alumni have spoken on what labor in Berea has meant to them. None of these speakers, however, have uttered words of greater wisdom than did Dean Weidler himself when in 1934 he gave the Labor Day address on "Labor, Learning, and Leisure."

The first labor procession was added to the day of awards and addresses in 1926. Dean Weidler in his report to President Hutchins in June, 1925, had made this suggestion: "I think that nothing would help the students to see the magnitude of our work better than by having a procession to the Chapel by labor departments. Each department could have some sort of a banner indicating the department, and the students might wear the costumes which they wear at work."

Immediately the idea captured the imagination of the students, and each Labor Day since that time has had its procession through the campus by way of the University Walk. This is no such train as the solemn academic procession in cap and gown which follows practically the same route a few weeks later. The labor procession is a joyous thing, reminiscent of the medieval craft guilds. The moving spectacle suggests labor taking its leisure with robust gaiety before the more serious speaking, the awards, and the contests take place.

The first labor contests were held in 1923 in the Tabernacle, then used as a gymnasium, and they were limited to the single class period customarily used for a lecture. In the next year a half day instead of an hour was given to the labor activities, and the time was changed to the afternoon because the cows' milking time in the morning was 4:30 a.m., too early an hour for any holiday. Outdoor contests were added this year, to take place on the athletic field, namely, milking (dairy), and hitching and sheepshearing (farm). In 1926 the procession, address, and awards were activities of the morning and the contests were held in the afternoon. In 1936 the chimes-playing contest, formerly held at 12:30, was scheduled for 6:30 p.m., after the evening meal, and there it has remained to the present time.

Among the Labor Day contests, held once a year for more than thirty years, ten have been selected as samples:

Boone Tavern: serving a meal;

Dental office: denture wax-up;

Fire Department: 2 teams, 5 men each, erecting ladder, mounting with hose;

Health Department: bedmaking with patient in bed;

Men's weaving: making homespun on fly-shuttle loom;

Music Department: writing manuscript;

Poultry: grading eggs;

Power and heat: pole climbing;

Printing: linotype operation;

Woodwork: stacking and measuring lumber.

Sometimes a zealous new teacher resents the academic loss of this day for Labor's hearty expression of joy in work; but the spirit of Labor, the good teacher, sitting invisibly among the professors adds materially to their accumulated wisdom on human relations.

By the close of 1954 there were sixty-three organized departments of labor on the payroll schedule, ranging from admissions office, agriculture, agronomy farm, to salesroom, treasurer's office, woodcraft. Some new departments are proliferations, as it were, of earlier departments. The bakery began as the boarding hall's baker. The farm has become, if one speak in organizational terms, agriculture, agronomy farm, livestock industry, poultry industry, garden, grounds, forestry, dairy, and creamery. Janitors-monitors' service showed the need for a department of properties. From Boone Tavern grew Boone Tavern garage. From the college store's lunch counter grew the student lunch counter and recreation room designated as Powell Hall. Out of the early woodwork has grown woodcraft, industrial arts, and the machine shop. Some departments of labor grew from the need for stabilizing industries, such as broomcraft, mountain weavers (using fly-shuttle looms), woodcraft, needlecraft, and the Fireside Industries. With the great increase of numbers in the College, there has been an almost incredible increase in student workers in the offices of deans and other administrators; student laboratory assistants in physics, chemistry, and biology; assistants in men's and women's physical education; aides in preschool, and specialized labor in music, dramatics, and art. The growth of labor departments making products for the outside market, Fireside Industries, woodcraft, bakery, candy kitchen, needlecraft, mountain weavers, and broomcraft, created a need for customers' service, salesroom, and gift shop as labor departments.

VIII

No two industries have passed through exactly the same cycle of growth. The life history of the bakery illustrates particularly well the experiences of a thriving Berea adjunct over the past half century.

When the Industrial Building was built so that Berea boys might be trained to make woodwork for Phelps Stokes Chapel, and the laundry was moved from the basement of Ladies' Hall, more room was made for the Boarding Department; so a large brick oven was constructed there in 1903. There was no bakery yet, but only a large oven and a baker who made two kinds of light bread, as well as cornbread, which he mixed by hand in a great bowl made from a poplar log.

Ten years later a boy from eastern Tennessee who had been reading a Berea booklet on *How College Students Earn an Education* came into the kitchen on opening day with a student guide. The baker in charge found an extra apron for the new boy, who worked the rest of the morning under the baker's direction. Later in the day it was found that Dean Marsh had already assigned the new boy to milk cows, but Clyde had milked all the cows he cared to milk in his young life. The matron arranged his transfer to the cumbersome mixing bowl and the brick oven. Clyde made a bad mistake in mixing his first batch of cornbread, for when the recipe directed the use of a cup of soda, he innocently used a *pint* cup. That mistake gave him an understanding of how a green boy feels when he is learning.

After graduating from the Academy and beginning College work, he joined the Navy soon after the United States entered World War I. He meant to go into hospital work in the Navy because he planned in the future to enter some medical school; but at the Hampton Roads base he found that a new naval bakery was standing idle for want of sufficient bakers. The young sailor used his Berea baking experience in the new shop and came out of the war a petty officer, baker first class. In 1921 he came to Berea as assistant to the baker, and five years later when the older baker was about to retire, Clyde Jones was sent on a six-months fellowship to the American Institute of Baking in Chicago for special training, just as though he were a promising young instructor in physics or history. From that time to the present he has been the superintendent of the bakery, too busy to study medicine. Like an ambitious professor, he has kept up with advances in his field, becoming a member of the American Society of Baking Engineers and attending annual meetings of the American Bakers' Association, always realizing that he worked in a technical and highly competitive field where, to use Chaucer's words: "The lyf is short, the craft so long to lerne,/Th' assay so hard, so sharp the conquering." In Berea he heard persistent talk about the need for more opportunities in which to use student labor. Instead of bringing in a new industry, he made plans to expand his old industry by developing new markets and new products.

Under the wings of the bakery tea-sugar decoration and candy making came in to absorb surplus labor of student girls. A friend with a creative imagination showed to Mr. and Mrs. Jones a small box of tea sugars which she had received as a gift. They were overdecorated in an uninteresting design by a heavy hand. Mrs. Jones and her friend saw the possibility of creating beautiful party sugars by hand-decorating them with delicate, recognizable designs. Soon there were student girls who became very skillful in tea-sugar work. Mrs. Jones in her own small home experimented with nut candies, in those days weighing out the requisite quantities on her baby's scales. The candy kitchen, which had grown up inside the bakery, by the end of five years (1937) was employing fifty-seven girls to make fruit cake, beaten biscuits, candy, and cookies, besides hand-decorated tea sugars.

Every labor department in the College was seriously affected by the Second World War, and the bakery was no exception. It normally employed about the same number of men and women students, the men being slightly in the majority. When the war came on, the men students month after month were called into service. Young women were used for some of the men's work in the bakery; but much of it was too heavy for young girls, and nonstudent labor was hard to find, especially such labor as would fit into a food industry. The rationing of the ingredients essential to a bakery, the shortage of sugar, fats, egg yolks, chocolate, cinnamon, cellophane, and wax paper, and the shift to enriched breads made it hard to plan either a production or a sales program. These problems were intensified by the difficulty in replacing worn parts in the bakery machinery. The candy kitchen, largely a girls' industry, suffered more from rationing and raw material shortages than from any lack of labor. Because of sugar shortage the girls for more than two years were unable to decorate tea sugars and made very little candy. They ran part time on decorated jellies, beaten biscuits, and cookies. The wartime problems of a college with student industries were difficult indeed.

For many years the superintendent of the bakery has been interested in the educational experience of the students under his direction. He has emphasized the social responsibility of his workers for the food that would be used by thousands of people, and for years he has been giving his experienced students assignments to train new students for work in the plant. He encourages his students to report ideas for better safety practices, timesaving devices, and new products, and teaches them that attitude is at least as important as skill. He does not expect to turn out many professional bakers in the course of the years, but a continuing succession of better citizens.

IX

WILSON A. EVANS in 1950 was appointed dean of labor. He has inherited a good organization and a priceless tradition. He worked in this labor program as a student for six years and as a labor supervisor for five years, when he was the alumni secretary. He took special training in personnel administration in Teachers' College, Columbia University, and wrote his doctoral dissertation on the educational values of the Berea College work program. Besides, he is a man of great patience, courtesy, and human sympathy.

This first century of "labor and learning" in Berea College has been attended by many problems. Some solutions have come through the inventions of dexterous men who never heard of Berea's work program, some through wearing conferences in Berea's offices, some through wartime experience, and some through sheer patience. Some urgent problems have not been solved, but at least they have not been left unstudied. To forsake such a labor program because of its irritating problems would be a betrayal of priceless educational experience in social democracy.

The problem of how to supervise student labor is the most pressing labor problem in Berea today. Already in 1894 it was a serious problem when President Frost wrote: "I do not think anybody in Berea has ever made a study of supervising, and yet we have a great deal of it to do, and ought to do more. It is a kingly art and one which there is a great pleasure in exercising, to transform the unskilled apprentice into the efficient workman."[26] A good supervisor on the campus today with a clear program of procedures soon trains an unskilled student into a productive worker without arousing resentment from his corrections; a careless supervisor or one who feels resentment that he must perform his duties with inexperienced help soon taints the student with irritation. Of course, a good printer may not be fitted to supervise; an excellent hospital technician may exasperate each student who comes within sound of her voice; and an excellent weaver may find it harder to direct the labor of student girls than to weave with her own hands the most intricate pattern of double weaving.

Another problem is the adjustment of labor to the class schedule. In most forms of work the superintendent finds that the fifty-minute academic hour is too short a work period, especially if the student must change his clothes or wash up within that time. Yet it may be difficult to make a student's schedule of college courses and still preserve a place for two consecutive hours of work. Many a student has found a solution for his labor troubles in a janitor's job, since janitor work, though it may seem the least interesting of tasks, is usually done after classwork in a room is ended.

The Berea work policy includes the idea that drudgery has no great value per se. If laborsavers by their introduction bring to an end some college jobs, the College will face the problem and provide some other work. Time was when sawing wood for college furnaces and stoves employed many men students, but central heating has long since eliminated the work of the sawyers. Class bells are now under electric control; so no bell ringer leaves his classes five minutes early to do his hourly labor. Janitors are no longer responsible for putting out campus fires by means of their water buckets. Instead, a preferred form of labor for a few spirited young men is to ride on the two red fire trucks and operate the up-to-date fire-fighting equipment by which both the College and the town are protected. The cows are milked by machine, the college store uses cash registers, and needlecraft uses electric sewing machines.

The labor program has had to keep pace with the increase in Berea's enrollment and with the increasing emphasis upon the College Department. In the early days when no student industries had been set up, the College simply offered institutional work, as much as was possible. This work was of two sorts: first, collegiate service such as library work, assistance in laboratories, and ringing the college bell; second, house work, such as janitor service, mixing bread for the boarding hall, and pumping water to the fourth floor of Ladies' Hall. Almost all the college labor of today has grown from those two types of institutional work.

Student labor still shelves books in the library and still cleans classrooms, but the boarding hall's baker now has an adjunct of his own, the bakery, which bakes the college bread, and some extra. In fact, many of the college industries, while performing indispensable services for the College, have enlarged their facilities for production because of the desire of people outside the College to share in college services and products. The laundry, the power and heat, and the dairy illustrate such enlarged production. Certain adjuncts are essential for teaching agriculture, such as the poultry farm, the livestock farm, and the garden; but they too produce essential products for the College and for others. Some students secure a desirable cultural experience from such an industry as woodcraft, which sprang from the old woodworking department, and from the new pottery, which still rests under the wing of a teacher in the Art Department. Finally, there are certain industries, such as needlecraft, which were begun as stabilizing industries to absorb student labor when other types of campus work were unusually scarce.

x

To READ SOME of the things that hard-working Berea students of the past fifty years have said about their "labor for learning" is to find reassurance that the effort put upon Berea's labor program has been worthwhile, even though new problems spring up before the old ones have been quite solved. While it is in the classroom and the college Chapel that the serious student becomes devoted to great ideas for the rest of his life, the place of his labor is likely to be where he becomes habituated to social responsibility and drawn to new interests that enrich all his mature life.

It was in her Labor Day address, 1952, that a senior said: "I began my student labor as a waitress in Boone Tavern. Some of my campus friends are janitors; some are gardeners; some are weavers; some are typists; and some are making dough at the Bakery. . . . The way we do a job is more important than the job because it indicates answers to so many of the questions that future employers want to know about us."[27]

A young man wrote on February 16, 1912: "I have been thinking what Berea has been to me. When I first heard of Berea, it was to me as a dream that was about to come true or a long wishful prayer that was about to be answered, for I had long hoped that there was some place where a young man could get an education regardless of his financial situation. . . . I have learned to do my part and trust in Berea College, and Berea College trusts in God, so I need feel no uneasiness about the rest. Some young men think they cannot work and do any good in school . . . but I say from experience he does not know how to enjoy life and make his joy pay him in dollars and cents."[28]

In 1928 a lad with fifty-one cents in his pocket stepped off the bus in Berea and inquired for the "Berea College schoolhouse." He spent three years in the Academy and four in the College, earning almost half of his school expenses through literary and oratorical prizes, and the rest through campus labor. When he was close to graduation in 1935 he wrote: "I like to feel that I have been living in a fairly normal way, instead of getting a theoretical preparation for living. Berea College, with its work for everyone, is a whole community in itself, and this fact simplifies our adjustment to the larger community of the outside world."[29]

A graduate of the class of 1925, who has become a professor in an outstanding medical school, wrote in 1938: "While at Berea I enjoyed the privilege of working with Mr. Fielder [garden], Mr. Goudey [painting], and Mr. Osborne, spending four years with Mr. Osborne and his associates . . . in the Treasurer's Office. To me this attitude toward work, that is, any task however menial or hard, when well done, is an honor, and the association with these men are by far the greatest things that Berea gave to me."[30]

Finally from a young woman who will graduate from the College in 1955: "The next afternoon I went to work in the College Store. Everyone was busy, but each person took time to show me the things I would need to know. Those first days were a mass of confusion, but gradually I learned the pattern of doing things. . . . I shall never forget the time I sold a customer a fifteen-cent paint brush and then put the whole box of four dozen brushes into her package. I went home that afternoon wishing I'd never have to return. . . . I lived that down in a few weeks. My labor experience has helped me grow toward maturity. The people who know me are not my roommates, nor my teachers or classmates, but the people with whom and for whom I work."[31]

XI

DEAN WEIDLER in his Labor Day address of 1934 quoted these words from Rabbi A. H. Silver: "Man must have more than one world in which to live. . . . Alongside of his job-world he must construct for himself a leisure world wherein he can live freely and joyously in the role of a creative amateur, pursuing objectives not out of economic necessity but because of his sheer love for them. This will enable him to remain young amidst the ageing toll of relentless years."[32]

Next door to broomcraft's building there is a brick building known as the Westervelt Shop, named from the friend in Texas who gave the building in hope that it might be a place where students would go in leisure time to do handwork not for credit and not for pay, but for the sake of learning how to make things for their homes.[33] The equipment now includes fine power tools as well as hand tools. While some secondary classes for credit are held there in the daytime, the shop is open evenings for extracurricular work. Faculty and students, men and women, work there in spare time while their friends resort to the gymnasium or to their gardens. The instructor is always present to help them with their designs, to guide them in the use of the machinery, and to show them how to finish their woodwork until it is "smooth as a minnow's tail," as he says. This work place bears witness to the fact that craftsmanship is at home on this campus without a pledge of pay or academic credit. Westervelt Shop is for many a person "a leisure world wherein he can live freely and joyously in the role of a creative amateur."

CHAPTER 7: Financing a
Private College

THE SITE, the boards, and the labor for the one-room district school that was to become Berea College were contributed by local men who wanted a school for their community. Cassius M. Clay showed his interest in the project by mentioning in a letter to Fee, dated December 18, 1855, that he was sending twenty-five dollars "to the schoolhouse." Another small gift for the schoolhouse was contributed by one of New York's outstanding philanthropists in the mid 1850's, Gerrit Smith. In his later years Fee liked to repeat the story of that donation. When he told Gerrit Smith of the work that he was about to establish in Berea, Smith replied: "It is impossible. They will not allow you to establish an antislavery church or school in Kentucky." "Well," said Fee, "I am going to try." Then Gerrit Smith said: "Here is fifty dollars to help you try."

The Woolwine tract which the trustees had arranged to buy before the Civil War and for which Fee had raised most of the necessary money during the war, and other land on the Ridge which the trustees had bought at the close of the war became their first source of income, for they sold building lots to newcomers who were attracted to the Ridge by the little college. This income, however, would not begin to satisfy the school's need for permanent buildings, current expenses, scholarships, and endowment.

Six months after the College opened in 1866 at the close of the Civil War, John G. Fee secured the offer of an endowment of $10,000 from the executors of the estate of the Reverend Charles Avery, a Methodist minister who had made a fortune from his investments. The executors proposed to invest the fund and pay the proceeds to Berea College on certain conditions. The first of these was that the proceeds should be used by the College "for the purpose of promoting the education and elevation of the colored people of the United States and Canada."[1] The second condition was that the Berea trustees should agree that the fund could be withdrawn from them in three years "if said executors decide that the college is or is likely to be a failure, or is not carrying out the purpose to which said fund is by will to be devoted, viz., the education and elevation of the colored race."[2] Eventually the College received this money, which became the foundation of Berea's general endowment.

The Freedmen's Bureau not only provided the money for erecting the first real college building, Howard Hall, but also provided tuition scholarships (1870-1874), which were especially necessary for the newly emancipated freedmen. The form of this business transaction was that the College sold fifty such scholarships to the Bureau, "each giving four (4) years' tuition to the holder in any Department of Berea College."[3] The Bureau paid forty dollars for each scholarship, turning over to the College the sum of $2,000 for them.

Between 1872 and 1876 C. F. Dike and his uncle C. F. Hammond deposited with the American Missionary Association considerable sums of money for Berea College, receiving the interest as annuity payments as long as they themselves lived. After their death this money, amounting to $30,000, became a special kind of endowment, for the income could be used only for tuition scholarships. These became available for students in 1877.[4]

In the college donation books the Avery and the Dike-Hammond funds constituted the main part of what was called the "Old Endowment." Between mid December, 1880, and April 23, 1881, a period of about four months, the "New Endowment" was raised largely through the efforts of President Fairchild's oldest son, Charles G. Fairchild, who besides being a teacher of natural sciences in Berea College for eight years was an unusually successful part-time financial agent for the College. Today his subscription book tells succinctly how the New Endowment came into existence.

Mrs. Valeria G. Stone was a wealthy woman of Malden, Massachusetts, who left her large fortune to educational institutions. She, like Avery, Dike, and Hammond, was in close touch with the A.M.A. The entry of her gift of $10,000 on December 13, 1880, was followed by this condition: "Already paid to A.M.A. to be held in trust for Berea College until $40,000 additional is secured." Four men and a family gave $5,000 each, another person gave $7,500, another $2,500, and the remaining $5,000 was raised in the last two days, most of it being contributed by two persons who had already given $5,000. Every man and woman named in this little subscription book as a donor to the Stone Fund had already given generously to Berea in past years.

The twelve years after the New Endowment was raised were critical years in the financing of Berea College, the only bright spot being Roswell Smith's gift of Lincoln Hall, accompanied by his devoted attention to its construction. The decline in Berea's financial prosperity was due to causes which are clearer now than they were at that time.

Many of the first generation of Berea's donors were dead by the mid 1880's, for example, such men as Gerrit Smith, Lewis Tappan, and C. F. Dike who had substituted the cause of Negro education for their prewar antislavery zeal and appreciated Berea's interracial work. In the 1880's the College was paying the price financially for having been remiss in making new friends. Moreover, Berea's relations with the A.M.A. had grown less close. In its early days the Association had been supported by various religious denominations; but when several religious bodies formed their own home missionary boards, the Association's work fell largely into the hands of the Congregationalists.[5] That was why the antisectarian John G. Fee in 1883 declined to accept a salary from the A.M.A. While the Reverend E. M. Cravath at the suggestion of the Association was elected to the Berea Board of Trustees in 1868, his place on the Board was not filled by an Association candidate after his retirement in 1879.

In the midst of this static financial condition, Berea's donations became entangled in a theological web for a few months in President Stewart's second year. The new president gave his attention to teaching instead of making an effort to revive old friendships and find new donors for the institution. He had been Fee's preference for president, and being a Baptist, he assented to Fee's latest theological writings. In November of his second year as president (1891), some anxious persons sent out a printed statement that Berea College was drifting into a narrow sectarianism that was offensive to many donors and was seriously affecting Berea's income. The signers asked that once more the friends of the College pledge a contribution, but make their pledges conditional upon the appointment of two new trustees who would be recommended by the A.M.A.[6] In other words, the donors had been invited to exert pressure upon the trustees. The Prudential Committee replied by asking that men cease their agitation until the following June, 1892, when the regular trustee meeting would be held. The intervening months overflowed with words, both written and spoken, the wisest of which were probably those of John G. Fee, then seventy-five years of age, who maintained "that Berea College should not be held responsible for the utterance of his principles as set forth in his *Autobiography*."[7]

The post-Commencement trustee meetings in 1892 lasted for three days instead of one. The two Association candidates were elected trustees, President Stewart resigned, and Professor William G. Frost of Oberlin was offered the presidency. The following week the *Berea College Reporter* gave what was in a sense the last word in the controversy: "The meeting was one of unusual interest. The past history of the College, its present basis and financial condition, and future prospects were fully discussed. . . . While some divergence of views as to certain lines of policy was found to exist, the meeting closed with harmonious feeling and unanimous action."[8] A crisis had passed. A new period in Berea's financial history was about to begin.

II

PRESIDENT FROST had little to say about finances in his inaugural address at the close of his first year in office; but in his annual report given the following day, June 22, 1893, he uttered such biting criticism that he had only a few of the milder pages printed for friends of the College.

He spoke of "an air of dilapidation about the place." He remarked that the newcomer was oppressed with a sense of decadence, although this decline had stolen over the College so gradually that some people might not be aware of it. He said that men talked about the work "which Berea *has* done," as though she were dead and buried. Referring to the fact that the endowment had not increased for twelve years, he commented that so long a period of standing still meant the disheartening of Berea's entire constituency. He reminded them that the debt incurred in building the Chapel in 1879 had never been extinguished, but had increased year by year until at the time he spoke it equaled a quarter of the entire endowment. He called attention to the fact that the treasurer was the only man on the staff who knew much about business and that his business experience was limited to his present field; nor could the College obtain much financial help from the trustees since there was not a single man on the Board who transacted a business of as much as $5,000 a year.

When he called upon former donors, he noticed their coolness, and realized that first of all he must build up a list of new donors whose interest was in the Berea of the present, his Berea. Yet the past had not quite deserted him, for at his hardest time a considerable bequest left by a past donor whom he had never seen relieved the pressure upon him. Fifteen years later President Frost in a public address expressed his gratitude when he said: "We should have been swamped in the panic of 1893 had it not been for the bequest of $6000 from Joseph H. Stickney."[9] In 1915 he again referred to the emergency of his first year when he said in reference to this bequest: "That money we used to live upon. From that good time we have never been obliged to eat our bequests. All the bequests since then have gone into permanent things."[10]

In midwinter of the year 1894-1895 President Frost had an intuition that he ought to call on Dr. D. K. Pearsons, a philanthropist who had already made generous gifts to numerous small private colleges. Without delay President Frost left his financial work in the East and secured an interview with the philanthropist in his Chicago home. In the end it was arranged that a ministerial friend of the doctor would deliver an address the following Commencement, 1895, and Dr. Pearsons would accompany him to Berea. This plan would give President Frost the opportunity to show Berea College to a rich man who was already interested in college education.

The doctor liked what he heard and what he saw on the Berea campus, even including the thin potato parings in the boarding hall kitchen. Commencement afternoon he gave a short address, at the close of which he handed President Frost a letter to read aloud. Dr. Pearsons offered to give Berea College $50,000 when the College had raised $150,000 for additional endowment. This was his customary pattern of donation, intended to encourage other donors to join in strengthening a college's financial basis. The Commencement crowd in and around the Tabernacle threw up their hats, yelled, and sang jubilantly. The band played "Hail Columbia." College boys hunted up two long ropes, and after unhitching the span of horses from the doctor's carriage and fastening the ropes to it, they themselves pulled the old doctor in a joy ride over the campus to President Frost's home. Everybody enjoyed this great day, including Dr. Pearsons. Fifty thousand dollars was the largest sum of money that Berea had ever been offered, to say nothing of the additional $150,000 that was in prospect. Forty-three years after the memorable day an elderly man wrote to President Frost: "I was one of the boys who hauled Dr. Pearsons and yourself about town in a carriage when he gave his first $50,000 to the College."[11]

Because so much effort had to be expended upon raising money for current expenses, three and a half years passed before the requisite $150,000 was raised to meet the doctor's offer. In the latter part of this financial campaign President Frost taught his wife how to raise money for the College, and in the last month of the drive she raised $30,000. For the next sixteen years she was his best financial assistant. The following selection from a letter to Mrs. Frost while the president was raising the first Pearsons endowment could be repeated from any of the first twenty years of his administration, though the sums grew larger as the years passed: "In the last 30 days have seen 93 new people and 36 old friends, visited 16 towns, made 15 addresses, sent home $760 while some $400 has been sent in by people I have seen, secured written pledges for $260 and verbal pledges for enough more to make up a total of some $2000. Besides, have made progress with Hospital . . . and access to Rockefeller, Carnegie, and C. P. Huntington."[12] Four months after the first Pearsons Endowment Fund came to a successful close, the old doctor repeated his offer, which was completed with a struggle in June, 1900.

In 1909 Dr. Pearsons gave $25,000 for building a men's dormitory, now Pearsons Hall, his gift this time being unconditional. Later in the same year he made his third endowment offer to Berea College, this time promising to give for endowment $100,000 when Berea had raised $400,000 of new endowment money. He had helped more than forty colleges with gifts of endowment and buildings, but now in his ninetieth year he chose Berea for his final donation, emphasizing in his offer the fact that he was particularly impressed by "the faithfulness which its officers had shown in the care of endowment funds." He closed his letter with the words: "I can think of no place where my last gift to colleges will be so well invested as there."[13] At this time President Frost was too much broken in health from his work in raising the Adjustment Fund to carry on another financial campaign, but the trustees took the burden upon their shoulders, and by the time the president returned from a year's rest in England, the J. S. Kennedy bequest of $50,000 and Mrs. Kennedy's promise of $250,000 had been made, so that the entire endowment was soon completed. By Frost's twentieth year in office (1912) the college endowment had been increased from $100,000 to $1,000,000.

From the time of his coming to Berea President Frost had pressed hard for more students, and the growth from 354 in 1892-1893 to 1,423 in 1912-1913 greatly increased the need for "more pillows and more plates." The more endowment he secured, the more buildings and donations for current expenses he needed. He personally wrote much publicity material, which his office mailed to a growing list of interested people.

He recognized the value of having distinguished persons as friends of Berea College, such outstanding persons as Theodore Roosevelt, New York's new police commissioner, who addressed a Berea meeting in Boston in November, 1896; Mrs. Julia Ward Howe, who presided over a meeting where Frost spoke (1899); Miss Helen M. Gould, who came to Berea with a party of lady friends to spend the Commencement season in 1900; Andrew Carnegie, who in 1907 pledged $200,000 to the Adjustment Fund; and Governor Woodrow Wilson, who in 1911 spoke at a great meeting in Carnegie Hall, New York, for the Pearsons-Kennedy Endowment Fund.

At the close of his fourth year in Berea (1896) President Frost wrote to the Berea trustees: "It is a disappointment to me and a loss to the school that so much of whatever gifts I have as an educator must lie unused while I am struggling for current expenses."[14] In 1911 at the close of a day in New York when he had finished mailing four thousand invitations to his great meeting in Carnegie Hall, he turned to his Berea secretary and said: "Think what will happen when we can work at the school work and the religious work like this! And really 'the good time coming' seems almost here."[15]

"The good time coming" had not yet arrived, however. President Frost, his wife, his faithful aide Professor Henry M. Penniman, and a new assistant carried on one more financial struggle, an "Efficiency Campaign" to raise a million dollars, half for additional endowment and half for the construction of permanent buildings for the five segregated departments. The College had never before set so great an amount as its goal, and this time there was no Dr. Pearsons to start off the campaign with a munificent initial contribution. Hopefully President Frost sought for a generous grant from the young General Education Board and the newly founded Carnegie Foundation through which Carnegie by this time usually gave his donations for education; but both foundations with courtesy deferred a final decision so long that President Frost set out upon his financial effort without their help.

In place of a large initial gift President Frost arranged a meeting to be held in the new D.A.R. hall in Washington, with Justice Charles Evans Hughes as presiding officer and the President of the United States as the principal speaker. More than two thousand invitations were issued, in the name of forty-eight friends of Berea College, including cabinet members, senators, distinguished ministers of various denominations, and outstanding businessmen. After Justice Hughes, President Frost, Professor Frederick G. Bonser of Columbia University, and Hamilton W. Mabie of the *Outlook* had given their interpretation of Berea's work, President Woodrow Wilson made his appeal for Berea College. His words, spoken in Berea's sixtieth year, form a memorable part of Berea's treasured past—the democratic ideal of Fee and Clay restated for a new generation of Americans. Wilson said that he was not speaking in his official capacity of President of the United States, but because of "his profound interest in Berea College." Presently he said: "Our nation is not fed from the top. It is not fed from the conspicuous people down. It is fed from the inconspicuous people up; and the institutions like Berea that go into the unexhausted soils and tap their virgin resources are the best feeders of democracy."[16]

The meeting received excellent publicity, but the harvest did not come until the following year (1916). An incredible number of calls and addresses were made to raise this Fund. Eventually Carnegie out of his personal friendship for President Frost made a conditional pledge of $63,000, a sum which was so figured as to make him the donor who had pledged the largest total sum to Berea College up to that time. It was very exciting to receive now the promise of a dormitory, now a new home economics center, now the money for a new hospital building, and now $40,000 for the endowment of mountain agriculture. A million dollars, however, is a very large sum of money to raise, and by the fall of 1916 Mrs. Frost was too near exhaustion to continue her work. President Frost, too, was drooping in health, but he continued at his work until early December, 1916, when he collapsed in New York. One hundred thousand dollars was yet to be raised. As some of the pledges had January 15, 1917, as their terminal date, he continued his work by mail and telegraph from his office in Berea, and by January 15 the goal of the Efficiency Fund was reached at least in pledges. President Frost never fully recovered from this overeffort.

III

CERTAIN GIFTS create in their donors an unusual glow of satisfaction. Such was the case with the college forest reserve and the college waterworks. Professor Mason, a forest expert, ac-

companied the students on their all-day picnic to Indian Fort
Mountain his first autumn in Berea (1897). He saw the breath-
taking views from East and West Pinnacle, explored Indian
Fort, and made up his mind that the College ought to possess
a forest for two reasons: first, to aid in teaching forest care to
his classes; second, to provide fuel and lumber for the College.
During the fall days after this Mountain Day, he rode much
in the forest lands and saw John Kindred's fine spring, about
which he wrote later: "It was then I gained the idea that this
spring and other springs lay at a considerable elevation above
Berea College and might be piped there by a gravity system of
water works."[17] His interest, however, was more in the forest
than in the springs.

Since the hills were covered with second growth and not
virgin timber, he thought that purchases of many small holdings could be made at a very low price if the buying were done
quietly. He had much of the forest surveyed under his direction by a young instructor in mathematics, who also tested the
water flow of each spring. As it was not easy for President
Frost and the trustees to buy forest land when every effort was
being made to raise money for the Pearsons Endowment and
for current expenses at the same time, Professor Mason personally bought both East Pinnacle and Indian Fort lest they
fall into other hands before the College was ready to buy.

Then one day in 1899 President Frost was invited to call on
a certain Boston woman of property who wished to make an
unusual donation. She had heard of Berea's interest in forestry
and wished to buy a forest for Berea College in memory of her
late father, who had dearly loved a well-kept stretch of woodland. By 1901 the College possessed eight hundred acres of
forest land, for most of which this woman had paid. In her
letters Miss Sarah B. Fay repeatedly reminded the president
that part of her check was to apply on the salary of the professor of forestry. When President Frost in a letter made mention
of a tract containing good springs, she replied in an undated
letter: "It seems to me at this distance . . . that it would be

desirable to secure that tract if really suitable before it is turned over to some other purpose." One day in 1903 she wrote from her summer home at Wood's Hole: "I sent you $2,000, of which I think $600 was for salary and the remainder toward woodland. Take advantage while you may of my having a fresh attack of what my father called 'land fever.' Gifts that grow are best. . . . Besides, an unbroken tract is so appealing to a land lover."[18] On a certain January day, year unmentioned, she wrote to President Frost: "I can probably manage to help out on that land. . . . I feel more like investing in land than in human nature. I have learned that I know nothing of human nature and would better stick to trees." She possessed a green map on which the various tracts, large and small, were indicated. One day in 1903 she wrote: "The tract marked B you ought to have to fill out, when you can get it. . . . I do love a handsome, well-bounded piece of land now better than a handsome boy."[19] In 1911 when Berea's forest contained more than four thousand acres, Miss Fay wrote with a vague desire for the silent woodland: "I'm just longing to buy those big oaks that Mr. Penniman can't get a clear title to."[20]

After 1900 the annual reports pressed for an adequate water supply, now that people knew the College owned some mountain springs. Since the trustees in 1902 and 1903 hesitated to incur the expense of piping water downhill and up again from springs four miles distant and two hundred feet above the Berea Ridge, the trustee committee considered the wisdom of placing a small engine in the bed of Brushy Creek to supply Ladies' Hall and Howard Hall with water at no great expense. In August, 1903, Dr. Pearsons wrote to Trustee Cleveland Cady in New York that he considered water the most important of all Berea's problems, but that he had so many pledges to pay the next year that he could not consider a gift of waterworks for Berea College.

It was Trustee Addison Ballard who took Berea's lack of water most seriously. He was a Chicago businessman, and a friend of Dr. Pearsons. In 1902 when the trustees hesitated over the expense of piping spring water from the hills to Berea, he suggested that they could avoid expense by following Chicago's pioneer example. They might cut logs out of the forest and make a four-inch bore lengthwise: "If properly buried, they will do the work for twelve or fifteen years. Do it all ourselves and have water and plenty of it without paying any interest money for drain pipes."[21] Late in 1903 after a trustee meeting in Cincinnati this tenderhearted trustee from Chicago wrote to President Frost: "There has scarcely been a day that I have not been thinking about that water supply at Berea, nor a night that I don't dream of it since I came home from Cincinnati."[22] Already he had told Dr. Pearsons that he had "no right to build up a school to the number of a thousand students and then let them choke to death with thirst."[23]

By this time the Reverend William E. Barton was pastor of a church in Oak Park, near Chicago. He knew the water need of Berea, and since he was a trustee, he was acquainted with Addison Ballard. In the fall of 1903 these two trustees, aided by Mrs. Barton, secured from Dr. Pearsons a secret pledge that the next year he would provide Berea College with waterworks;[24] and on June 22, 1904, the doctor sent his pledge for $50,000 to the trustees, adding in the fourth paragraph: "Mrs. Pearsons and I make this gift to promote the cleanliness, good health, and permanent prosperity of Berea College, and of the village, especially the families who have moved there to educate their children, and of the young people boarding themselves."[25] It was Addison Ballard who dug the first shovelful of dirt for the water pipes in October, 1904, and Mrs. W. E. Barton who on Commencement afternoon in June, 1905, at a hydrant near Lincoln Hall "officially started water flowing upon the college campus. The student fire company was there in readiness to give a short display of the height and volume of the stream of water for fire purposes."[26] Dr. Pearsons often said that the gift of waterworks to Berea College was the best investment he had ever made and that "he had never done a thing in his life that gave him so much fun."[27]

IV

IN LATE OCTOBER, 1914, President Frost made a special trip to call on Charles M. Hall, first vice-president of the Aluminum Company of America, hoping to secure $1,000 for the Efficiency Fund. He was disappointed to receive only $500. This quiet industrial chemist, Charles M. Hall, who had invented an inexpensive method of extracting aluminum from clay, had known about Berea College for many years, for when he was a little boy back in 1872-1873, his eldest sister had taught in Berea. Also, he had known President Frost as a Greek professor who had helped him to make up some Greek lessons one Christmas vacation in Oberlin. Hall never came to Berea, but he made donations to the College that ranged from $50 in 1903 to $5,000 in 1910.

When he sent a check to Berea, he usually accompanied it with a personal letter to his former teacher, President Frost. This correspondence is of peculiar interest from the fact that this Charles M. Hall who never saw Berea donated the largest block of endowment that Berea has received up to this time (1955). In 1906 he assured President Frost that he was a firm believer in the importance of Berea's work. In 1910 when he pledged $5,000 he added in a postscript: "My interest in Berea College is largely on account of your personality and your work. I should like to see you again perhaps sometime when you are in New York, and learn a few things about the college itself."[28] A few days later he mentioned in a letter that he had been greatly interested in the *Berea Quarterly*, and that he wanted to ask the president a few specific questions about Berea. In October, 1912, he wrote: "If I should continue to prosper, I hope to do more for you in the future."[29] He made no mention of having written Berea College into his will the preceding July. In August, 1914, his letter expressed his expectation of helping Berea in the future, though the war situation had temporarily embarrassed him.[30] Hall died on December 27 of that same year, 1914. On January 15, 1915, the president noted in his diary: "News of bequest of Hall, whom I had seen in October last."

By this will Berea College was left one-sixth of Charles M. Hall's residuary estate. While this property, consisting largely of speculative stocks, would not come into the possession of the College for a considerable number of years, some income from it might be expected within a few years. Such income began to be paid to Berea in 1918, $72,000 the first year and $98,000 in each of the two following years.

President Frost feared certain ill effects from the prospect of future payments from the Hall estate. In the last financial survey of his administration he warned the trustees and faculty of this danger: "The Hall Fund does harm as well as good. It is easily assumed that this income will be permanent, even enlarged, and should be used not to reach farther into the mountains, but to embellish and pad our life here in Berea! . . . We have kept the Hall income separate from our 'chief revenues' to pay debts, erect buildings, and provide for forward steps. Its first service has been to help meet the extra expense entailed by the war."[31]

                                 v

WHEN WILLIAM J. Hutchins became president, he found Berea College encumbered by a debt amounting to a quarter of a million dollars. This was a respectable debt, but it was a debt, nevertheless, and one which in time might hurt the College in the eyes of its donors. This debt had not been incurred for current expenses and it was not an old debt. It had been made in wartime and when President Frost was in poor health. This borrowed money had been spent in buying land for college expansion and in providing much-needed new buildings and equipment in a period of great expansion of student attendance. A large part of this money had been borrowed from college funds, not from outsiders. These college funds, however, consisted of money that had been given for some future use other than expansion in land and buildings.

It was assumed that such loans were not undesirable, for they were more than covered by the wills of friends still living and by the expectation of continuing income from the Hall estate. Moreover, the president expected to raise money for repaying much of this debt from certain "great friends of the Institution" when he was in a better state of health for presenting the College's needs.[32] Finally, however, the trustees in their meeting of June, 1919, voted to cut every possible expenditure for expansion.

Five months before President Hutchins took office in June, 1920, the treasurer of Berea College warned President Frost that the College was following a poor financial system: "Our expenditures have no relation whatever to our income, and our attempts to run on a budget plan are more or less of a joke. We have followed this method of spending money before we get it, trusting to our prospective bequests, funds we administer, or our borrowing power, until we have almost reached the point of disaster."[33]

When the Berea trustees' committee urged William J. Hutchins, for thirteen years a professor in the Oberlin Graduate School of Theology, to accept the presidency of Berea College, they assured him that he was entering upon educational rather than financial duties inasmuch as the Hall bequest would doubtless bring to Berea at least the same amount as in the two preceding years; but in his first summer after taking up his new duties, President Hutchins found it necessary to join in signing a personal note in both July and August so that teachers' salaries might be paid. He learned also that at the preceding trustee meeting teachers' salaries had been raised 25 per cent, the new rate to begin with September, 1920.

In late August, 1920, a member of the Board of Trustees wrote to the new president a five-page letter by hand, frankly explaining the seriousness of Berea's recent method of financing expansion and asking for more respect for the endowment and the budget. To this letter President Hutchins replied with an earnest letter of appreciation, saying that he agreed with the idea that bequests should be used only as endowment and that he welcomed a mandate of the trustees to this effect. He asked, however, for a short breathing space to extricate the institution from its "staggering debt." Three days later the president wrote to one of the oldest and most devoted trustees:

"I wish first to remove the present indebtedness and then I wish to present to the Board of Trustees the recommendation that hereafter we shall live within a carefully prepared budget and use bequests exclusively for endowment and similar purposes. Now . . . I need the backing of those trustees who have been working at the great task during the past years; who know what has taken place, why it has taken place, and how to devise ways and means by which we may escape from our present situation. . . . Personally I am full of hope. I believe we are working in a deep hole, but a hole which shall prove a tunnel and not a grave."[34]

On the following October 20, 1920, two days before the formal inauguration of President Hutchins, the Board of Trustees took action providing that the Prudential Committee should prepare a formal budget, to be presented to the Board at their annual spring meeting for approval. "After the adoption thereof by the trustees, the budget may not be exceeded by the Prudential Committee except in special emergencies when the majority of the Financial Committee shall be required." In his annual report of 1923 President Hutchins included a summary of the budget that had been adopted by the trustees for the year 1923-1924, and this practice of printing the budget in the president's report has been continued up to the present time. It is, in a sense, a mark of the respect which Berea College pays to the endowment and to the principle of a budget for responsible living.

The $100,000 of endowment held by Berea College in 1892 had increased to $3,500,000 by the close of President Frost's

administration. Since 1920 this endowment has been aug-
mented largely through the addition of bequests to it. When
Berea's share of the bequest left by Charles M. Hall at the
time of his death in 1914 was transferred to the College in
1929, it was gradually reinvested in a diversity of securities
which were credited to the endowment. By 1930 President
William J. Hutchins in his annual report was able to state that
endowment funds amounted to a little more than $9,000,000.
In President Francis S. Hutchins' first annual report in 1940,
he reported Berea's nonexpendable funds as amounting to about
$10,500,000. By 1955 this mainstay of Berea's economic life
amounted to $16,000,000.

The endowment is rightly called the lifeblood of Berea's
financial structure. It takes the place of annual legislative
grants to state colleges and universities, and of Board grants to
colleges under church management. Berea's nonexpendable
endowment is what gives stability to this nonstate, nondenominational college. Since 1920 this fact has been more than ever
recognized and respected by Berea trustees and administrative
staff. The vital function of the nonexpendable endowment in
supporting the existence of Berea College may be realized from
the fact that 70 per cent of Berea's annual income is derived
from endowment, 20 per cent from donations, 2.5 per cent from
laboratory and similar student fees, and the remaining 7.5 per
cent from rentals and student industries.

Strangers often ask why people give so generously to Berea
while they live, and write Berea into their wills, whether their
estate is large or small. The answer was well expressed by
Zenas Crane, Sr., a very generous donor to Berea in the first
half century of Berea's existence. Professor Fairchild had begun to thank him for another gift when Crane interrupted with
the words: "Don't thank me. I thank you and your father from
the bottom of my heart for doing exactly the type of work
which I want to see done in the South."[35] These words from a
man who gave by the thousands of dollars apply likewise to
the many donors who for a century have given by the hun-

dreds, the fifties, and the tens, because they believed in Berea's program of education. The words of these donors show their desire to be continuing partners in Berea's "allegiance to humanity."

Bruce Barton in a letter asking for $1,000 for Berea from each of twenty-four friends expressed in another way the answer which many people give to the above question: "A couple of years ago I said: 'I'd like to discover the one place in the United States where a dollar does more net good than anywhere else.' . . . I believe I have found the place." After telling about Berea he continued: "Most of the activities to which we give our lives stop when we stop. But families go on. And young life goes on, and matures, and gives birth to other lives. . . . Honestly, can you think of any other investment that would keep your life working in the world for so long a time after you are gone?"[36]

Historically Berea's financial support comes from individuals rather than from the great foundations. The family foundations, however, and the foundations that reflect personal interests have been of very great service to Berea in recent years, enriching the College with improved equipment, financing educational projects for an initial period of years, adding to scholarship funds, providing series of lectures, and giving aid in emergencies.

VI

BEREA COLLEGE in many ways shows its concern for the financial life of its students. The cares of the administration would be lessened if a tuition fee replaced the no-tuition policy of the College, but even a low tuition charge would defeat the fundamental purpose of the institution to bring education within the reach of promising students who have very limited means. Every possible effort is made to keep the price of board and room low, though the boarding halls and dormitories must cover their operating costs from student payments. The College makes emergency loans available at the recommendation of the deans of men or women. If a student finds it impossible to bring cash even for his first term bill, he may receive a loan from the College, to be repaid by earnings from his labor. If a student chooses to stay for full-time labor in the summer or the winter vacation, he receives a considerably higher rate than during term time, and also under certain conditions a 10 per cent bonus upon his summer vacation earnings.

The salaries of Berea's faculty are not large, but at least they meet the requirements of the Southern Association; and fortunately there are highly trained teachers in the prime of their professional life who help to make Berea's no-tuition program possible by adding to their modest pay checks the satisfaction which they find in Berea's educational and social pattern.

Since 1920 the College has added some services which are especially helpful to the staff. In 1923 the annuity service of the Teachers Insurance and Annuity Association was provided to the teaching and administrative staff with the College contributing 5 per cent and the staff member the same share of his salary for a retirement income. Twelve years later the same service was extended to nonacademic college workers. In 1947 the College made group life insurance available to all college workers, in 1951 federal social security was introduced, and in 1952 participation in the College Equities Retirement Fund of the T.I.A.A. was extended to the Berea staff. The College Credit Union, for which the administration furnishes an office and part time of a secretary, makes loans on character reference to the faculty at very reasonable rates. The faculty have the benefit of low rental if they live in college-owned houses, and reduced rates for hospital care. A limited number of grants are made each summer for faculty study and travel, and a decennial leave of absence for these two purposes is given with full pay for half a year or half pay for a full year.

Berea's work program necessitates certain activities seldom recorded in the financial reports of a liberal arts college. Before pay-up day every half term each superintendent of student labor, the librarian for example, prepares a report from the student time cards. This shows the total number of hours worked by each student worker, his rate of pay, which rises with increased experience, and his total earnings for the past nine weeks. This report is sent to the labor office to be added to the student's labor record, and is then transferred to the treasurer's office for use on pay-up day. The business manager must order supplies for the dairy and the Fireside Industries as well as for the library and the registrar's office. Tables of net loss or gain of the utility adjuncts, for instance broomcraft and the creamery, must be prepared. In the financial report for the fiscal year ending June 30, 1954, the schedule of the equipment, fixtures, merchandise, and supplies for the enumerated utility adjuncts amounted to a little more than $1,000,000. The schedule of college buildings in the same report included among others such buildings as the cannery, the piggery, the trades building, two imperishable silos, calf barns, brooder houses, a dry kiln, and a cattle shed. All this and more is essential to the working of the labor program.

Berea College also has interesting business relations with the town of Berea. Soon after the College built waterworks in 1905, it began to sell water service to the town, and still with increased facilities continues to do so. Therefore the income from water must be included in the fiscal report of the College. The College holds a twenty-year franchise from the city of Berea to sell electricity to the city and the citizens. Town and College share in the same sewer system, though for many years the College had its own sewer lines. The College and the town share equally in the cost of the two Berea fire trucks, and they also share equally in their operating expenses. The College provides the service and salary of two staff members as fire chiefs, and the labor and living quarters of young men students as firemen, while the city pays the College twenty-five dollars for each call made by the town.

BEREA COLLEGE before 1890 might have done well enough without a Board of Trustees, but since that time trustees have been absolutely essential to the welfare of the College. The Board of Trustees of Berea College consists of thirty members and the college president. These trustees hold office for a term of six years. The Board is a self-perpetuating body, and it is accustomed to select new members who shall represent a diversity of interests. Some are skilled lawyers, a few are bankers, some are industrial executives, some are educators, some are ministers of various denominations, and now three are alumni nominated by the alumni organization. At the present time ten are from the East, six are from the Middle West east of the Mississippi River, three are from the trans-Mississippi West, and eleven are from the South, seven of these being from Kentucky.

The Board of Trustees holds two meetings a year, one in New York in the late fall, the other in the spring at Berea. Much of the trustee work is done by committees, which meet as suits their convenience during the year. One of the most important committees is the Finance Committee, which in collaboration with the fiscal agent of the College, now the First National Bank of Chicago, handles the investment securities. Other important standing committees are those on Student Industries, on Buildings and Grounds, and on Educational Policies, while special committees are formed to meet particular situations.

Over the years the trustees have been men of unusual social conscience, and they give their service to Berea as to a beloved cause. Most of them have served for several terms and have gained a deep understanding of Berea's problems. Thompson S. Burnam said in 1916 in his second term: "As the years roll by, Berea grips me closer." When William A. Julian, the treasurer of the United States, died in 1949, he was in his thirty-fourth year as a trustee of Berea College; and although the property which came to Berea from his will was the second largest bequest ever made to the College, yet the value of his service as a trustee and especially as a member of the Finance Committee over a long stretch of years may have been worth fully as much as his final bequest.

No man is elected to the Board of Trustees because of his wealth. Each trustee shares as he is able in carrying the college burden, whether by priceless legal advice, by financial service, by finding new friends for the institution, by defense of a fundamental principle when it seems to him endangered, by giving encouragement to a burdened president, or by calling to mind the importance of spiritual values.

The well-being of Berea College depends not only upon what is done with the College's endowment, but also upon the kind of men who are chosen as trustees. President William J. Hutchins expressed this with clarity in saying to the trustees when they were considering the election of a new member to the Board: "I sometimes think of Berea as a beautiful and precious vase, in which are stored certain spiritual essences, which, quite without our knowledge, may escape. One day they may disappear; the vase will be here, all the buildings, the endowment, the students; but the Berea which you and I love, and for which we would gladly die, will be lost."[37]

CHAPTER 8: A Century of
Sharing

FOR A CENTURY Berea College has faced urgent social needs that have weighed upon its conscience as a community of faculty, students, and neighbors. For a century it has been clear that the College would fail of its best intentions if it were only a recipient and not also a giver. The more freely Berea College has received, the more strongly it has felt the duty to give in increasing measure.

From the beginning Berea's "chivalry of education" has found expression in many outlying communities. This sense of widespread social needs that the College ought to meet has always been a source of strength, sustaining the institution in its hardest years. When this sense of social duty fails, Berea College as the past has known it, as the present knows it, will cease to exist; and Berea will be only buildings, books, and credit.

II

IN THE EARLY DAYS Berea teachers and students were sometimes invited to mountain communities for the purpose of organizing a Sunday school which in a superrural area without a minister served almost as a church. President Fairchild in 1875 spoke of twenty such Sunday schools having been founded in a single year in this way, and added that they were organized largely through the influence of used books brought from Berea.[1] In 1880 when he spoke of his experience at a neighboring county seat in establishing a Sunday school which soon grew to a membership of seventy-five persons, he said that a good library from Berea had been of great help to him in this success.[2]

These Sunday school libraries were succeeded in the 1890's by teachers' "traveling libraries," each one containing from fifteen to twenty books sent in a wooden box which could be set up as though it were a bookcase. A student going out from Berea to teach in a district school would borrow such a library for a term. Of course no charge was ever made for its rental. Already in 1897-1898 the college librarian reported that twenty-one such libraries had been borrowed by outgoing young teachers.

As time passed, Berea's book boxes were made larger so as to hold more books, sometimes as many as fifty, and they were sent farther back into the hill country. As recently as 1933 Berea's extension librarian wrote in her annual report: "The mode of reaching their destination varies from mail train to river boat and from private car to mule back. One teacher in the mountains wrote to ask if she might keep her box of books a little longer 'until the roads get better, as the mail carrier has to go on a mule about twelve miles.' A wooden case containing forty-five books would make quite an addition to the mule's load of mail!"[3]

Thanks to friends who became interested in Berea's extension work with books, the library presently was able to buy new books to replace the used books of earlier days. The librarian's report in June, 1954, showed that the Berea College library had circulated during the past school year 161 traveling libraries, containing a total of 6,872 books, and that these libraries were placed in the schools of twenty-three counties.

The need for this service is suggested by the fact that seventy-five of these book boxes were placed in one-room schools. County bookmobiles have not yet superseded Berea's traveling libraries in schools at the head of the hollow.

For twenty-seven years (1916-1943) the college library also shared its resources of books by means of a book wagon or, later, a book car. Miss Corwin had read of book-wagon service provided by public libraries in communities of Maryland, Delaware, and Connecticut. Could not the library of a college with cultural *noblesse oblige* in its heart set up a similar service for its timid country neighbors? Miss Corwin secured the gift of two book wagons—one of them built by the dexterous father of a Berea student—as well as a small sum of money for operating the roadside service.

In the early years of this adventure in adult education the assistant librarian, Mrs. Florence H. Ridgway, directed the book-wagon service in person with the help of student boys chosen for their ability to handle mules and horses on deeply rutted roads, their understanding of books for book-famished people, and their grace in meeting people.

Mrs. Ridgway saved some of the choice words of appreciation spoken by her patrons. One man upon returning Nicolay's *Boy's Life of Abraham Lincoln* jocosely remarked, "I got so interested I like to have sot up all night reading, and my woman mighty nigh whupped me." An old lady who on the book wagon's first trip refused a book because she was too busy studying "Revelation," compromised later with a book of Spurgeon's sermons, and finally asked for *Ben Hur*, though adding quickly, "But I don't believe much in reading the works of man." The words of an illiterate woman whose husband read the library books to her reflect the common appreciation of the book-wagon service: "It's the nicest thing I know, the way you folks haul around books for us to read."

When this kind of extension work was carried on after 1922 by book car instead of by book wagon, a librarian could cover more miles and visit more schools than formerly, even though her "bookmobile" was the town taxi with no conveniences for dispensing books. Although this book-car service became increasingly more concerned with book reading in the rural schools, it remained to the last also a means of adult education.

In Mrs. Ridgway's 1926 report she spoke of visiting twenty-one schools with books and pictures. The time of the book-car visits was the school's term from July to Christmas. In this year the third book-reading contest was carried on during the entire term, fourteen schools with an approximate attendance of five hundred children participating in the contest, which was intended to guide children into desirable habits and tastes. Also, Home Reading Circles were set up in certain homes, from which the books circulated. In 1926 Mrs. Ridgway reported nine circles, with four hundred books from the book car passing from one member to another.

When Miss Alice Kirk took up the book-car work in 1931, she reported visits to twenty-nine schoolrooms, seventeen of which were one-room schools, making about six calls at each school during the term. The Berea extension service in 1938 furnished books to nine workers in the W.P.A.'s Pack Horse Library Project, sponsored by county boards of education.[4] With gas and tire rationing and the shortage of labor in wartime, Berea's book-car service ceased in 1943 and it was not revived after the war because much of its work could be done through traveling libraries and through the extension office in the Berea College library.

This extension office eventually outstripped in circulation the book wagon, the book car, and even the traveling libraries, and occasionally exceeded the circulation of all these services combined. The first step toward this additional service was the desire of one of the librarians (1914) for an extension room where books for the traveling libraries might be kept. Presently (1916) Miss Corwin secured a "Director of Library Extension," with her office in a basement room which had an outside entrance separate from the students' entrance. She meant to make it easy for country people to come to the library for books during the long months when the book wagon was not running.

By 1922, when the book-wagon circulation was 3,200, the extension room charged out 302 books directly. In 1923-1924 the extension library added to its service "package libraries" sent out by mail in response to a direct request, often expressed in vague terms, such as "some books for my little boys," or "a good book about canning and sewing." The extension librarian was kept in good spirits, however, by confidence that this work was part of "a great vital movement for the betterment of American rural life,"[5] and this faith seemed justified when the circulation from the extension room rose to 995 books in 1930, and 5,183 in 1935, exclusive of book-car and traveling library service. In the year ending in June, 1938, when the over-all extension service was 10,636, the extension room's service amounted to 5,945 of this total. There was, as one mountain man said, "a powerful mess o' larnin' and lookin'" going out to country people in the hills near Berea. In 1954 the extension library showed a total circulation of 11,445 books, 4,573 of which were charged directly from the comfortable, well-lighted extension room with its east basement door.

This survey of the library's extension work would be incomplete if no mention were made of the "extra mile" extension service. The extension librarians rendered many another kind of aid besides taking books, magazines, and pictures to outlying schools and families. They helped country women to find a market for their walnut meats and for their Christmas mistletoe and saw brier greens. They listened to the mother's sorrow, the father's defeat, and the children's unsatisfied desires.

A mountain woman begged to be taught how to write her name, so that hereafter she need not feel embarrassed in the presence of the mailman when he asked her to sign her name. Miss Pearl Durst, like an understanding librarian, taught her this simple thing, and the woman was proud and happy. After some time the mountain woman reported with an unsmiling face that she was now married. Miss Durst tried to congratulate her, but the woman only shook her head. "You're going to be happy, I know," said Miss Durst. The woman sighed: "I never thought of it before I married him. I can't write my name now."

III

IN THE FAIRCHILD administration Berea teachers occasionally rode deep into the hills to lecture on educational subjects. For example, in 1877 Professor Le Vant Dodge was excused from teaching during the fall term so that he might do educational work in the mountains. In 1883 he traveled in twenty-five counties. This kind of work was continued during President Frost's twenty-eight years of administration; but he had the dream of a larger service in his mind. In 1897 he proposed that "this university extension lecturing should be recognized as a regular department of our work."[6] In the fall of 1896 he sent into the hills a young Oberlin graduate, C. Rexford Raymond, whom he described as "a remarkably fine speaker, a master of the mountain dialect, a genial, faithful, winning young man";[7] but at the end of the first month of extension work Raymond was taken sick with typhoid fever and had to give up the promising plans which he and President Frost had made.

In 1899 when Raymond had recovered his health and had completed a theological course at Oberlin, he returned to Berea as the director of extension work. The college catalog of 1900 contained several paragraphs about his new work: "The College reaches out to the surrounding region with benefits of libraries, institutes, lectures, and Sunday schools, as an organized extension for humanity's sake." It explained that Berea College desired "to bring as many as possible of the advantages of learning and the gifts of science to all the people of this region."

In addition to outlying work in rural churches, Sunday schools, and county institutes, the Extension Department offered two new services. One of these, called extension tours, was a slate of five professors, any one of whom would go into the mountains to lecture on certain listed subjects. One of the five was Professor Mason, whose proffered subjects were full-flavored of the good earth: 1. Why our forests should be preserved. 2. Raising more and better stock. 3. How to preserve the fertility of the land. This, you recall, was before the days of county agents.

The other new service was called a "people's institute," in contrast to the familiar teachers' institute. In the late summer and early fall of 1900 Director of Extension Raymond and his young wife, in company with the Normal dean and his wife, carried on such a people's institute, and Professor Raymond left an account of this experience. The party, including the two Raymonds, the two Dinsmores, a cook, and drivers of the two baggage wagons, traveled more than three hundred miles in rugged mountain country, sometimes fifty miles from a railroad, carrying with them tents, sleeping accommodations, an acetylene gas stereopticon, a baby organ, and cooking equipment. They held their five-day institutes in ten counties. Their schedule of meetings began Thursday and closed on Monday or Tuesday, after which the party would drive for two or three days by way of creek beds to the next place on their institute route. Professor Raymond at the end of the trip wrote: "With our tents and baggage wagons our approach doubtless produced quite a circus effect, for one man frankly put his head into our living tent and asked: 'Have you all got any livin' beastes in the tent?' "

Though the extension party twice traversed the belt where there had recently been feud warfare, the meetings were undisturbed. In each place they found earnest people in the valleys "eager to know us and get our message. . . . And when, as often, our newmade friends besought us to come again and said, 'We all never have been fed like this before,' we felt rebuked at the knowledge that what seemed so little in our sight was so much in their lives."[8]

Within eight months after the return of this extension group, two significant comments were passed upon the experiment of a people's institute. In December, 1900, President Frost received a warning from Berea's chief donor that he should not waste money on extension work, which he characterized as "humbug."[9] Fortunately President Frost was not the man to be frightened by a mere six-letter word.

In the following June, Professor Raymond, in commenting upon his experience in the preceding autumn, wrote: "It will make a great difference fifty years hence in all this great territory, and through its influence, in the whole nation, whether our extension workers penetrate one hundred or two hundred miles further into the mountains, and whether eight hundred or sixteen hundred students are in attendance at Berea."[10]

In 1902 President Frost wrote an illuminating message on the subject of planting ideas of progress in the mountains: "To the dwellers on the headwaters of the Kentucky River it is a far cry to Berea, and all the voices of civilization sound faint and indistinct. We propose to go out and make friends with these isolated people, and bring them a few seed-thoughts. In this work we have had no forerunners or examples, and we are feeling our way. . . . The starting of these people toward greater light is so urgent a matter that we cannot wait for them to come to Berea. Indirectly our extension work will bring many students, but the immediate object is to benefit those who may never come."[11]

In the history of the people's institutes there were four very successful leaders, C. Rexford Raymond, John W. Dinsmore, James P. Faulkner, and Charles S. Knight; but none of these men served in the field for more than a few years.

The Reverend James P. Faulkner was the director of extension work from 1908 to 1911. He came to Berea fresh from study at Harvard University; but he was a mountain man who had returned to the land of his birth to work on its problems. With his tent and stereopticon he often forded rocky streams, and in remote valleys he frequently addressed an audience which had come entirely on foot or on horseback. He talked about mountain agriculture, better homes, temperance, improved rural schools, and most of all, sanitation and health. He gave help to young teachers in little slab and log schools. Miss Katherine Pettit wrote from Hindman that his message was the best thing that as yet had come to the mountains. "I hope Berea will keep him in the mountains all the time."[12]

The Reverend Charles Spurgeon Knight began his three-year service as superintendent of extension work early in 1912. His outfit consisted of one wagon, two mules, one tent, one folding cookstove, a stereopticon, and a "talking machine," as well as three helpers. His series of meetings in one place lasted three days, and he lectured on sanitation, better schools, better roads, consumption, cure of hookworm, and bad habits, but always ended his series of meetings with a rousing evangelical sermon and a call for Christian commitment. He reported in 1913 that he had traveled nearly one thousand miles and had spoken to more than eleven thousand people.

When Knight retired as a field leader with wagon and tent, no one was ready to take his place, and the college secretary, Marshall E. Vaughn, who was also the director of extension work, handled speakers' service from his office. The full-page catalog statement of the Extension Department remained unchanged until 1921, but in reality new ideas of extension work were quietly maturing. For example, the introduction to the Extension Department's statement of offerings in the catalog of 1921 contained a new idea: "Berea proposes to co-operate with and supplement the work of individuals and organizations that are doing constructive work in the Southern mountains." That statement expresses what has been the very core of Berea's extension policy since the beginning of President W. J. Hutchins' administration (1920). The days of isolated pioneering in progress had passed. Great organizations like the United States Department of Agriculture, the United States Office of Education, the University of Kentucky, the Red Cross, and the Conference of Southern Mountain Workers had their minds on mountain problems, and Berea College was ready to co-operate with them, giving and receiving ideas and service.

In the catalog of 1921 the services formerly offered by Berea's extension service were condensed into very brief statements, and a new service was added: that Berea College would furnish "demonstrators to co-operate with state and local organizations in putting on school fairs, stock shows, and educational rallies." Another difference is to be noted in the 1921 statement of Berea's extension offerings, namely, the assumption that local communities would take the initiative in arranging for any of these extension services. The team-and-tent days had passed. The days of 4-H Clubs, Future Farmers of America, and county agents were at hand, the days of county consolidated schools, the days of telephone and radio in the country home, and the days of cream cans at the gate; and the extension work was affected by all these movements.

IV

When Berea College in 1899 organized its Extension Department to send speakers into the mountain counties, it set up another "sower of progress," a weekly newspaper called the *Citizen*, to spread good ideas about agriculture, forestry, homemaking, and the children's schools. The *Berea College Reporter* had been a campus publication, but the new *Citizen* was an independent fireside paper that in its early years bore on its masthead the words: "Devoted to the interests of Home, School and Farm." It was not a political sheet, but was "designed to teach when and where there was no voice." The people's institute with its speakers, its stereopticon, and its organ could be with a community for only a few days in the summer or fall; the *Citizen* could come to help them every week in the year.

The *Citizen* in several of its early issues published "Our Platform," saying in substance that its aim was to bring the best reading to every fireside, giving weekly a few new ideas to lighten the labor of housewives and some valuable hints which would enable the farmer to make more from his land and cattle. Some subjects treated in the *Citizen* before the time of the earliest county agents were: Value of fruits as breakfast food; Keeping food clean; Measurements in cooking; The teacher and the first day; Education that educates; Some experiments for boys and girls; Cultivation of memory; Value of absorbents in stalls; How to get good seed corn; Need of a National Forest Reserve in our mountains.

The first page would contain a column of national and state news, some Berea personals, a report of outstanding campus events, and the dates of county courts, county fairs, and teachers' institutes, as well as a few town advertisements. The two inside pages in the first two decades usually consisted of syndicate plate material such as a study of the Sunday school lesson, temperance notes, and the next installment of a serial story.

The fourth page was sure to contain at least three full columns of news items from mountain counties. The flavor of country life was expressed with uninhibited frankness by the *Citizen's* country correspondents. The following communications are selected from the county news items contributed during the first thirteen months after the *Citizen* had been established in 1899:

"Disputanta, Rockcastle Co.: Miss Johnson of Tanyard School was tried for whipping one of Wm. Gadd's children and was acquitted. Good for our citizens. The teacher must be protected."

"Miller's Creek, Estill Co.: Uncle James Smith was bitten by a mad dog on the 17th inst. He went to the madstone at Foxtown in Madison County, and the stone adhered only once. He returned in the full hope that all danger is over."

"Pineville, Bell Co.: G. Taylor was in town recently and the deputy sheriff levied on his mule. There was quite a tussle before he got the mule."

A correspondent from Hyden, Leslie County, wrote: "Some politicians criticize the L. & N. Railroad. They don't live in this part of the county. We believe in the L. & N. If they will build a branch out this way, we solemnly promise that we won't sue the company even if the train should run over our jersey calf. We won't steal rides in boxcars. We'll be good. In default of railroads why not have good district roads? The farmers will make better fences and clean up their farms, when good roads run through the county."

From 1907 to 1924 the *Citizen* bore at its masthead the words: "Devoted to the interests of the Mountain People," and it was altogether suitable that men who were active in mountain field work should also contribute to the *Citizen's* pages. Dinsmore wrote many articles on school improvement for the *Citizen*. Between 1910 and 1913 Faulkner was editor of the *Citizen* in addition to his strenuous speaking tours with wagon and tent. In his three years as editor, the voice of the *Citizen* made very challenging demands for improvement in Kentucky, for better parents, better officials, better schools, and better farmers. This highly educated mountain man had much to say to mountain people, and he spoke with fearless words that commanded attention. Each week for three years he cleared a two-column lane down the middle of his six-column front page for his forceful words. He printed his titles in large type. A random selection from his headings in the five months between July 21 and December 22, 1910, gives the reader some idea of his strong moral and social appeal: "Real coward, the moral one." "Your job, Mamma, not the Lord's." "It's up to the parents." "15 minutes of friendship and the result." "Eyes too sore to see eye sores." "Death's toll in the mountains from criminal indifference." "Folly of ignorance among farmers." "An eight-headed dragon." "Make room in the inn" (December 22).

The state of Kentucky needed Faulkner to carry on extension work against tuberculosis, and the state's gain was Berea's great loss. Soon after Faulkner left Berea, federal and state concern over better roads and schools in the hill country, and the increasing importance of the county agent and the home demonstration agent made it obvious that the *Citizen's* best service could be rendered by close co-operation with these new "sowers of progress." Therefore the pages of the *Citizen* became the organ of the local county agent and home agent. By this time most mountain counties had their own county papers and hardly needed the *Citizen*. On the other hand, both College and town had made very rapid growth in the twenty years after the *Citizen* was established, thus creating more demand for the Berea paper's attention. Since 1925 the *Citizen* has been largely a local paper, serving the interests of the town, the College, and the closely adjoining rural area.

v

THE UNITED STATES Department of Agriculture in 1912 made public a plan to demonstrate to the farmer on his own farm the value of knowledge in practical farming. Immediately President Frost secured this service for Berea, and signed a contract to co-operate with the U.S.D.A. in their plans. Frank Montgomery, a trained agriculturalist, was employed to teach a winter term in animal husbandry in Berea College and to spend eight months of the year in demonstrations to farmers in parts of five counties adjacent to Berea. This was the first such federal appointment made in the state and the fifth in the United States as a whole.[13] This "Special Investigator for Berea College and the U.S.D.A." was what is now a county agent.

In Montgomery's first annual report of his work as a farm demonstrator he wrote that in his first four and a half months in the field (August to the end of the year 1912) he had visited 282 farmers to study the needs of their locality and select the men best fitted to carry on demonstration work the following spring. He reported also the selection of a piece of land near Berea for experimental work, on four acres of which a soil fertility experiment would soon be tried in co-operation with the Kentucky Agricultural Experiment Station. "It is believed that the publicity given this strictly scientific work by State publications and our own literature . . . will give a dignity and prestige to our agricultural course."[14]

In 1914 Montgomery reported that in the past year he had worked with 110 adult farmers and 49 boys and girls, had held 73 public meetings, and had traveled 1,052 miles by rail and 3,129 miles by horse. With genuine insight he wrote to Berea's president: "The true missionary spirit is required for this work. It means much for a mountain man to break away from traditions and take up new methods. Progress must begin with the young, so much of my time was spent in boys' and girls' club work."[15] After two years in Berea's work Montgomery too, like Professor Mason, went into government work.

In 1914 Montgomery was succeeded in his agricultural extension work by a young Berea College man, Robert F. Spence, from a farm in neighboring Laurel County, Kentucky. To an unusual degree Spence's life was rooted in Berea's tradition. His maternal grandfather had been a defender of John G. Fee and Cassius M. Clay in the abolition struggle before the Civil War. Robert Spence himself had begun his student life in Berea while there were still Negroes in every class. He had shared in Berea's work program by labor in the horse barn and in Professor Mason's office. He had taught school in the hills, and had also taught in Berea while still a student before completing his normal and agricultural course in 1914. His profound understanding of the mountain farmer was shown by his common saying, "I believe in working with the farmer, not for him." His love for boys and girls was shown in the fact that his first project was with their clubs in his district, which was southern Madison and the adjoining Rockcastle counties, both of them seeming by nature unpromising for farming.

Forty years he worked with the people of this district, retiring in 1954. His task was to make a better living possible through better farming, and this work never grew stale to him.

He was in the employ of Berea College, the University of Kentucky College of Agriculture and Home Economics, and the U.S.D.A. in co-operative extension work. Berea College not only paid a share of his salary, furnished him with an office and part time of a secretary free of charge, the free use of college rooms for his various projects, and the columns of the *Citizen,* but also showed a warm interest in his work because he was serving the common good in a much-needed field of the mountain area. This county agent was not looked upon as an ordinary federal-state employee. He was Berea College sharing with its neighbors, and it was not by accident that President W. J. Hutchins in each of his annual reports from 1922 to the end of his administration in 1939 wrote appreciative words that showed his interest in County Agent Spence's work, just as though it were in a department of Berea College. After a home demonstration agent began work with women's Homemaker Clubs in 1928, Berea College treated her with a like interest and practical co-operation.[16]

Robert Spence always centered his club work for boys and girls around the schoolhouse, for he knew that when the organizer had left, the teacher was still there to press home the new ideas. He talked to them on a great variety of exciting, grown-up subjects, as one girl wrote in her report, "seed corn, fertilizer, Liberty bonds (1919), and club work." A boy who had recently won a first place for his club project wrote thus about Spence: "Our County Agent is a sticker and helps us do things we think we cannot do."[17] In 1918 one of Spence's club boys wrote a statement that makes further words about this live leader superfluous: "When a county agent influences a boy to burst clods with an ax and manure land by carrying manure in an old dishpan to put on his corn, and roll rocks off the hill, he is worthy of being called a county agent. This is what the county agent is doing that is behind me, and you see we are beginning to go somewhere."[18]

This pioneering county agent was impatient to arouse the adult farmers in his sleepy district as well as the boys and girls.

It was not enough for him to chat in a friendly way with a farmer about better calves, more fertilizer, and poultry that would pay more. He must blow a loud horn in their ears, and blow it over and over. That horn was a slogan, "Paint the county red." Soon people called him "Red Bob"—and not because of his sandy hair. He wanted to sell the county on pure-bred cows—but red cows, Shorthorns. They ought to be raising better hogs, pedigreed red Durocs. Did the barn need painting? Paint it red. And the gates? Paint them red. More silos? Paint them red too. This county agent was not a bookish professor nor an office sitter. He was a picturesque fieldman who made the people listen to him. Soon he had the women raising Rhode Island Red hens. When they were troubled over a way to get settings of eggs for purebred Rhode Island Reds, he secured the co-operation of first one bank and then of both banks in Berea, which agreed to invest in settings of such eggs, selling at the bank for cash or for a promissory note (printed in red) payable without interest in six months in cash or in poultry.[19]

When this farm agent began his work in 1914, only one carload of limestone was used in his territory. Five years later fifty-four carloads of it were used. He was interested in everything that concerned his farm families, the roads, hog cholera, better marketing, water piped into the house, hybrid corn and lambs, improved pasture, sweet clover, rural electric power and telephones—everything. He often held a week's night school (we might call it a workshop). Instead of introducing an expert to lecture in the schoolroom, he used his expert to draw out the farmers' problems in a round-table discussion. Always back of him was Berea College with its resources at hand for his agricultural fairs, demonstrations, and conventions, for he was a means by which Berea shared with the mountain people.

"Red Bob" Spence's successor is a graduate of Berea's four-year College course in agriculture, and through him too Berea shares for the common good.

VI

A COUNTY ACHIEVEMENT Contest was initiated in 1922 by
Berea College through Secretary M. E. Vaughn, with the aid
of Professor Everett Dix, a special supervisor of social service
under the Red Cross, and sponsored by Berea's trustee Judge
Robert W. Bingham, publisher of the Louisville *Courier Journal*, who offered two prizes, one of $3,000 and the other of
$2,000, to the counties of eastern Kentucky showing the great-
est progress in the seventeen months (later changed to two
years) of the contest.[20] A manual was prepared by Vaughn in
collaboration with the Red Cross and the Kentucky Department of Education, Agricultural Experiment Station, and Board
of Health. This booklet listed the ten branches of the contest
and the natural leaders in each of these departments, county
agents and home demonstration agents, health officers, county
superintendents and boards of education, county judges and
fiscal courts, local editors, Red Cross and club leaders, as well
as committees of religious leaders. A maximum of 10,000 points
was assigned to the ten projects: 2,000 points for improvements in the school system; 1,000 each for health and sanitation, home and farm improvement, church and Sunday school,
agriculture and livestock, community clubs, junior clubs, roads
and public buildings; and 500 each to community clubs and
to newspaper circulation. This free manual which Berea College distributed to the project leaders contained the rules and
the score sheets.[21]

Ten counties entered the contest, which "quickened seven
of the competing counties to undreamed of co-operative effort."
This contest harnessed the social forces of the county to the
common good. If a farmer put screens on his windows or built
a sanitary privy for his family, if a congregation painted its
church, if a county employed a county agent, issued bonds for
a new county courthouse, or employed a county nurse, points
were scored for the county.

In seven counties more than 20,000 man-days of free labor were given to road building, and more than 2,000 team-days. In one county five Sunday schools with 409 pupils were increased to twenty-three Sunday schools with 1,950 pupils enrolled. Lee County won first place, and Jackson and Rockcastle tied for second place; but it was clear that whether or not a county shared in the prize money, it had won in reality because so much progress had been made and so much cooperation had grown up among the people of each county.[22]

VII

COUNTY AGENT SPENCE in his annual report at the close of the calendar year of 1930 noted in a few simple words that a butter and cheese factory had been established on a small scale by Berea College and that farmers that year had received $13,000 for milk sold to the College. In the annual reports for the succeeding years of his work as county agent he never failed to express his appreciation of the college creamery's service to his farmers in buying their cream and whole milk to make into butter and cheese for the market.

From its beginning the creamery has been unique among Berea's industries because it has served as a laboratory for training agricultural majors in the practical and technical business of dairy manufacture rather than as an absorber of student labor in general and because it has supplied a better market for farmers' milk and cream than had existed previously in Berea's larger community. From the latter service it has touched in an economic way an astonishingly large number of farm families in five adjoining counties.

The first year of its operation was a drought year in eastern Kentucky with cash very scarce. In June, 1931, President Hutchins wrote in his annual report: "The Creamery has bought from neighboring farmers in this year of their great distress more than $19,000 worth of milk." By the sixth year of its operation (1935-1936) it was buying cream and whole milk from 562 farm families.[23] The number of farmers who sold to the creamery was really more important, especially in drought years, than the total amount paid out to them, because it was the small farmer who most needed such marketing aid and a cash income. In the year 1953-1954 some 850 farm families sold milk and cream to the college creamery.[24]

Under the wise direction of Howard B. Monier, superintendent of the dairy and the creamery, the latter has been a means of adult education as well as a cash resource. Until recently Monier provided his farmers with mimeographed material to show them the importance of raising the best stock and to give hints on feeding. As President Hutchins expressed it: "He sends out with the college checks little sermons on sanitation and milk production."[25] In recent years Monier has sent every two weeks an excellent printed dairy newspaper with the milk check. He used to call upon his farm patrons so as to talk over their dairy problems, but now uses half the time of an assistant to visit his farmers.

VIII

IN THE YEARS between 1925 and 1950 Berea adventured in an "Opportunity School," a unique form of adult education intended to appease "the other kind of hunger" among young adults who were dissatisfied with the dullness of their lives, for plain young people who were not illiterate nonthinkers, but who vaguely craved stimulation and guidance to new interests, though they could at that time attend school for only a few weeks.

Miss Helen H. Dingman had learned from Mrs. J. C. Campbell the advantages of the Danish folk school as a pattern for adult education, and secured not only the consent, but also the enthusiastic co-operation of President W. J. Hutchins. The first such school in Berea College was held for three weeks in

January, 1925, with twenty-three students in attendance, thirteen men and ten women, coming from fourteen counties in Kentucky, one in Virginia, and one in Tennessee. It was not easy to adapt the traditionally informal procedure of the Danish folk school to a college campus where classes were fitted into a fixed daily pattern; but it was possible, and so it was done.

This school continued to meet each January with the exception of 1929, when influenza was rampant. Although these students were usually assigned to vacant dormitory rooms, they always ate together in one of the college dining rooms, and they always had a "home," a room of some size, preferably with a fireplace, and equipped with easy chairs as well as straight classroom chairs, plenty of tables large and small, and books in abundance within arm's reach. This room was open for their exclusive use at any hour of day or evening, and it played an important part in speedily welding two or three dozen young strangers into a group. "We at once realized . . . that we were in a place where we need not be afraid to express ourselves," wrote a student regarding the first morning's session of the Opportunity School in 1941.

The Opportunity School in Berea followed closely the principles of the Danish folk school. There was no scholastic requirement for entrance, and there were no tests of knowledge anywhere in the course, the only requirement being that a student must be over eighteen years of age. All teaching was by use of the "living word," and so the students had no assignments in textbooks, though every encouragement was given them to read books in the home room or in the library. Some students took notes studiously, while others listened without writing a word. One farmer of sixty, a most eager student, constantly took notes in slow, cramped writing. Miss Dingman had helped him to complete a thought after class, and then had asked what he was going to do with his notes. "Well," he said, "I have promised to tell my old Pap all that I have learned here. When I get back home, we'll sit by the fire and talk it all over." His "old Pap" was over eighty.

The men and women who attended Opportunity School were likely to be farmers, carpenters, miners, lumberjacks, rural teachers, rural ministers, housewives, weavers, and youths who had not yet found their way of living. The morning talks were from such fields as literature, home science, child care, biology, music, Bible, history, and social problems. The afternoon's work might be in the loom house, the woodwork shop, the printing office, the sewing department, the plumbing department, or some agricultural adjunct such as the dairy barns, the farm, or the poultry houses. After a visit to the dairy barns, one of these men remarked, "Berea is the durndest place you ever saw in your life. They won't even let you spit in the barn!"

At the Chapel assembly there was at least one treat for them each year, such as the music of the Stradivarius Quartet. One year there was a demonstration of the color organ, and at another time a demonstration of liquid air. President Hutchins usually invited them to spend an evening at his home, and the comments afterward show their sincere appreciation, even the outspoken words of one of these guests: "We sat in President Hutchins' chair at his desk, talked on his dictaphone, and played skittles in his sun parlor." Music from first to last was one of the most vital parts of each Opportunity School group. They delighted to sing "Whenever God doth let us see His treasures," to the music of Sibelius. In the evening recreation hours there was always music, sad, gay, moody, and reminiscent. One student wrote in 1940: "Not the least of our music hours were our own songs around the fire, whether old songs, hymns on Sunday night, or Jim lining out 'Old Mossy Mountain.' "[26] It was 1945, the twentieth year of this institution of Opportunity School. The school had come to a close, and the young men and women were going home, the songs of their Berea fireside echoing in their hearts. One of these students wrote back for the annual prepared by the Opportunity School students, the "Echo": "The train that carried these last 1945 members from Berea whistles back the refrain, 'Live and learn -j-u-b-i-l-e-e.' "[27]

An institution of self-expression that gave added value to this three-week experience in Berea was the annual Opportunity School banquet, served in a small dining room of the boarding hall. The tables, arranged in a rectangle, were decorated with flowers, lighted candles, and interesting place cards made by the students. The menu was that of a holiday. At one end of the room exhibits of the students' handiwork were on display—weavings, woodwork, printing, millinery, handbags, designs for family conveniences, and sometimes even designs for plumbing. One of the students acted as toastmaster, invariably with dignity, humor, and originality. In 1926 President Hutchins wrote in his annual report: "I attended the final 'banquet' of the school, and heard boys and girls, who had never dared to stand and speak before; I heard a song which two of the students had written; I saw a light never before seen on the faces of the men and women; and I am grateful." The banquet came to an end. The term was over. "And common folk like you and me are builders of eternity," wrote one of these students on the title page of the last "Echo," 1950.

The registrar's records show that during the twenty-five years of this adventure 679 students were enrolled in Opportunity School, and that at some later time 111 of these enrolled for regular course work. These figures, however, have nothing to say about the warmth of friendship pervading the group, "better to me than the world's gold or silver," wrote one young woman; the revival of hope that led more than a hundred of these students to return for long-term courses; the creativeness that surged in them as they returned to their homes; the rhythms that they hummed in later days.

Three years after the first Opportunity School was held on the campus, an urgent request came for a week-end school in the mountain community of a man who had gained much in the three-week school in Berea. Plans were carefully laid, and the experiment was a success, though the weather was uncommonly bad. The attendance averaged about 100, though at the climax 168 were present.

Until war came on, it was the custom for several such extension schools to drive out to the hills in October or early November, after the crops were in and before rough weather came on. No group went out unless urgently invited by the community, which provided hospitality and half the transportation cost. The term of the school was a week end, the place a schoolhouse, a settlement house, or occasionally a church. It became the custom to include in the extension group an experienced and versatile song leader, a minister who would lead the morning devotions and preach on Sunday but could also present some secular interest, a storyteller who could hold in his grasp both children and adults of all ages, a speaker on social problems, history, or government, and a speaker on some phase of agriculture, homemaking, or a natural science. A mountain man who wanted to express his appreciation of the extension school summed up his thoughts in 1944 when he said in his words of farewell: "You've left us many a thought and dropped us many a hint." "Child, this is better than a revival," said another man to Miss Dingman.

The evening meeting had begun about six o'clock, as was the country custom. After a song and a story the speaker had talked almost an hour to an audience that drank in every word. It had been planned to close the day with a marshmallow roast around a bonfire. A man in the audience walked deliberately forward and said to Miss Dingman, "Do you reckon that man would give us another talk? We could just sit down and begin all over again."

The extension Opportunity Schools which had become possible because of the automobile and somewhat improved roads necessarily became fewer in wartime because of gas rationing and tire shortage; and after the war they were slow to recover. No Berea teacher who participated in even one of these extension experiences would ever forget the challenge made to him by the sight of his soul-searching audience, or the questions put to him at the fireside of his host.

IX

IN 1943 AT THE invitation of Kentucky's State Department of Education, Berea College became a partner along with six state and municipal colleges in a rural school improvement project. Each college was to work with some Kentucky county on developing and putting into practice some plans for improvement. The Pulaski County Board of Education in the mountain field invited Berea College to adopt that county for its study. At once the Berea-Pulaski Co-operative Enterprise was formed.

At that time there were in Pulaski County 111 one-teacher schools, now reduced to 93. The teachers were greatly underpaid; the shabby little school buildings were in a bad state of repair, many of them without a teacher's desk or even a manmade toilet. The teachers were deeply discouraged, and the people in general indifferent to the rural child's welfare.

Berea furnished three-fourths of the time of a professor, Dr. Charles C. Graham, to serve as co-ordinator of the project. "He is our spark plug," one of the county officials remarked. His greatest service was to interest people in plans for county progress not only in school but also in social welfare. Besides teachers and parents, the service clubs of the county, the county Board of Health, the county agent, the home demonstration agent, and the two county newspapers took an active part making improvements. "Actually," said Dr. Graham in 1946, "we had and have but one aim, and that is to improve living throughout the county." Through the county superintendent he secured the appointment of four of the best rural teachers in the county to act as supervisors, "helping teachers," as they were called. Berea College from special funds given for the purpose financed the traveling expenses of these helping teachers, as well as providing small subsidies for them and money for working materials. Berea also furnished about forty traveling libraries, and each year offered prizes for the rural schools that made the greatest improvement in various lines.

In the first year 103 schools were painted inside, outside, or both. By 1946 county teachers' salaries had been increased by 77 per cent. A hot lunch program was set up to provide half the vitamin and caloric content necessary for growing children. Some of the clubs arranged to pay for a dental trailer's service for six weeks. As time went on, the people in the county carried more and more of the burden, so that Berea's help finally became unnecessary.[28]

In 1949 the Pine Mountain Settlement School became financially unable to carry on its former work in southeastern Kentucky, and Berea was urged to continue this superrural work. After much deliberation an arrangement was made with the Harlan County School Board to turn the Pine Mountain high school organization into a consolidated elementary school, the county to pay the teachers, provide buses for an eight-grade school, and pay a small rental for the use of the Pine Mountain classrooms, library, and lunch rooms. On the other hand, Berea College would share with Pine Mountain in maintaining the buildings and grounds and in providing medical and agricultural work for this greatly needed school in the heart of the mountains. The College received the right to recommend well-qualified teachers to the county superintendent for the school and to use the school for rural teacher training, if it wished.

The two hundred pupils in this elementary consolidated school are residents of what were formerly one-room school districts in an area twenty-five miles in radius. Their parents are disadvantaged, for they live by lumbering and mining, since there is a lack of good bottom land for farming. The districts here consolidated are ones that are unusually isolated by the mountain walls. They need the medical service, the hot lunches, the discipline of a well-managed playground, the improved schoolroom equipment, the records of good music, and the science that is skillfully taught from the surrounding hills. It is interesting to see Berea a partner of Harlan County in enriching a school in the heart of the Kentucky mountains.[29]

After eight years of dreaming, Berea in 1953 found a way to carry on another sharing project. This venture is financed by the Fund for the Advancement of Education, established by the Ford Foundation, and is directed by a Berea professor, Dr. Luther Ambrose. The plan is to train teachers in such a way as to make them regard rural teaching even in the most remote mountain valleys as a profession and a challenge to a college graduate, regardless of low salaries and isolation. Neither the sponsoring Fund nor Berea College pays the salary of these teaching fellows; that is the responsibility of the public school system, as in the Pulaski and the Harlan County projects. The Fund does, however, finance the selected teachers in addition to the county's remuneration. Since the philosophy of the program is that material improvements should come from local effort, the teachers strive to stimulate such local effort, and the helping teachers furnished by the Fund guide the teachers in this work. In the summer these teaching fellows are given the privilege of travel in America or in Europe at the Fund's expense, and the chance to do graduate study in the summer at the college of their choice, besides having their expenses paid at conferences of the group.

The valleys are very isolated, the communities are underprivileged, and the teacher's life is lonely enough. A visitor from Louisville was taken by means of a jeep to Forkéd Mouth School, where a man and his wife taught under the new project. The man explained to the guest: "I am trying things I never tried before, instead of just going on teaching the same old way."[30]

The project is financed for three years. The director, the experts who brave the deep roads to visit these schools, and the chance visitor fortunate enough to accompany the little party that goes out from Berea at least once a week when school holds raise many questions as to the next step that should be taken in order to make the most of this pioneering experiment. This much at least is certain, that Berea College still has the youthful spirit of a young adventurer. The light in Berea's tower still throws a shaft of light along the rough road that leads to Pine Mountain and Middle Squabble.

Berea College in 1955 as in its early days strives to meet urgent human needs, especially when they are in the field of education. The Berea pattern of college life tends to leave in the graduate a permanent sensitivity to social needs and a desire to share in the betterment of some precinct of his world.

CHAPTER 9: Into a New
Century

IN HER EIGHTH chapter, "A Century of Sharing," Elisabeth
Peck comments: "When this sense of social duty fails, Berea
College as the past has known it . . . will cease to exist; and
Berea will be only buildings, books, and credit." Berea College
in the fifth quarter of its history has been more than buildings, books, and credit. In a steadily rising national economy
it has continued to offer its students a chance to earn a good
degree at low cost. It knows that in a democracy the minds
of *all* citizens should be developed and so should democratic
social conscience. It proposes in many ways a consideration
of the human condition and the assumption of responsibility
by those who know the problems and some of the solutions.
The Berea College work-study system is a good system for
producing effective citizens.

In the quarter century since 1955 momentous technological
changes have been made in the whole world. Nations are no
longer private or isolated. Now young people who come to
college take for granted space flight, heart transplant, computer competence. Tempos and technology are different from
what they have been, but the basic needs of human beings
remain the same. There is much work to be done, essentially the same work.

WHEN BEREA COLLEGE set out in 1939 to find a fifth president to succeed President William J. Hutchins, it found him in a corner of China and relayed its invitation to him by way of a British gunboat. The new man was Francis S. Hutchins, son of William J. Hutchins and director of Yale-in-China, which he had been serving for fourteen years. Francis Hutchins was educated at Oberlin and at Yale. At Yale he received a master's degree in international relations. He had been reared in a family personally and professionally concerned with education, religion, and citizenship. On all counts he appeared to be a fortunate choice for Berea, which was already known for "its distinctive and unorthodox approaches to education."[1] And that he proved to be for the next twenty-eight years.

Soon after President Francis Hutchins took his new office, the United States entered World War II, and he found himself with the hard job of presiding over a college where most of the men students, many of the women, and many of the faculty had gone into the military services. But, like other institutions and American citizens generally, the College set out to do its share of the difficult national task. That share was large. According to the President's Report, 1943-1948, there were 1,386 Berea men and women who went into the Army, the Navy, the Air Force, the Women's Marine Corps, the WAVES, the WACS, or military nursing. There were fifty-three Berea College casualties. A story came back to the College hospital that increased pride in the nurses Berea had trained: In one military camp the surgeons, when faced with an emergency, would call for their "hillbilly nursing team."[2]

On the campus, Berea College welcomed a V-12 Navy unit, a total of 782 sailors, who came in shifts between July, 1943, and October, 1945. The group was one of many units stationed across the country, to be trained during the interval when the United States was recovering from the effect of Pearl Harbor and rebuilding its Navy ships. The V-12 unit brought financial assistance in lean times to the College, and the sailors entered into naval discipline and special training, and also into social life with the College girls, deprived by the war of other male students. At that period in the 1940s, Berea's social rules were rather restrictive. So, in order to be hospitable to the sailors, the College eased some of its regulations—on dancing and the number of social events, for instance—and life for the undergraduates and the visitors flourished. During the "occupation" of the Navy unit, it was pleasant for the College people and the citizens of Berea to watch the sailors drill each morning with increasing exactitude, to see them salute their officers so stylishly, to hear their rueful boasting about Navy ways—for example, white-glove inspections of quarters that extended even to dusty bed springs under mattresses. The sailors called their Berea headquarters the Ship, and they always addressed a woman instructor as Ma'am. The V-12 unit added color and vitality to a lonesome campus.

The Executive Officer, John Kessler, and the Commanding Officer, Homer Dunathan, respected Berea and appreciated the College, its president, and his helpers, particularly Louis Smith, Department of History and Political Science, who saw to it that the Navy "sailed old Brushy Fork Creek without a ripple."[3] For a while the sailors, stationed forty miles from the nearest urban lights, were not enthusiastic about their "boondocks" campus. Most of them, gradually or later as they looked back to the experience, felt friendship for its way of life. The mountain climbing, the girls, the good food, and the Berea faculty helped to win them. At the end of the war some of the sailors asked to be allowed to complete their degrees at Berea. Ordinarily, because the young men were not from the Berea territory and usually came from families with high incomes, they would not qualify as Berea applicants. But the College made an exception for thirty-five "Berea sailors." They received their Berea degrees. Today, Berea prizes a photograph of the S.S. *Berea Victory*, a ship named in recognition of the college that did a war job well.

After the war the veterans came back, undergraduates with their caps at a different angle of experience, eager to get their degrees, some with families to be accommodated in College housing, one with a group of fine short stories which he had written in the Philippines. Berea provided 114 apartments, a few in a remodelled frame building, many in quonsets and prefabricated units prepared by the College. In the year of 1947–1948 there were 143 married veterans. Living in College quarters there were 115.[4] Among them there were seventy-two children and babies whose diapers, white flags flapping in the wind, could be seen from the windows of classrooms. The total enrollment of veterans for Berea was 504. They were valuable additions to college classes, were mature, serious, diligent and, in general, set a fast academic pace for the young undergraduates who had been in high schools during the war and who labelled the hard-working veterans DARS, meaning Damned Average Raisers. Perhaps this return to college of the veterans marked a psychological watershed of change for Berea. One Berea veteran, who had been a bombardier, spoke in a Berea College chapel. He said: "The greatest changes are within us. Our minds have discovered a world that lies beyond the point where the earth and the sky once met. We are bigger men than the men who went to war; perhaps not better men but nevertheless bigger men. We know now things we once suspected, and things we never questioned before are now questioned. We know for one thing why we are in school again."[5] That veteran received his Berea B.A. degree in English, later a Ph.D. in philosophy and, in time, became the chairman of a department of philosophy and religion in an eastern college.

Berea administrators also recognized postwar changes. President Francis Hutchins once said: "We know that the society we serve and the institutions in which we work are in continuous change and our programs may lag behind the new conditions they should meet."[6] Dean Louis Smith warned: "Berea must be *and* become. If we hold only to what has been, we achieve a high degree of obsolescence and produce in all likelihood ill-prepared mediocrities."[7] There were many changes in the Appalachian region as well as in the country as a whole. Blacktop roads pushed into the mountains; in the region, consolidated schools, usually with yellow buses and libraries, began to replace one-teacher and two-teacher schools. Public institutions of higher learning increased in the southern states. Television changed the air and also the minds of those who listened and watched. In 1957 American high school teachers across the country considered the significance of Sputnik sailing across a quiet evening sky and encouraged their best students to go into the sciences. Berea made careful changes in curriculum, sometimes in institutional structure and in academic regulations, but held to its basic purpose—the education of capable students willing to help educate themselves, particularly those from the Appalachian region, on a campus interracial and Christian in emphasis.

After the tide of veterans the new freshmen, mostly from Appalachia, increased in number. Then a quiet but important re-entry took place. In 1950, as a result of accumulated protest—from blacks who sued the University of Kentucky for entrance into its graduate schools and also from the city of Louisville that had sought unsuccessfully to support two equal universities, one for blacks and one for whites—the state altered its Day Law, which from 1904 had prohibited the education of blacks and whites on the same campus. Berea at once reopened its doors to all students, regardless of race. The Dean of Berea College wrote: "In September 1950 Negro students may again enter College. After an interruption of almost half a century, the College will resume its historic position in interracial education."[8] This major change took place in Kentucky and in Berea College four years before the United States Supreme Court, in *Brown* v. *Board of Education,* outlawed segregation in the nation. In the first year three black students applied to Berea and were welcomed cordially. Black enrollment from the Appalachian region gradually increased. The black students entered smoothly into campus life, held campus political positions, acted in plays, won college awards. But race consciousness accelerated on campuses across the land. When President Hutchins retired in June, 1967, one of the problems he passed on to his successor was the black-white relationship and the black insistence on more recognition for black students among a white majority.

Between 1967 and 1972 the percentage of black students among entering freshmen grew from five to thirteen per cent, as a deliberate and active search for qualified black students became effective. Except for Kentucky State College, the traditional public black college, Berea came to have the largest percentage of black students of all the Kentucky four-year colleges. In the curriculum of 1970 a Black Studies course was included; the new interdisciplinary courses, required of all freshmen, had units that dealt with the interracial problem. Also, elective courses in various departments gave academic attention to black culture. Gradually, such electives as Problems of the South, Afro-American Music, A Survey of Afro-American History, The Black Experience in American Literature attracted students, regardless of their own race and culture. A Black Student Union was formed that gave black students a campus base and pride in their group. A Black Ensemble singing group was organized. Bereans recognized the acute race problem and its dangers, even on a campus that from 1855 had been committed to interracial education. Two divisions of thought on the problem existed among staff and students: those who supported the necessity for black self-assertiveness and those who held "that the emphasis should be on people and not on color."[9] The latter felt that stress on differences in race—and by that time Berea had a considerable enrollment of Oriental, South American, African students—could reduce unity and negate the insistence of Berea on the value of *all* people, whatever their racial identity. The new president set up a black-white central committee to confer, to talk out some of the issues, to reason together, to be patient and listen to one another.

Despite these efforts, in December, 1971, there was a threat of violence, and the College closed three days early for the Christmas holidays. Several events contributed to the trouble —an episode involving two black students and the town police, a dormitory happening that seemed threatening to some black students, the departure of a black counsellor whose contract was not renewed. On one occasion black students occupied the president's office for one night. President Weatherford talked long to the protesters, then went to attend to other presidential duties. No administrators were personally threatened, no files disturbed. Before the students left the office, two of them obtained brooms and dustpans from an administrative closet and swept up the traces of their visit. It was thought by Berea staff that only Berea students, white, black, yellow or brown, would characteristically know where Berea institutional dustpans are to be found.

There were continuing efforts by the administration to reduce tension and friction, to bring tolerance if not friendship. Many staff and many students, black and white, worked at the task. Progressively the black students developed their own leaders, and, as the number of black students from the Berea territory increased, confidence and cooperation increased. Berea has consistently searched for black staff and has had some success, but not enough to meet its own commitments. The College employs black staff, both academic and administrative. The Campus Christian Center is operated by two ministers, one black, one white. For recruiting, Berea uses both black and white admissions counsellors. It is anticipated that with the recent widening of the Berea territory to include all counties in Kentucky and nineteen Appalachian counties in southern Ohio, there will be a larger number of qualified black students available from Kentucky and Ohio cities.

The parts of Berea's present student body seem to be reasonably cohesive. Approximately one hundred foreign students—from Asia, Africa, and other parts of the world—encourage the emphasis on international and racial unity. In

1979 Berea College enrolled two students from Mainland China, in 1980 three more. All these young foreigners have much to add to Berea's campus. They have an international background, frequently are multilingual. They see the world and its problems differently. Many are especially good in science. They usually work hard in classes and in labor assignments. Many carry the maximum hours of Berea labor. There are good personal friendships across race and national lines. In general, students on the campus smile readily and are courteous to visitors, to staff, and to one another.

II

As an experienced teacher and administrator, President Francis Hutchins was curriculum conscious, encouraging improvements, urging achievement of academic excellence. In 1939 he inherited a curricular organization which separated the first two years from the last two. After five years it was deemed awkward and divisive, unsatisfactory in many ways to both students and faculty. Dean Charles Shutt, with the cooperation of the president, studied and recommended curricular plans being used then in Michigan State University and in the University of Chicago. The Berea administrators involved the whole teaching faculty in the project; they created a central committee and gave it two years to build a curriculum which would be tailor-made for Berea College. The resulting curriculum, called the General Education Curriculum, was in use for the next twenty-two years.

In the new plan, the freshman and sophomore years were rejoined to the junior and senior years of college. The intention of the required program of the first two years was to provide all students with a common body of knowledge, a liberal arts foundation. In the two semesters of the freshman year, every student took composition, history of western civilization, an introduction to the physical sciences, psychology, Old Testament, physical education, hygiene, and a few electives. In the two semesters of the second year, every sophomore took an introduction to the biological sciences, a survey of social sciences, a humanities course (which integrated literature, art, and music), New Testament, speech, physical education, and six hours of electives. For graduation a student was required to take a philosophy course in the junior or the senior year and to demonstrate proficiency in a foreign language. On that liberal arts base, a student specialized in the last two years in a major, B.A. or B.S. Available were twenty-three B.A. major departments and by 1958 five B.S. major departments.

The General Education Curriculum did its work well, and increasingly it won the approval of most students. At first, some of the B.S. candidates protested the eight-hour humanities course. But graduate schools and business employers appreciated the results of the general education foundation which Berea graduates had. And, with accumulating experience, students and alumni found that the liberal arts foundation not only was useful socially but also gave extra dimensions to understanding human experience and enriched daily personal living.

There were, of course, problems. Berea was realistic in analyzing them and practical in solutions. Dean Shutt used to say that a main problem at Berea was distinguishing between the poor student poorly prepared and the capable student poorly prepared. The College had two ways of dealing with the difficulty: first, a flexible, exploring system of testing new students and, second, a pre-freshman preparatory program, called the Basic Program, for freshmen who on tests indicated ability but who clearly needed more work in fundamental skills or subject matter before being allowed to enter the regular freshman courses. The basic courses at Berea were mathematics, composition, literature (which trained in reading also), American history, and world geography—all non-credit, all required if needed, and all taught by College faculty. Sometimes much assistance and encouragement were needed to keep basic students from giving up and going home. Help was available from teachers and also from other students who had themselves successfully completed basic courses.

In the 1950s and the early 1960s other educational changes began, some large and expensive, some small, but all directed to increasing academic quality. The report of Berea College to the Ford Foundation in 1962, when Berea applied for funds to strengthen its educational program, lists several changes.[10] The Office of Guidance, established in 1947, was enlarged gradually to allow extensive, speedy testing and to insure accurate placement for entering students, who were no longer selected by the pattern of high school credits but were chosen on the basis of their overall general records. In 1950 the speed and dependability of the testing were increased by an IBM scoring machine, which made possible the processing of large numbers of tests in a short time. It also permitted the expansion and refining of a variety of achievement tests to be applied at academic check points through the four college years. In 1959, the Audio-Visual Service was detached from the Office of Guidance and made into a separate department. In addition to its standard services to the campus, it operated a twelve-place foreign language laboratory, which expanded in 1961 to eighteen places.

The Ford report states also that in 1960–1961 all students were required to take six hours of composition, including a unit of library science.[11] The library science block was taught by the library staff. An indication of increasing academic quality came in 1953 with the establishment of the national honor society, Phi Kappa Phi, which recognizes scholarly achievement of both B.A. and B.S. candidates. Austin Awards and Austin Scholarships, made possible by generous friends, encouraged sophomores, juniors, and seniors to achieve high academic standing.

From the beginning of the College, the teacher-training program has had special importance. The leaders of the Berea Department of Education worked especially to put good teachers into the classrooms of the region, encouraged an increase in their numbers and in the quality of their training. In 1956 Berea College was accredited by the National Council for the Accreditation of Teacher Education. In 1953, because the State Hotel Association had asked for a hotel management training course in Kentucky, Berea College established a hotel management major in its Department of Economics and Business. A special advantage is the use of Boone Tavern, the College hotel, for training experience. By 1979 seventy-four men and women had completed this major. In 1956 Berea's nursing program, which in varying patterns for eighty years has been a strong concern of the College, changed from a three-year diploma to a full-fledged baccalaureate program, offering a four-year Bachelor of Science degree. The Berea program is the oldest nursing program in a college west of the Allegheny Mountains. It is fully accredited by the National League for Nursing. Like all other Berea majors it has the liberal arts foundation. Berea nurses, male and female, are being trained beyond medical skills. The belief of the department is that nursing of the future will require not only a knowledge of medication and precise medical procedures but also an understanding of the complexity of human beings. Also, a strong emphasis is on teaching people how to stay healthy.

Berea established in 1958 its fifth Bachelor of Science degree, that of Industrial Arts. One of the original purposes was to provide skilled teachers to the numerous vocational high schools of the state and of the widespread Appalachian region. Another selection of courses prepares graduates for positions in industrial technology. The youngest of the five B.S. departments, Industrial Arts has graduated two hundred majors, who in this technological period have quickly found employment.

The departments of Agriculture, of Home Economics, of Economics and Business offer both B.S. and B.A. degrees.

Berea values its five Bachelor of Science majors: Agriculture, Home Economics, Business Administration, Nursing, Industrial Arts. By requiring the same liberal arts foundation that is required of the B.A. majors, the College deepens and expands professional training. The two patterns, B.A. and B.S., co-exist well and often overlap to the advantage of the students, whether B.A. or B.S.

One of the major changes in the structure of Berea College came near the end of the presidency of Francis Hutchins in 1967, to be effected in the first year of President Weatherford's succession. That change was the elimination of the Foundation School, the Berea College high school, and of Knapp Hall, the Berea College elementary school. For many productive years, with a devoted faculty and effective deans, the Foundation School served well a host of young people from the Appalachian region who sought in Berea more extensive education than they could get at home. But the region itself changed. Consolidated schools and blacktop roads made good training accessible in the mountain counties. Berea's Board of Trustees and its president, at last, acted to eliminate the Foundation School as well as Knapp Hall and to join with the Berea community in the building, the financial support, and in the overall encouragement of a new Community School, which now enrolls approximately 1,200 students.[12]

In 1967, when Willis Weatherford took office as the sixth president of Berea College, only the College itself remained of the five original schools that made up the Berea under William G. Frost. It was a strong college, absorbing in its departments many of the functions of the original schools, adapting to new conditions, but maintaining its democratic and Christian intentions. Willis Weatherford brought varied experience as an educator. For seventeen years he had taught in Swarthmore College, and most recently he had served for two years as Dean of Carleton College. He was a specialist in labor economics with a master's degree and a doctorate from Harvard University. Also, he had a theological degree from Yale.

One of the first administrative acts of the new president was to open an examination of the curriculum. The General Education Curriculum had helped to develop many able graduates—private citizens, public servants, and Ph.D.'s—but campuses in the United States in the late 1960s and early 1970s were reacting strongly, sometimes violently, to national circumstances, to the Civil Rights movement, the Vietnam War and its protest, later to the Watergate cabal; and the quiet campus of Berea College also was feeling the stir. The president and many of the faculty felt that a new academic wind was blowing, that a curriculum with fewer rigid requirements and more room for individual preferences was needed for the new decade.

Berea College has always carefully scrutinized any curriculum it is using, adjusting details and parts as experience indicates. Sometimes, as in 1938 and again in 1947 and in 1969, it has abandoned a curricular structure and built a completely new one. The president and the new Dean of Academic Affairs, William Jones, appointed committees, encouraged the project, and joined in the planning. In January, 1970, a new core curriculum was officially adopted by the Berea College faculty. Adjustments were made to fit the major departments to the new requirements, which provided a foundation for all Berea degrees, Bachelor of Arts and Bachelor of Science. In September, 1970, the first freshmen were enrolled under the new plan.

One purpose of the planners was to have a curriculum both liberal in content and liberating in approach. Also, the committee wished to reaffirm within the curriculum Berea's historic dedication to the liberal arts in a democracy, to interracial education, to appreciation of cultural heritage, to the dignity and worth of all good labor, to nonsectarian Christianity. Berea College has always undertaken more than the training of minds. It wants its graduates to be intellectually exploratory but also to be spiritually aware.

In the new curriculum students are given greater responsibility for their own education. Requirements are distributed so that in a year a student can use one-third academic time for the required courses, a third for major courses, and a third for intellectual or creative exploration. For graduation a student has to have a total of thirty-three courses. Nine are required. Three of the nine—Issues and Values, Man and the Arts, Religious and Historical Perspectives—are interdisciplinary and are to be completed in the first two years. Each academic department determines its own requirements for a major, subject to the approval of the College Curriculum Committee and of the College Faculty. A student is required to complete at least eight courses in a major, with a maximum of twelve courses plus collateral courses to total no more than sixteen. Area majors and independent majors can be substituted for departmental majors.[13]

The academic calendar is structured in a four-one-four sequence with a fall term of four months, a January short term, a spring term of four months. The short term can be used in many ways. It allows concentration on one academic course or experiment in a new area. Each year during January there is the possibility of an academic exchange with students from some other colleges. Independent study is encouraged and often leads to the development of independent majors. It is now possible for a foreign language major, with the assistance of the College, to study for a semester in Europe—in Germany, Spain, or France, possibly in Italy for classical studies. Following a trend in the whole country, the new grading system records success rather than failure. A No-Record (NR) is used instead of the F for failure. Berea has always offered special noncredit classes, with instructors and tutors, to entering students who are deficient in academic preparation but who are able, if given help and time, to do college work. But whatever the deficiency, a student to be graduated must catch up and meet the quality standard of Berea's B.A. or B.S. degree.

This curriculum has been in use for twelve years. From

time to time students and staff have been asked to evaluate the program. Generally students approve the overall flexibility of the curriculum, the opportunity to develop their own academic interests and competencies. The gifted students like the independent study and the independent majors. Because of parallel changes in the Berea Labor Program, a student may overlap a labor assignment with a major so that practical experience for a profession or for graduate study can be accumulated before graduation. Examples are science majors who are laboratory assistants; English majors, mathematics majors, language majors who tutor; economics majors who work in the accounting office and who often appreciate the opportunity for apprentice experience acquired as they are getting their degrees. Berea has always used small classes, and the 1970 curriculum continues them, with a faculty-to-student ratio of 1 to 12. Students and staff value the close student-faculty relationships that are common. Other advantages are the diverse offerings in both B.A. and B.S. curricula; the opportunity in the January short term to focus on one class or one project, with relief from multiple academic pressures; the possibility of a permitted leave-of-absence for a student who, for personal or family reasons, needs a respite.

There are some negative opinions on the 1970 curriculum from both staff and students and some important academic reservations. Both groups in considerable number have leveled criticism at the interdisciplinary courses, especially Issues and Values and Religious and Historical Perspectives, which, in addition to specific subject matter, have been assigned the main responsibility in the core curriculum of teaching communication skills.[14] Critics say that writing and speech are neglected. In the years since 1970 the staffs for Issues and Values and Religious and Historical Perspectives have worked to improve the quality of instruction in writing and speaking, and tests show improvement. There are other complaints. Teachers often are required to teach out of their own fields. Some object. Some staff believe that the curriculum is not suited to the academic preparation of typical freshmen coming out of the high schools of the 1970s. Scrutiny of grades indicates that, as is true in many colleges across the country, overall grade point averages have risen and that the unusual increase of A grades has distorted the grade curve so that the normal number of C grades is reduced.[15]

But Berea College continues to examine its curriculum and to adjust and make changes. Under the leadership of its academic dean, William Stolte, the faculty is in the process of revising the curriculum to be used in September, 1982, with changes particularly in science, mathematics, and written English. Meanwhile, a Berea student with purpose and persistence has the opportunity to use the flexibility and the substance of the Berea curriculum and to get a good B.A. or B.S. degree and a good start on postcollege living.

III

LIKE THE ACADEMIC curriculum and organization, the Berea Labor Program has developed in stages, an evolution within an institution that itself has evolved. In its earliest days, Berea had no established labor program in which all students were required to work. The institution undertook "to furnish the facilities for a thorough education to all persons of good moral character at the least possible expense," and the Board of Trustees undertook, as far as was feasible, to supply "inducements and facilities for manual labor," either in the school or in the community.[16]

In 1859 "inducements and facilities for manual labor" meant, according to Professor John A. R. Rogers, that "Almost all wrought with their hands, as well as brains, cutting trees, grubbing roots, and, if at all skilled, shoving the saw and swinging the hammer."[17] On the college level many of the shovers of the saw and swingers of the hammer were reading Latin and Greek in their academic classes, studying higher mathematics, history, philosophy, English literature, and rhetoric. But at that time the institution undertook to provide as far as possible manual labor to those who needed it. Many needed it. In the early years of the 1900s the emphasis shifted to include not only low costs and manual work but industrial training—brickmaking, bricklaying, stone cutting—work that could be useful in continuing vocations. Under Miles Marsh, the first Berea Dean of Labor, the Labor Program enlarged its purpose: to get the necessary work of the College done without losing money but also, when possible, to place students in assignments suited to their special interests.

During the presidency of Francis Hutchins, Berea had the services of two unusually capable deans of labor. The first, Albert Weidler, both an effective administrator and a scholar with a Ph.D. in economics, came to Berea in 1918 and served with three of its presidents. He believed that labor can do more for a student than pay school bills. He believed that labor produces a balanced life. He said of Berea College: "Probably education has lost contact with life less here than in any other college, since there is less of a break with normal living."[18] Dean Weidler strengthened the organization and operation of the Labor Program, dramatized and rewarded good labor, underscored the importance of labor supervisors, and, in order to give more varied work experience to more students, increased the number of the industries from seventeen to thirty.

Wilson Evans, a graduate of Berea College, succeeded Dean Weidler in 1950. He was a good example of what he advocated. He believed in the system, was effective with both students and staff. During his period of service, the following statement of the broadened purpose of the Berea Labor Program was made by the Berea College Board of Trustees in 1951:

> Berea has never believed and does not now believe that education is a matter of training the mind alone. Berea believes that skills acquired through all forms of constructive labor are an essential ingredient of real educa-

tion. . . . Labor is introduced into the wider curriculum
of the campus, not only as a way of paying expenses
while getting an education, but as education itself. . . .
Therefore, both the Educational Policy Committee of
the Board and the Student Industries Committee would
recommend that every student coming to Berea should
be thoroughly informed as to the unique educational
value of our Labor Program, and should also be urged
to participate in, and elect as part of his or her campus
activity, those arts and crafts which demand the highest
skills and therefore offer the maximum of educational
value.[19]

At Berea College all students work in the Labor Program.
If there are 1,514 students enrolled, as was true in 1980, there
are 1,514 jobs, with a margin for those who need to carry more
than the minimum. Each student works a minimum of ten
hours a week, two hours a day. Some carry fifteen hours a
week. A few, who financially need still more, may carry
twenty hours a week, if they are in good academic standing.
The College employs a number of professional workers, such
as electricians, carpenters, plumbers, and with these long-term
expert employees mixes short-term workers, who are students.
In the first year all new students, freshmen and transfers, are
assigned by the Labor Office to their labor positions. Most
do the work created by the presence of students themselves,
work necessary to the basic maintenance of the College—in the
Food Service, in the housekeeping of public buildings or
dormitories, in the Boone Tavern Hotel, in the maintenance
of the campus grounds, in the College offices and the Student
Industries. Berea students pay no tuition except through their
labor, for which they receive hourly wages at special rates.
Berea College could not operate as a low-cost quality institution without student labor. By their work, students help the
College to keep costs down, and the College is thus able to
help them educate themselves and achieve their degrees.
Berea students, though they traditionally grumble about

the first-year labor requirement, seem to recognize its fairness. Sometimes they have utilized the first required jobs advantageously. One student, who worked his first year in the Berea paint department, then majored in physics, went to Yale for study in graduate science. There he was able to get much-needed supplementary employment painting the Yale Faculty Club walls in a special blue shade. He got the job over other applicants because he had acquired skill in mixing paints at Berea and could mix the special Yale blue. Recently, a foreign language major, who had stayed with her first labor assignment in the Berea Broomcraft, needed a complete academic and labor recommendation for a desirable financial grant. She got it. Her academic grades were high, and her labor superintendent recommended her in standard terms, said that she was reliable, punctual, productive, worked well with others. Then he added, "And she makes a good broom, too." After the first year, a student, who usually by then has Berea "sea legs" and knows the campus labor possibilities, is free to seek another job or, if doing satisfactory work, to stay with the first position and accumulate more skill, greater responsibilities, and higher wages. Some set out to explore new creative or intellectual areas.

In 1955 there were sixty-seven labor departments in the Berea Labor Program. In 1967 there were seventy-eight, in 1972 there were ninety-four, and in 1979 there were 110. Students have a variety of experiences to choose from—five general categories of jobs: basic services, academic offices, College offices, the Student Industries, community services. Employment figures appear in a Summary of Labor Assignments issued by the Berea Labor Office in 1978.[20] The campus jobs that serve the physical needs of the College—food, cleanliness, order, health—used approximately 300 students. The academic offices, including the Hutchins Library, employed about 485 students as secretaries, tutors, teachers' assistants, laboratory assistants, farm managers. About 200 more worked in the College offices, such as Admissions, the Registrar's

Office, the Labor Office, the Accounting Office, the Development Offices, Student Health. The Student Industries—Weaving, Woodcraft, Needlecraft, Ceramics, Broomcraft, Lapidary, Wrought Iron, together with Boone Tavern, the College Press, and the Laundry—employed perhaps 360 students. Community services used 75-100 students, giving help of different kinds to people needing help. Some of these community projects are Students for Appalachia, STABLE, in which undergraduates teach adults to read and write; People Who Care, dealing with hospitalized patients, disabled veterans, prisoners; off-campus assignments with community agencies such as Save the Children Federation and Mountain Maternal Health League. The presidency of the Student Association, the editorship of the College newspaper, and the editorship of the yearbook are labor assignments with wages. Students often choose jobs as janitors in public buildings or dormitories or as supervisory monitors. On the Berea campus a monitor or a janitor job is sometimes preferred because the hours are flexible and can be adjusted to the academic schedule of the student. Since 1967, when Berea College acquired its first computer, twenty-five students work each year in the Computer Center as keypunch/verifier operators, computer operators, and programmers. But computer programmer or janitor, T.A. or weaver, broommaker or laboratory assistant, student instructor in physical education classes or Resident Assistant in a dormitory, one job done well is as respected as another.

The public often know Berea College first through the Berea College Student Industries, which not only provide creative work in the crafts but encourage the interest of students and customers in some of the traditional skills of the Appalachian region. The weavings and the stuffed toys and the hearth brooms sell in shops across the country and in the shops on the Berea campus. The gleaming furniture—desks, tables, chairs, four-posters—is of high quality, perhaps heirlooms of the future. Craftsmen supervise students who may become craftsmen. Recently the superintendent of the Student

Industries stated with pride that in the Woodcraft Department, which employs forty-eight students, there were five students able to assemble furniture from blueprint to finished product without supervision.

Through its years, Berea has had student industries that grew, flourished, then in time, for various economic reasons, were eliminated. Some of the older industries, such as the Creamery, the Dairy, the Bakery, the Candy Kitchen, for many years supplied the College and retail outlets with their products, and also gave practical labor experience to students. Then, as economic conditions changed and automation for competitive market production became more and more necessary, the College eliminated certain of these service industries and introduced new craft industries—ceramics, lapidary, wrought iron—that could operate as teaching laboratories. In former days the older industries were often financially profitable. Sometimes the new ones make a little profit. The aim is, at least, to break even. The primary purpose of the Student Industries is to give work to the students which will help to support the cost of their education and to provide them with educational work experience—all this at a minimum cost to the College.

In 1964 the Berea Creamery, which had supplied the College itself and the Berea College Bakery with milk, butter, and cheese, was eliminated. Even on a small scale the College could not compete economically with the big commercial milk companies. In August, 1970, the fine Berea herd of Guernseys and Holsteins, butter-fat rich, was—to the sorrow of Bereans— sold. Many of the eager buyers were Berea alumni. As undergraduates they had worked in the Berea Agricultural Department, and they knew the quality of the prize-winning animals. The Candy Kitchen closed December 31, 1970, and in June, 1974, the College Bakery likewise closed, because of the increasing commercial competition, the unsuccessful effort to develop a local retail market, and the necessity for expensive automation which, if adopted, would have reduced the number of students employed.

But all these industries, during their long life, produced more than milk, cheese, butter, salt rising bread, cakes, and tea sugars. Dean Albert Weidler, Berea's second Dean of Labor, once said that it is as important for a Berea student to have a good foreman as it is to have a good teacher in the classroom.[21] Though double-duty supervisors, who can both produce and teach, are hard to find at any time, there have been through the years many excellent supervisors in the Labor Program. They have influenced students, not only by instruction in specific work procedures but by personal advocacy and example of ethical values. If labor supervisors do what the College hopes they will do, they will teach more than work procedures. Often the result for the student is an established preference for quality work of any kind and sometimes for quality living. Much good teaching has taken place in the barns, the Loomhouse, the Needlecraft, the shops, the academic offices, the College offices, the printing press, the laboratories.

The Berea Labor Program, at its best, can add power to a college degree. It provides a controlled apprenticeship in work. It asks for much, but not too much, and it gives much. It is carefully fitted to the academic curriculum, is subject to adjustments, but it is firm and is as purposeful as scheduled classes. The program has many benefits. The obvious one is that it allows students to get a quality education at a low cost. They study, they work in the labor system, and they receive wages for their work. A portion of their wages is an in-kind payment in the form of a tuition-free education. In 1978–1979 the annual education cost of approximately $3,900 for a student represents more than $9.00 an hour in student wages for that year. But aside from economics, Berea students value the independence of helping to put themselves through college. They often discover their own unrealized strengths and weaknesses in the labor discipline and in the competition with other students. Most take pride in personal accomplishments. In addition to opportunities for success in academic work, in athletics, in campus leadership, the Labor Program offers students another route to personal achievement in which courage and confidence are bolstered. Students especially like the fact that on the Berea campus everybody works, that everybody has the same chance to develop. For four years a student is a part of a democratic community in which social and economic distinctions are minimal.

In the Labor Program an exploring student can discover enriching areas outside a major that will add interest and pleasure to postcollege living. Berea believes that the arts improve doctors and lawyers. A history major, whose labor in Berea was ceramics, now operates a fine pottery in Georgia. Recently he went to Africa to lecture and to find new designs. An agriculture major, whose labor was in the Berea hospital, returned after graduation to Berea for science courses, then went to medical school, and is now a doctor, practicing in West Virginia.

Berea is realistic in the operation of its Labor Program. There are many difficulties, many problems in such a complex project. By accumulated experience, the College knows the variety of undergraduate abilities and limitations—of the wise and the diligent, the slow, the shy, the reluctant, the immature, the eager, also the sluggish. But it has years of success with the program and many methods of instruction and persuasion. Its classroom faculty, who frequently supervise academic labor, and its supervisors in the Industries and other labor assignments generally believe in what the system can do for a student. They also believe in the potentiality of most Berea undergraduates. One highly effective supervisor, whose discipline is firm and who consistently gets good results from the students she trains says: "The funny thing is that when you expect people to amount to something, they usually do."

There are supervisory headaches in the system. One is

the mobility of the labor student, a mobility necessary sometimes for maximum learning experience. After the first year of assigned work, collegians must find their own jobs. A superintendent perhaps has trained a freshman to a reasonable competence. In a second year the student may choose to move to another assignment, sometimes to reinforce an academic major, sometimes to explore an attractive creative activity. The supervisor must then train a new worker.

Another major problem for supervisors, particularly in the Student Industries, is producing quality furniture or brooms or stuffed toys or weavings that will sell on a commercial market and also teaching students in limited time blocks to produce quality furniture, brooms, stuffed toys, or weavings. But year after year, the miracle is accomplished. Beautiful items are produced, and many students learn valuable work procedures. In an enrollment of 1,400–1,500 there are sure to be some drones. But in a system where everybody works and where what one student does or does not do affects others quickly, there is usually pressure on the reluctant one that spurs effort as much as do the standard penalties that may be applied. Some supervisors complain that a student who loafs on a job and is fired simply applies to another department and is taken on. Actually there is a practical limit to job hopping, and there are serious consequences to persistent loafing. A few students have been asked to leave the College because their labor was consistently unsatisfactory. But the College works especially to develop the individual student and is patient with late bloomers who eventually may blossom and with sleepers who may wake. A professor in the Department of Agriculture summed up the aim of his own department and perhaps of Berea College. "We end up," he said, "with trained students, not pigs, chickens, and eggs."

In the long run, the results are good. Recently one alumnus who knows many Berea graduates said: "The typical Berea graduate may not be able to tell you a specific course grade he made, but I guarantee you he can tell you where he worked, the number of hours he worked, the time of day he worked, and the pay rate—and he'll tell you with a sense of pride, too." He added: "And the feeling of pride and accomplishment will carry over to other activities." That is what the College intends.

In the 1960s, although it continued its steady support of the curriculum and taught students many lessons outside classrooms, the Labor Program was increasingly secondary to the academic program. The early death of the new Dean of Labor, Douglas Massey, brought the issue to the fore of administrative consideration. President Weatherford, himself a labor specialist, turned major attention to the Labor Program. In 1970 William Ramsay, a graduate of Berea College and also a specialist in management and organization, was invited to take the position of Dean of Labor. The president asked the new dean to find ways to strengthen the Labor Program, to make clear to participants that the system not only supports the academic curriculum but that it provides an important part of Berea's whole philosophy of education, that of head and hand, of mind and muscle, of perception and practice.

The Labor Office of Berea undertook to make a study of alumni attitudes regarding the labor experience in Berea. With the approval of the Labor Committee of the Board of Trustees questionnaires were sent out, inviting alumni opinion in perspective on the College Labor Program. What had graduates learned? Was it worth the learning? The information which was returned was coded by student research assistants and key-punched by student operators at the Berea College Computer Center.

Eighty-four percent of the responding alumni valued the Labor Program, both its intentions and its effects. Many noted, of course, the considerable financial advantages and said in various ways: "I could not have attended college without it." Then they recommended refining and upgrading the program, enlarging its educational intention but continuing its insistence

A FORMATION OF THE NAVY V-12 UNIT

VETERANS' HOUSING

Top: Chemistry Laboratory
Bottom: Art Studio

AGRICULTURE

COMPUTER LABORATORY

INDUSTRIAL ARTS

BASKETBALL IN SEABURY GYMNASIUM

COUNTRY DANCERS

CHAPEL CHOIR

THE HUTCHINS LIBRARY
Dedicated to two Berea Presidents,
William J. Hutchins and Francis S. Hutchins

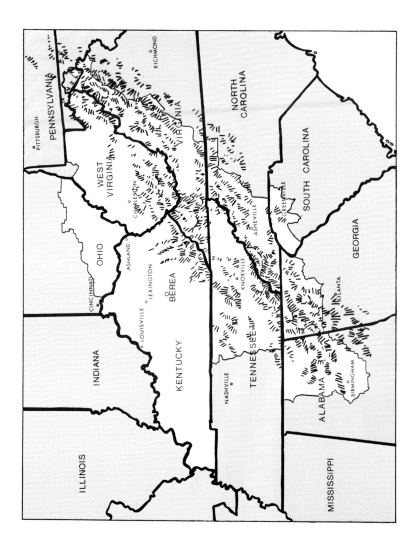

THE BEREA TERRITORY IN 1980

that all good work of any kind has value and dignity. They emphasized that Berea students should understand that labor experiences go beyond the financial purpose, that the program should integrate work and learning "by preparing students through a practical combination of academic *and* work experiences for careers or vocations after graduation."[22] They stressed their own personal growth in the system, some attributing much to the particular effect of individual labor supervisors.

In the revision of the Labor Program two new categories were added to the kinds of labor available to Berea students: service jobs in the community and the county, in the hospital, the churches, the schools, which provided practical experience in civic and social work; jobs linked directly to academic majors and academic programs, which provided apprentice professional experience and often helped a student in applying for employment or graduate study. Now all jobs in the Labor Program are organized into a progression of five grades, indicating progression in responsibility and skill. In the earlier years of the Labor Program a student was paid according to length of service in a job. The range of pay rates was narrow. In the new plan, in addition to length of service, wages are determined by accumulated skill and assumption of responsibility. The range of rates is wide. Students are encouraged to move up the grade ladder. In the four-year college stretch, students reach at least a top level of Grade 3, but a limited number are able to handle both academic classes and labor of Grade 4 and Grade 5, which involves major responsibility, high technical skill, and maximum independence. Beginning in 1977, the Poultry Farm of four thousand birds has been managed and operated by students only. There a Grade 5 student is in charge, with five other students on lower levels of responsibility. In the central Labor Office undergraduates handle the big student labor payroll. Audio-Visual Service depends heavily upon its students and is really managed by students. During the sickness of a superintendent in one of the Industries, a student, who was a business major, successfully directed the department of twenty-seven workers.

There have been other changes in the operation of the Labor Program, generally a consolidation of all labor services to students. In 1975 Berea labor procedures, financial aid, and the placement functions were merged into one office. Here, at the opening of a semester, all Berea students receive their labor assignments. A cumulative work record for each student is kept on file—the jobs held by each with a rating sheet from each supervisor. Records of labor payments, of rates, of financial aid and grants to each student are filed. In recent years government assistance to college students such as Work-Study, Basic Educational Opportunity Grants, Nursing Scholarships, National Defense Loans, and Nursing Loans is handled by this central Labor Office. Financial aid and the Labor Program are administered jointly toward a common end, with emphasis placed on self-help through work.

An important service of the Labor Office is job placement. A full-time Career Coordinator helps Berea students to find summer jobs and Berea seniors who are not going to graduate school to find employment after graduation. Generally, because of the four years of supervised work within their degree programs, Berea graduates are highly employable. In the spring, job recruiters come in numbers to interview Berea seniors. The Career Coordinator for the Labor Office gathers records, academic and labor, instructs the seniors to be interviewed, arranges time schedules so that the project goes smoothly for the interviews. Business and industries, like Montgomery Ward, Ashland Oil, Kobacher Shoes, General Motors, duPont, the fast-food chains, Goodyear, Dow Corning send interviewers to the Berea campus, and often they find there their new young employees. Representatives from the companies emphasize the advantages of the Bereans' combination of a liberal arts education with a four-year supervised work experience. Each year superintendents from public schools find many of their teachers in Berea College. For years the North Carolina Agriculture Department has employed Bereans as county agents. A Berean often succeeds a Berean because the early Berean did good work.

The trend today for many students in the Labor Program is preparation for careers, for a profession or a vocation or graduate school. But Bereans still do much manual work. New machinery has eased muscles and quickened tempos. In the 1930s students raked and piled the millions of October leaves and hauled them with mule teams to be used on the College gardens. Now gasoline blowers send fall leaves into high piles, to be packed by hay balers and taken by truck to the same gardens for spring enrichment. Berea agriculture majors fill most of the labor positions on the 1,100 acres of the College farm system. The "Aggies," as they are known to their friends, tend with care and skill twenty-four sows that produce around four hundred butcher hogs a year. A horticulture program, using ten students, produces vegetables, fruit, and ornamental plants for sale. Young women like this unit. Today one-third of Berea agriculture majors are women, and they weed, mulch, transplant, right along with their male partners. In the Loom House college students throw the shuttles on fourteen looms and weave steadily. A team of fifteen students started in September, 1979, the renovation of one of the college dormitories, to be completed before the end of the school year. Those students rewire, lay tile, replace doors, and plaster and paint. Physical work is taken for granted in the Berea system, but modern machinery has changed procedures. Air-conditioning, trucks with high-rise lifts to trim tree tops and wash windows, electric typewriters and Xerox machines, gasoline mowers are a normal part of the Berea scene today. Berea students do old things in new ways.

In 1967 Berea College acquired an IBM 1130 computer system. It had 16,000 characters of main memory. In March, 1979, the IBM was replaced with a Prime 400 time-sharing computer system. At present it has 640,000 characters of main memory and can handle thirty-one time-sharing users simul-taneously. Both capacities can be considerably increased. This computer is primarily for instructional work but is also used for administrative work, for grades, payrolls, accounts receivable, journal ledger for the College, utility billing, and a few payrolls for local nonprofit organizations. In the Labor Program the twenty-five students with jobs in the Computer Center are often mathematics majors or business majors, but majors in biology, physics, chemistry and psychology also find these jobs professionally useful, leading sometimes into lucra-tive positions in the computer/data processing field.

One walks the Berea campus in its 125th year and thinks of those early 1859 shoving saws and those swinging hammers, coupled with Latin and Greek, higher mathematics, history, philosophy, English literature and rhetoric. Today, the Hutchins Library on the quadrangle symbolizes campus scholarship. It houses many academic treasures—perhaps 230,000 books—and the Weatherford-Hammond Appalachian Collection that is a joy to many researchers. It holds special treasures like Cradle Books of the Aldine Press, books from the Plantin Press, the Elzevir Press, rare Bibles, Eastman John-son's "Boy Lincoln." The academic buildings form the other three sides of the quadrangle, and students go in and come out on the hour. Contemporary undergraduates still study Latin and Greek, mathematics, both low and high, history, philosophy, and English literature. But on the Berea campus in its 125th year there are sounds and sights not usual on a college campus: the fierce whine of electric saws, the smell of cut woods, revolving clay under skillful undergraduate palms and fingers, the ring of iron on iron, the rhythmic thumping of flyshuttle looms, the electronic silence of the Prime 400 computer in its airconditioned laboratory. Berea still aims for the old union of head and hand, for the educational con-cept that the Ph.D. may well have callused hands, that the blue collar worker may well enjoy Shakespeare and know the text of the Constitution of the United States. It is a high aim but surely a worthy one for a democratic society whose destiny depends on the ability of its self-governing people both to know and to do.

IV

IT HAS BEEN SAID that Berea College is not only an educational institution, it is a state of mind. To implement effectively its special responsibility, the College must seek teachers— the Berea term is "workers"—who understand or come to understand the central philosophy of the College; who accept the possibilities and the difficulties of the undertaking; who are willing to invest their lives and professional abilities in the Berea project. In Berea the term "teacher" includes not only the faculty who instruct in the classrooms but also superintendents and supervisors in the Labor Program—every worker who has direct contact with students.

Berea College has always asked much of its staff, and the staff has given much. In the 1930s and 1940s a tight economy necessary to keep the College going provided a discipline for the whole campus. Those were the years of low salaries, of low rents that somewhat eased the salaries, of classes on Saturday and at 7:30 in the morning. Many teachers, particularly women, were asked, in addition to their teaching assignments, to serve in dormitories as supervisors of students. In general, in those days, Bereans made one simple choice between what was essential and what was not. Values and patterns of living were clearly defined for both students and staff. Missionary stamina was an asset.

President Francis Hutchins in 1939 inherited a dedicated staff. In the next twenty-eight years there were valuable additions to it. Many of them became veterans of the institution. The Berea staff was characteristically made up of strong-minded educators who somehow subordinated individualism to the overall purpose of the College. Freely, in committees or in private groups over coffee, they discussed campus issues and problems, curriculum matters, changes in campus social regulations; they wrote explicit reports to administrators, spoke their minds to peers and to president. The curriculum committee, the admissions committee, the scholarship committee were vigorous and effective. In the early 1950s the College faculty shaped a new curriculum that did good work for twenty-two years. Berea staff members were as concerned with the principles, the practices, and the effects of the College program as were the president and the Board of Trustees.

President Willis Weatherford of Berea College has sometimes been congratulated by other college presidents because he heads an institution that so definitely knows the service that it wishes to give. The task has always been hard, but it has been performed successfully for 125 years. There are many reasons for the accumulated success of the century and a quarter. One is that Berea workers typically give their major attention to students. Primarily Berea's is a teaching faculty which focuses attention on the college students, what they are and what they may become.

A second reason for institutional effectiveness may be the chain of leadership and standards established in key programs and projects. Berea has been generally fortunate in major functions in that capable people have been succeeded by capable people and standards of work established in one cycle have been maintained in following cycles. Berea employs a wide variety of staff—usually 125 teachers in the academic area, perhaps 450 more workers, who serve the College in the Labor Program and in other functions. These bring diversified training, points of view, and experience from other institutions and other occupations, all to the benefit of the college students. Berea also employs a number of its own graduates, who after acquiring experience elsewhere choose to return to the campus as workers, sometimes as teachers, often as administrators or supervisors or key office employees. As alumni they know the work-study system from the inside;

they believe in its efficacy. They value the established standards. They also have in mind ideas and suggestions for future development. As a group they are pillars of strength to their college.

In Berea's fifth quarter there have been many examples of constructive linkage between generations of work.

Adelaide Gundlach, Registrar of Berea College from 1924 to 1955, guarded the academic standards of the College diligently and successfully. In the Labor Program she trained Virginia Auvil, a Berea undergraduate who, in time, became Registrar and from 1960 to 1976 gave the same firm guardianship to the academic standards of the institution. Britisher Frank Smith, after World War I, went to Denmark to study the cooperative recreation movement at the Danish Folk Schools. Later at the John C. Campbell School in North Carolina he learned folk dance patterns, brought them to Berea College (1940–1957), and set Berea students to dancing them. He was followed first by Ethel Capps, who on a Fulbright polished techniques of folk dancing in England, and then by the present director, a Berea graduate and former director of the John C. Campbell School. Both of these successors expanded the Berea folk dance program but retained the standards of discipline they had inherited. Elizabeth Gilbert, Berea graduate, did her undergraduate labor assignment under the supervision of Euphemia Corwin, early Librarian, then in 1944 became Librarian of the old library, later of the new Hutchins Library. Miss Gilbert served for twenty-nine years. Wilson Evans, Dean of Labor, followed Dean Albert Weidler who established the basic philosophy and structure of the Berea Labor Program. Dean Evans was succeeded by Douglas Massey, who died in office, and then by William Ramsay, the present Dean of Labor. All three were Berea graduates who as undergraduates had worked in the Labor Program. As deans, they with their associates adapted the program to changes in the Berea and the American economy, carefully expanded its educational and professional opportunities, but maintained the philosophy and the structure of the program.

Like most campuses, the Berea campus has local giants. Helen Dingman (1924–1952), once called Mother of the Mountains, and Perley Ayer, a New Englander (1947–1967), gave their professional lives in service to the Appalachian region, both on and off the campus. Julia Allen, graduate of Mount Holyoke and Dean of Women in Berea (1937–1959), modified institutional discipline, encouraged the social and personal development of college girls. Under Miss Allen students assumed greater responsibility in the campus matters which affected student life. Also, she was an early promoter of professional equality for women staff members of the Berea faculty. Mary Ela (1933–1952) established a distinguished department of the visual arts, passed its direction and its philosophy to co-chairmen, one a graduate of Oberlin, the other a graduate of Berea. The present dramatics division of the Department of English was created in the early 1930s, a period when theatre on a conservative campus was still somewhat suspect. James Watt Raine, Chairman of the Department of English, was farsighted, bold, and persuasive. He used dramatics as a technique of education to expand imaginative experience and stimulate personal growth of college students. Major successors, Earl Blank (1939–1949) and Fred Parrott (1953–1965) kept the organization vital. The present directors, one a Berea graduate, the other a graduate of the University of Michigan, recently supervised moving the dramatics laboratory into a new theatre. The science departments—chemistry, physics, geology, biology—under the former leadership of Julian Capps, Waldemar Noll, Wilbur Burroughs, and John Bangson passed their standards and their academic persuasiveness to the current staffs. These staffs continue to train young scientists who are unusually successful in graduate schools and professions.

Today Berea College has a well-trained faculty. Fifty-five per cent of the full-time faculty have doctoral degrees. The

College helps its teachers to advance in their disciplines; it grants leaves of absence after seven years of service rather than after ten years. There is an active Professional Growth Committee and a prestigious Seabury Award for Excellence in Teaching, given annually by the Charles Ward Seabury family. Since 1971 there have been seven new endowed scholarships, four of these from the family of Foster G. McGaw.

In the current Berea faculty there are the usual groupings: the senior faculty who have served Berea for eight, ten, or more years and who give major leadership; those who will do good teaching for four or five years, then leave for other academic or personal advantage; and the new young teachers who were educated in the 1960s. Often today new teachers are attracted to Berea College by its differences and its multiple educational purpose. Their own idealism reacts warmly to institutional idealism. Perhaps the old missionary zeal is reduced, but there is undoubtedly considerable humanitarian zeal.

In recent months a number of Berea staff members—classroom faculty, labor supervisors, and administrators—were asked for comment on their own work and on the effectiveness, as they saw it, of the Berea work-study system. It was clear that these educators like and respect the Berea students whom they instruct or supervise. Here are some of their comments. One young teacher said: "I am totally committed to what goes on here. These students are super." Another, who values the interest Berea takes in the individual student, said: "With the diminution of family influence, young people need parental attention. They want to be warmed and helped." Still another said: "Faculty are held here by the type of students. It is a pleasure to take to the Grand Canyon thirteen students who have never been west of Louisville." Some modify blanket approval. One observed ruefully: "If students don't throw Molotov cocktails, don't block the streets and vandalize, then the system is working." A classroom instructor said: "A quality faculty member to *stay* good must have some A students." Another said: "We give them a sense of self, a positive feeling of identity, but we are not demanding enough of them or of ourselves."

On the Berea Labor Program and its value, comments were favorable. One said: "Labor gives students stability." Another noted that in the Berea Labor Program a business major does not learn principles of management from textbooks only. He or she can learn principles and procedures of management by carrying complete responsibility for the production of one of the weekly plays in the College dramatics department or can learn work strategies as an observant employee in the College cafeteria. The chairman of a science department said that experience in the Labor Program gives Berea students an edge of advantage for graduate school. A labor administrator said that on the big employment market Berea's required labor is considered a valuable apprenticeship for jobs after graduation because Berea students not only work every day under supervision but learn early to take direction and criticism and to be evaluated. Several of those who were interviewed believe that Berea College should look ahead to a radically changed national economy, should begin now to teach its students to deal with entirely different conditions of living, conditions that will be permanent. A scientist said: "We pioneered once. We can pioneer again."

There were general comments. One said: "We are too conservative for liberals, too liberal for conservatives." Another complained: "We are blamed for not being already what we want to be." Some philosophized. "Tradition," said one, "permits me to survive in time of turmoil." Another warned: "Attenuation of high ideals will surely come with time if not checked. The danger can be a gradual shifting of emphasis to policy and organization. In Dante the organization of the church takes precedence over Jesus, the genesis of the idea." And still another: "Christianity's definition is what you do."

One speculates on what will be Berea's task in the next

twenty-five years, on whether its educational philosophy can continue to be implemented in a society which is already considerably changed in economy and technology and in social patterns. Will inevitable social changes bring diminution of institutional purpose and effect? Major responsibility for the future special identity and well-being of Berea College depends mainly on the group ability and the group conviction of the Berea staff.

v

BY TURN OF MIND, by education, by accumulated experience, Francis Hutchins was fitted to implement the special responsibilities of Berea College. In 1939 he came out of a turbulent China to lead the American college through a stretch of years filled with international and national turbulence. Berea under his guidance went through the periods of World War II, the Cold War, the atomic confrontation, two undeclared wars,, the early stages of the Civil Rights movement, and the first half of the national student unrest on American college campuses. Francis Hutchins had spent his early professional years in the Orient, but he learned his new job quickly. Philosophically he accepted completely Berea's central commitments—service to the Appalachian young people and to the Appalachian region, the interracial dedication, the obligation for service, the blend of mental and manual labor as a method of education.

President Hutchins set out to strengthen and expand the quality and the influence of the College. He combined idealism and practicality, insisted on accomplishment, then judged the result by its quality. He dealt with issues realistically, thoroughly, and speedily. In planning committees he often urged: "Let's stop describing problems and start solving them." In his twenty-eight years of service, many problems were both described and solved. No part of Berea College was more important to this new president than the soundness of its academic offering. In his inaugural address President Francis Hutchins said: "We rightly believe that the faculty is the crux of the entire educational process. It is our hope that we may provide these men and women with the requirements for their best work—libraries, laboratories, and freedom."[23] And that implied promise was kept. Able teachers joined the staff, and, in spite of relatively low salaries, the College retained many strong faculty. Like his father before him, President Hutchins worked to improve low salaries and increase long-term economic protection for Berea workers. He and his administrators developed an excellent housing program that allowed faculty to have inexpensive building sites and to use low-interest mortgages. Such practicalities helped to retain good teachers. Also, as the new president had proposed, the College provided more of the facilities necessary for good teaching. The Library grew; the laboratories were increased. And President Francis Hutchins never sought to curtail faculty freedom of expression, even during World War II, when some Bereans were unpopular because of their political views.

President Hutchins recognized basic changes in the country, in the patterns of American life, and in the resulting attitudes of young Americans. He encouraged the liberalizing of early Berea social regulations for student conduct, and he sought hard to accommodate physical living conditions on the campus to the needs and comfort of the undergraduates. Housing for war veterans and their families, later two new dormitories for women, improved lighting in the study areas, modern fire escapes—he knew their importance and worked to get them. The president was one who went to bed early and who rose early. Usually he walked the campus at 7:30 in the morning, checking with a sharp administrative eye. What he strove for was quality, all the way through the institution, in large or small part.

In financing a college that charged no tuition to 1,400–1,500 students, President Francis Hutchins and his assistants demonstrated not only competence but what seemed in unruly economic times like a fiscal miracle. The president insisted on conservative management of the College's resources, avoided red ink budgets, and would not permit new financial ventures, however desirable, unless there was assurance of proper financing. During his service of twenty-eight years, the Berea College budget and the endowment increased five-fold. The College was freed of debt incurred during the war years, and the policy of putting all unspecified bequests into endowment was firmly maintained. In this period ten major buildings were added to the campus: an addition to the Science Building and one to the Berea College Hospital; four dormitories—Anna Smith, Seabury, Bingham, and Dana; the Alumni Memorial Building; the Danforth Industrial Arts Building; the Harrison-McLain Home Management House; an organ, a lounge, and a music listening room in Presser Hall, gifts of Mrs. Margaret Allen; the Hutchins Library, dedicated to two Berea presidents; also the beginning of a nursing building that would be completed in the term of President Weatherford. There were many generous gifts that helped to keep the College in business, not only funds and buildings but tractors for the farms, station wagons to take apprentice nurses into mountain communities for trial nursing, and also things of beauty—two Greek vessels, probably of the fourth century B.C., fine music recordings, Doris Ulmann's photographs to the Art Department. In 1963 the Berea College Library was listed as one of the 119 college libraries in the category of "excellent."[24]

In 1962 the Board of Trustees revised the Bylaws of the College to establish standing committees of the Board and to create the position of Board chairman, separate from that of the president of the College. This was done under the leadership of T. J. Wood, who became the first Chairman of the Board. Since 1962 there have been five chairmen: T. J. Wood, Madison County and Cincinnati; Edward Dabney, Lexington, Kentucky; Barry Bingham, Sr., Louisville, Kentucky;

Edward Cooper, Newark, Delaware; and Kroger Pettingill, Cincinnati, Ohio. In 1968 the Board of Trustees recognized the need for a formal policy on academic freedom and tenure which was enacted after consultation with the faculty. For a long time the commissioned workers of the College had been employed "with a view to permanence," but this action of the Board of Trustees established a formal tenure policy for teaching faculty after a six-year probationary period.

President Hutchins was people-minded. He thought in terms of what is good for people, whatever their color or the shape of their eyes. He wanted college students to know how life is, including its grimness, but particularly how it can be. He believed in equal opportunity for all but also in equal obligation, the civic and moral obligation of the educated man or woman to contribute to the well-being of other people. He valued young people for themselves, for their vitality, their beauty, but especially for the promise of what they could be. As president, Francis Hutchins spoke often to undergraduates and alumni. He had a way of saying important things plainly. In one baccalaureate sermon, he said to the graduating class: "I do not believe that it is the function of Berea College to present you to the world 'smoothed up.' "[25]

In another he said: "The College would stir you up intellectually and spiritually. It would have you tremendously troubled by injustices foisted by man on man. It would have you concerned deeply and personally with cruelty and thoughtlessness, which in many situations mark our way of doing things."[26]

And again he said: "The real test of whether you are prepared for your diploma or not, the real test of the College's success in advancing your education lies in the answer to this question: As a county agent, a doctor, a nurse, a school teacher, as a homemaker, a clergyman, a mechanic, a dentist, as a citizen and a neighbor, is it your intention that God work through you that His kingdom may come?"[27]

Berea College and Francis Hutchins were both fortunate

in having Louise Gilman Hutchins as the president's wife. The daughter of an Episcopal bishop who worked in China for forty-two years, she is herself a pediatrician, the mother of four children, a charming hostess, who served fried chicken, hot biscuits, stimulating conversation to hundreds of Berea seniors and campus visitors. Daily she rode a bicycle to the hospital and to the pre-school, where she gave her medical services to the children of the community. When President Hutchins retired in 1967, Berea College gave to him an honorary degree of Doctor of Humane Letters and to Dr. Louise Hutchins an honorary degree of Doctor of Science. The Hutchinses spent the next three years in Hong Kong—he in administrative work for Yale-in-China, she in maternal medical service. Then they returned to their Berea home, located on a hill of Scaffold Cane Pike. Dr. Francis Hutchins for a limited period helped his successor in raising funds for the College. In some second semesters he teaches a class on Chinese culture. Dr. Louise Hutchins accepted a position with the Kentucky State Department of Health, where she does clinical work in maternal care and teaches methods of family planning in eight rural counties.

At the time of the Hutchins' retirement and the departure for Hong Kong, the Labor Department and other staff members of Berea College presented to Dr. and Mrs. Hutchins a gift of tulip, crocus, and daffodil bulbs which were planted by Berea workers in the large area around the Scaffold Cane residence. Also, a Japanese maple tree, given to Dr. Louise Hutchins by the children of the community, was planted so that it is always visible through the big window of the living room. Certainly the campus, the church, the town, and many educational and medical centers in the state are grateful that Dr. Francis Hutchins and Dr. Louise Hutchins have chosen to live where they have done much of their good work.

Willis Weatherford, like Francis Hutchins, has both an international and a regional background. During World War II, he did relief work for the American Friends Service in

Europe and in Africa, later spent a year in India for the American Friends Service, and another for the Ford Foundation. He worked a year in rural economic development in Malaya for the United Nations. From his father he inherited a special dedication to the Appalachian region. Dr. Willis Weatherford, Sr., for nearly five decades a trustee of Berea College, gave a large part of his life to finding ways and means for young people from the southern Appalachian mountains to be educated. He was wonderfully successful. In 1967 his son came from a career of college teaching to the presidency of Berea College.

President Willis Weatherford moved naturally into the service of the institution, brought his own competence and individuality. He had some hard problems early. The country and its campuses were deeply troubled. President Weatherford's double training as economist and theologian seemed particularly useful in circumstances that needed a blend of realism and faith. Also he was a teacher.

The first acute campus problem for the new president came in the early 1970s, the protest of the black students who asked for more black faculty, a larger enrollment of black students, more courses treating black issues. President Weatherford and his staff dealt sympathetically, patiently, steadily, and finally successfully with the problem. The event undoubtedly bruised the self-esteem of a college which from its pre-Civil War beginning had been committed to interracial education and which had suffered many penalties because of that commitment. But, in general, the black protest in the 1970s helped to re-educate Berea College, both black and white.

Out in the Appalachian territory there were changes in educational circumstances that affected Berea College. The number of regional institutions of higher learning was increasing, especially two-year community colleges that allow students to live at home, sleep in their own beds, commute to classes, and get a two-year start on degrees that can be completed by transferring to four-year colleges or state universities. Because of their convenience and low cost, these community colleges began to attract many of the students who in an earlier time would have applied to Berea College only.

Another change, affecting all colleges across the United States, and certainly Berea, was the multiplication of federal and state subsidies, grants and loans, available to low-income students—not enough to pay all educational costs but decidedly helpful to many students in the democracy. Berea students use these subsidies, grants, or loans, plus their own labor and the considerable assistance of the College. And, of course, students who once applied only to Berea often use these subsidies in other institutions. Nationally, fewer students are applying to colleges. Young people under pressure to ready themselves for employment on a narrowing job market are often choosing quick training, technical and vocational skills rather than the broader intellectual development possible in a four-year college program. Berea College has always undertaken to educate generalists who have skills but generalists who have much more than skills.

In earlier decades Berea chose a freshmen class from many applicants who were in the upper academic third of their high school graduating classes and often the lower third of the national family income scale. Now it is estimated that by 1987 the number of high school graduates from the eight mountain states that made up the Berea Appalachian territory will shrink by fifteen per cent. The Berea Long Range Planning Committee studied the problem, and the College in 1979 made changes. It throws its recruiting net out farther. It has expanded the Berea territory to include the whole of Kentucky and nineteen counties of the Appalachian area of Ohio. It reserves eighty per cent of its places for qualified students from Appalachia and the state of Kentucky. It allows five per cent for foreign students, fifteen per cent for qualified students from states not in the Berea territory. It seeks students of ability whose families cannot afford the educational cost of residential colleges. Berea uses admission counsellors who look for the kind of students the College wants to serve: those who are capable and ambitious, who have leadership potential, who prefer a Christian community, who lack funds but are willing to work in order to help educate themselves.

Demographic and societal changes in the Appalachian area have influenced programs in all colleges in the region. Migration from Appalachian counties to industrial cities, increased means of communication, more sophisticated high schools, changes within the typical mountain family—all these made differences in the outlook and susceptibility of all the Appalachian young people who left home for any college. President Weatherford and the Berea faculty recognized these changes, developed a new curriculum, which still insists on the liberal arts foundation for all majors but which increases choice and academic elasticity for the students and puts more responsibility for their education on the students themselves. Built into the curriculum are the basic commitments of the institution, treated in various ways. A student must recognize them as major emphases of Berea College. The Labor Program was restructured to encourage and increasingly reward quality work. Students now serve on College planning committees; social restrictions have been eased; undergraduate social events have expanded and are promoted largely by students under a trained supervisor.

From his own professional experience, Willis Weatherford knows well that "the heart of a college is learning and teaching."[28] He knows too that an effective teacher for Berea must, sooner or later, be willing to go beyond competence in an academic discipline. He says, "We seek faculty of high professional standards who have themselves inquiring, stimulating minds. We want faculty who are interested in students as persons, who wish to spend time in personal encounter with students outside the classroom. We seek staff members who are sympathetic with the purposes of the College, are willing to work to achieve them. While welcoming some of other religious persuasions, we seek faculty, most of whom are committed to a Christian way of life."[29] The president works hard at finding staff for a college that undertakes a multiple function.

When President Francis Hutchins retired, he passed on to his successor a financially sound institution. President Weatherford and his associates have kept it sound. In a period of ballooning national inflation, Berea College has enlarged its endowment and has avoided deficits. It has stayed ahead of inflation, though each June 30, when the fiscal year closes, is a time of anxiety and suspense. Sometimes the margin is small, but so far it has been in the black, not the red, and administrative breath has returned to normal on July 1.

President Weatherford has seen many new buildings rise on the campus and some old buildings, useful for decades and dear to many Bereans but beyond economical repair, come down. In the last dozen years there have been several handsome structures: the completed Hafer-Gibson Nursing Building; two dormitories, Danforth and Kettering; an addition to the Alumni Building; the Traylor wing to the Rogers Art Building for modern studios and classrooms; four racquetball courts. In 1980 the new Jelkyl Drama Center, McGaw Theatre, replaced the ancient beloved Tabernacle, which was the dramatics "home" that burned in 1973. A new Woodcraft building will be completed in 1982.

Two of President Weatherford's dominant concerns are the necessity of a vital Christian faith and the conviction that, if America is to remain free, its colleges and universities must be free to serve the young people of the country in many diverse ways. He is particularly concerned with education for young Americans who have college ability but lack educational funds. The president is deeply religious, and he would have those who work for Berea College and those who attend Berea College make the Christian ethic a directing, active part of their lives. His Christianity is pervasive but not intrusive. He advocates "a passionate but practical Christianity" and states for the College that "today we encourage students to remain active in their own churches while on the campus, but we continue to stress the basic principles of faith on which all can unite."[30] He warns that "an educational system which neglects the values upon which man's most profound decisions are based will likely develop an amoral citizenry."[31]

Early in his service President Weatherford foresaw the dangers to American colleges in federal grants that result in progressive federal control. As government regulations increased, his opposition in speeches, articles, testimony before committees in Washington grew stronger. Especially does he resist the increase of federal restrictions on the numerous private colleges of the country. He has warned: "The trend of federal regulation of colleges and universities of America continues strong and dangerous."[32] And again: "The formation of the minds of the coming generation is one of the most crucial tasks undertaken by our society. If America is to remain free, the institutions which undertake this task must remain free."[33] As an officer of the National Association of Colleges and Universities he has worked to reduce government control of colleges.

On the campus, President Weatherford uses participatory governance and encourages faculty cooperation in establishing policy, but he also works hard to keep the College directed to the accomplishment of its central purposes, which are expressed explicitly in its basic commitments. Early in his service, in 1969, the Berea Great Commitments, which had generally directed the institution throughout its history, were newly formulated and officially recognized by the faculty and the trustees as the goals of the College.[34] President Weatherford is an effective interpreter of Berea College. As an advocate of a special kind of institution that must have much public support in order to implement its responsibility, he is unusually successful in presenting to others the purpose and the work of Berea. Because he so completely believes in its intention and also knows the result of what it does, he is convincing and can engage the attention and often the assistance of many who want such a system of education to succeed.

Willis Weatherford is a good steward. He knows what is happening on the campus, whether he is in the plain, high-ceilinged presidential office, furnished with Berea student-made furniture, or in Florida or San Francisco on development business. One professor ruefully but admiringly noted that he never loses touch with the campus, always knows what is happening, will telephone from New York to add an item to the agenda for a Tuesday committee meeting. The custodian of Campus Security hastens the repair of a rip in the smooth grass, cut by a heavily loaded truck off its track. He orders: "Get that mended this afternoon or the president will telephone me before night to ask who did it and why it isn't repaired."

President Weatherford deals easily and naturally with principles and policies, but he also likes facts. He knows how many meals the Berea cafeteria serves in a year, how many brooms the Broomcraft has produced, how many people attended the Berea outdoor drama, *Wilderness Road*, in a summer. He knows the capability of a new Boller and Chivens 16-inch reflector telescope, a gift from friends of the College to the Berea Science Building, and he writes hundreds of letters thanking people for their generosity to the College.

As a private citizen, Willis Weatherford has many interests. He is a seasoned camper who casually carries a big camping axe over his arm to the airport, turns it over to the officials for the flight, to reclaim it when he lands. Students admire his expert rappelling. He uses hammer and saw skillfully, mends horse stalls, raises bees and roses, knows the difference between a Kerman and a Sarouk rug.

Like Louise and Francis Hutchins and their children, Anne and Willis Weatherford and their five children set a strong family example before the campus and the community.

Anne Weatherford, like Louise Hutchins, rides a daily bicycle on presidential business. She is an expert hostess, is deep in church and civic activities. Sometimes she teaches basic mathematics to freshmen; sometimes she enrolls in graduate courses in religion at a nearby theological seminary; sometimes she presides over a hearing for the State Human Rights Commission. Often she gives help to students or staff in personal difficulty. Her children and her husband are clear proof that she is a successful mother and homemaker.

During its 125 years Berea College has had six presidents. Four of these served a term each of twenty years or more. Now the sixth is in his fifteenth year. In many ways the College has had good fortune, not the least being the men who have been its presidents.

VI

BEREA COLLEGE works in a large perimeter. In its 125th year, it is not the same island institution that it was in its older decades when it welcomed the majority of its students from a culture that was generally not in the American mainstream itself, an Appalachian culture, often familial, parental in authority, and frequently religious in emphasis. The purposes of the College today, the basic philosophy are the same, but the times and the tempo of American living are different. Many students from Appalachia come now to Berea with ideas and attitudes shaped considerably by changes—good and bad—in the greater society. The dominant technology, the chain of recent wars, increased federal assistance of many kinds, the powerful influence of omnipresent television, the persuasion of the new youth culture which promotes both independence and self-indulgence—these make a difference in the pre-college experience, in the attitudes and the values of all freshmen entering any college. Today, one of the major functions of Berea College is to help its students sort out conflicting values and personal choices.

In Berea, students live unusually busy days, weeks, semesters. Academic classes, required labor, and preparation for upcoming classes make a tight daily schedule for each undergraduate. The Berea system requires that all students have these same obligations. There are no layers of privilege. But the problems of most contemporary colleges are to be found on the Berea campus also. The College explicitly prohibits the use of drugs and alcohol. In addition to the prohibition there is a concerted effort by the College to educate the student community on these issues, to promote understanding not only of the consequences, legal and personal, but also of the necessity for longtime choices. Hard drugs are rare. The College deans and their helpers steadily combat, with considerable success, the use of marijuana, though each year there are a few disciplinary cases involving the possession or use of "pot" that end in probation or suspension. As is true with colleges across the country, a bigger problem is alcohol. Residence hall managers and student personnel deans work hard to keep alcohol out of the dormitories and off the campus. As long as possible the College uses counselling and medical and psychiatric assistance. Most violations are dealt with by Student House Councils. A few cases require the action of formal College judicial bodies. In general, the overall policy of Berea is to use educative methods, although suspension may result.

Social life on the campus includes dances, parties, movies, such specials as pig roasts, turkey shoots, and Mountain Day to supplement the semicurricular events of drama, music, art, that also enrich the campus experience. Dormitory life seems to be reasonably satisfactory. Each dormitory has a Head Resident in charge, sometimes a faculty family with a child or children. The duties of the Head Resident are to supervise the management of the dormitory and to be available for counselling and emergency situations. There are two arrangements for student living in the residence halls: the standard two-occupant rooms or small single rooms, and in the two newest dormitories suites of six rooms each, accommodating twelve students. A few seniors and all married students live off campus. There are no coed dormitories. In the residence halls, visiting hours in the lounges are managed by elected student officers, subject to the vote of the residents of the hall. For social purposes and late entrance, students use, under regulation, dormitory keys. Because Berea is committed to keep the cost of a college education low, it discourages the possession of cars on the campus. Seniors who do not receive College grants and who are in good standing may own and use cars in the Berea area. Freshmen, sophomores and juniors may obtain permission to own and use cars in extenuating circumstances as established by the College. In general, the Berea way of personal living, as alumni of earlier decades knew it, puts more responsibility on the individual. There are rules, and they are known, enforced, and respected to a degree not enjoyed by many institutions of higher education today.

Beyond its academic program and its Labor Program, Berea College offers a variety of curricular, semicurricular, extracurricular projects that claim much undergraduate time and work and that give much pleasure and skill in return. Both presidents, in the last twenty-five years, have believed in putting before college students the best of cultural good things that the College could afford—music, drama, speakers on major issues—whatever in the arts is illuminating, whatever in intellectual exploration is stimulating and expanding. During the 1950s and 1960s, Berea College had such cultural imports as the Louisville Orchestra, the St. Olaf Lutheran Choir, the pianist Gina Bachauer, a performance of Aristophanes' *The Birds,* such speakers as Reinhold Niebuhr, Arnold Toynbee, Thornton Wilder, Robert Frost, Norman Cousins, Jacques Barzun. In the 1970s the Louisville Orchestra came again, also the Cincinnati Ballet, the Freiburg Baroque Quartet, the Don Redlich Dancers, a Japanese mime, and African dancers to supplement campus emphases on special cultures. There were Alex Haley and Julian Bond, a team of Danish gymnasts, the

United States Marine Band, two performances by travelling companies of Shakespeare's *Twelfth Night* and *A Midsummer Night's Dream*. Berea welcomes a series of Lilly professors of Christian thought who live on the campus for extended periods each year and lecture and teach. In the early days the famous visitors had often heard of the distinctive purpose and program of Berea College and, in order to see the campus firsthand, came for token fees or for a piece of Berea woodcraft. Fees in recent years are much higher, but Berea still offers generous extracurricular enrichment.

In the Berea program there are always semicurricular projects that allow students to test theory by practice, to produce music, plays, dances for campus and other audiences. The Berea Players is one of the most active small college theatres in the South, teaching dramatic techniques and giving dramatic experience on many levels to actors, to undergraduate producers and technicians, and to audience. In the spring there are individual recitals by graduating music majors and individual art shows by graduating art majors. Close campus attention is always given to good creative work. Also, faculty members of the departments of music and art are generous with their talents in public recitals, lectures, and seminars. The Berea Chapel Choir has a long, lovely history. Under a gifted conductor, Rolf Hovey, it dates from the wish of President Francis Hutchins to put into chapel services religious beauty to move both singers and audiences. The Chapel Choir goes on annual tour, has sung in many of the cities of this country, and also in England's Coventry Cathedral, in Holland and in Germany, and most recently in Russia and Poland. Then there are the well-known Berea College Country Dancers, who have danced across the United States, under the big oaks of their own campus, in the White House garden on the invitation of President and Mrs. John Kennedy, on an NBC national television program. In 1962, sponsored by the State Department, they toured in nine Latin American countries and served as attractive ambassadors for the United

States. Frequently they go to Denmark and Great Britain to dance in the market places and the town squares and to resharpen for themselves the old dance patterns, modified on this side of the Atlantic.

Both the athletics program for men and the athletics program for women are strong and keep the undergraduates moving. Berea College believes wholeheartedly in amateur athletics. Often the "Mountaineers" basketball team and the soccer team bring game success to the campus, but there are no subsidized athletes. There is no football team. Physical education classes, general and specialized, are required of all students. In them and in cross-country running, soccer, volleyball, field hockey, swimming, tennis, track, and baseball, the aim is healthy bodies, minds, and nervous systems for all Berea undergraduates.

Berea College and the town of Berea have been interrelated since the establishment of the College. Beginning in 1853 as a small church and a one-room subscription school, Berea College was built on the Ridge when the community was a village. As the College grew, the town grew. Now its population, excluding the College students, is about nine thousand. Through the years there have been many intertwinings and overlaps, many cooperative projects between the town and the institution, generally to the benefit of both. The College still owns and operates for itself and for the city the local water and electricity systems. A part of the 7,000-acre Fay Forest, a valuable gift in early days to Berea College, is reserved for the watershed that supplies both College and town with water. That supply is controlled by four dams, three erected through the years by the College alone, the fourth by the College and the Soil Conservation Service. In 1898, soon after Harvard University built the first college hospital in America, Berea College started its hospital. It served the College students and the staff and, increasingly, the people in the area, particularly in maternal health and pediatrics. In 1967 the Berea College hospital was turned over to the town of Berea and is now called the Berea Hospital. It is used by local physicians for general practice and also by the College physicians for the particular care of the College students and staff. Berea College nursing students do some of their training in the Berea Hospital. The payroll of Berea College, which employs approximately six hundred people, puts into the community about $6 million a year. In the last ten years, the town of Berea, under the leadership of its far-sighted, careful mayor and city council, has acquired six nonpolluting industries that have added economic strength and many good citizens to the area.

There have been other cooperating projects. Until 1966 Berea College students manned the fire department which served the whole community. Then the city acquired a fine firehouse, professional fire fighters, and even a coach dog mascot. Citizens of Berea are invited to use College facilities —the College Library, the College Bookstore, the College tennis courts—to enroll in College classes and to attend without charge the many cultural programs brought to the campus.

Another valued College-community relationship is that of Berea College and the Northeastern Forest Experiment Station. For many years the Forest Service had an office on the Berea campus. Recently it built on land provided by the College an expanded new research center and ranger station of the Daniel Boone National Forest System. The Service provides information and practical assistance for a large region and advises in the care of Berea's wooded hills. Sometimes the Experiment Station has employed the College specialists in biology, in economics, and in strip mining geology. Sometimes the president of Berea College invites the forestry staff to meetings of the College General Faculty. Near Berea, the Experiment Station assists with a plantation of yellow poplar and red oak and another of black walnut, perhaps fifteen hundred to two thousand trees.

In 1955, as a part of its centennial celebration, Berea College built an outdoor theatre in its forest, three miles from town, and staged there an outdoor play, *Wilderness Road*, written by Paul Green, winner of a Pulitzer Prize. The play presented a story of regional Civil War history and vivified principles of living that Berea College as an institution advocates. The drama was given in the summers from 1955 through 1958, then was revived in 1972 and performed through the 1980 season when it was discontinued. For three of its latter years it was a joint responsibility of Berea College and the Berea Chamber of Commerce, then of Madison Drama, Incorporated, a local sponsoring group that included the College. The play brought 25,000 or more visitors to the community in a season. In all its seasons it was seen by nearly half a million people.

Perhaps the most unusual cooperative project is the Berea Community School, established in 1968 when the College eliminated its private high school and its elementary school and joined with the town to build and support a new community high school and an elementary school. Under an agreement with the Berea Community School the College provided $300,000 toward the construction of the new public school building and in addition arranged to provide $1,048,000 over a thirty-year period toward various general and operating expenses of the school. The College pays the salaries of two teachers in the Community School. College education majors often do their practice teaching in the Community School. High school students may use the College library, and some of the advanced high school students take College classes before their own high school graduation. In 1974 President Weatherford was given the award of Man-of-the-Year by the Berea Chamber of Commerce to recognize his help in maintaining the independence of the Community School.

At times, there have been differences of opinion between the College and the town—utility bills, undergraduate high jinks or blunders, differences of social and political opinion. During World War II the College defended a group of American-born Japanese students from local suspicion. During the campus turbulence in the late 1960s and the 1970s, some citizens considered the College soft as it dealt with campus black students who occupied the president's office for a night. But patience, basic good will, mutual dependence, and much consultation have brought peaceful conclusions.

From its beginning Berea has reached out into the Appalachian territory with varied services. Before state bookmobiles, when there were few books and fewer libraries in the schools of the rural southern mountains, Berea College shipped out by mule, then by car, hundreds of boxed travelling libraries. In later decades, on invitation from remote communities, it sent out Opportunity Schools, groups of College staff who on a Friday gave practical assistance in home economics, agriculture, the arts, hygiene, and health, and helped to provide a Saturday night social and a good Sunday preaching service. In the 1950s the College conducted workshops for teachers in the small, rural schools. Sometimes it joined with Eastern Kentucky University or the University of Kentucky in education projects. In 1953, with the assistance of the Fund for the Advancement of Education, Berea conducted a four-year Rural School Improvement Project, which set out to improve thirty-six rural schools—buildings and school rooms, the morale of the teachers, the health, the teeth, and the minds of many children.[35] The overall objective was to reduce the inequality of educational opportunity in rural communities of eastern Kentucky.

Berea College has always had a strong interest in the Appalachian settlement schools that out in the region encourage education, community improvement, physical and spiritual health, and effective leadership. In 1976 Berea joined with fifteen church and community schools in a cooperative association, Settlement Institutions of Appalachia (SIA). The central office of the consortium is now on the Berea campus, and Berea cooperates in the support of the program and of the staff. For many years Berea College has worked with the settlement schools at Hindman, Hazel Green, Oneida, Red

Bird Mission, and others. It has had a long, close relationship with Pine Mountain Settlement School, which now specializes in programs in environmental education. Bereans serve on its Board of Trustees, and the president of Berea College is the chairman of the board.

In many ways Berea encourages interest in the Appalachian region and concern for its heritage, its culture, and its people. One of the important units of the College is the Appalachian Center. This Center provides courses, information, lectures, programs on the history, the economy, the crafts, the music, the literature of the Appalachian region. The Weatherford-Hammond Appalachian Collection in the Hutchins Library is the oldest and one of the largest mountain collections in the nation. The College also operates on the campus the Berea College Appalachian Museum, opened in January, 1971, which displays samples of authentic southern Appalachian culture—tools, furniture, utensils, over two thousand items gathered from the Great Smokies area. Thousands of visitors have been able to *see* here a way of life, now largely gone, and to glimpse the early rugged living that went into the building of this country.

Berea goes out into the mountain territory, but it also reaches out and brings to the campus young people from small high schools. It operates a project, Upward Bound, which is supported by federal funds and which provides on the campus in the summer basic studies, motivation, and encouragement for disadvantaged high school students. College undergraduates often teach in this project and learn much themselves. An eight-year-old program for Rising Seniors offers intensive courses for students of high ability who have completed the junior year of high school. Berea also invites its alumni to return in the summer for a refresher course, taught by College faculty. In addition to its customary honorary doctorate degrees, Berea College gives each year Service Awards—sometimes one, sometimes three—to individuals who have rendered outstanding service to their communities and who in their daily lives exemplify the ideals of Berea's Great Commitments.

The State Department has long known what Berea may offer to foreign educators who come to this democracy, seeking model institutions whose methods can be adapted to the needs of their own people. Though situated in the Midwest, Berea has served as an educational outpost of internationalism. Along with the University of Michigan, Cornell, and Columbia University, it has acquired a world reputation for educational ideas and techniques. Educators and consultants through the years have come from many countries, and the president's guest book is always an international roster.

Berea has welcomed many foreign visitors, and under the auspices of the State Department or of foundations interested in international problems it has sent its own specialists, administrators, and lecturers to foreign countries—to India, Paraguay, Japan, Pakistan, Thailand, Liberia, the Sudan, Taiwan, Egypt, Iraq. Dean Louis Smith worked for two years in the Middle East for the Ford Foundation as an advisor on rural education. Later he went to India for the Ford Foundation and a United States development agency as consultant for ten new colleges. Dean Kenneth Thompson had direct responsibility for a year for the Fulbright program in Pakistan. Lester Pross, Chairman of the Art Department, on a Fulbright grant lectured for a year at the University of Punjab. Dr. Thomas Kreider, Chairman of the Department of English, on a Fulbright grant taught American literature for a year at the University of Karachi, Pakistan. Several staff members in the Department of Education, Dr. Luther Ambrose, Dr. Pat Wear, Orville Boes, served as consultants in various educational institutions of Africa. In 1960 Virginia Auvil, Registrar of Berea College, was acting registrar at the American University in Cairo, Egypt. These travellers—in one decade forty-one Berea faculty lived or worked overseas—have brought back to the College their enlarged experience. For the undergraduates whom they instructed the American horizon was widened.

In 1980 there were on the campus ninety-two foreign students from forty countries. They helped to reduce national provincialism and increased world consciousness for undergraduates. Foreign visitors in lectures and seminars come to Berea frequently. Students listen to a Buddhist monk in orange robe and sandals and note not only what he says but that he wears wool socks within his sandals because Kentucky weather is too cool for sandals alone. A Moslem is a tenured member of the history and political science faculty.

Berea is regional, but it is also world-minded.

VII

THE EARLY BEREA presidents, year after year, battled for enough money to pay the monthly bills of the institution. They were remarkable men, pioneers in education, valiant, dedicated, and they were successful in their main purpose, which was establishing a college that would last. It was President William J. Hutchins, scholar and minister, who in the 1920s recommended to the Berea Board of Trustees new principles for Berea's monetary operations. Those principles hold today and continue to make sense. They are: Remove or avoid indebtedness. Live within a budget which is carefully prepared and published annually. Use undesignated bequests exclusively for endowment, to be invested carefully. President Francis Hutchins and his associates accepted the fiscal formula. President Weatherford and his associates use it. Berea's present Vice-President for Finance was asked recently how many deficits the College has had since the 1940s. He examined the records and said, "Five, in thirty-eight years." That period included the hard war years. Then he added, "There have been none in the last fifteen years." Why not, one wondered. His answer was, "We do not spend what we do not take in."

A journalist visitor on the campus in 1957 speculated on the same matter. He wrote: "A major part of Berea's income is from its endowment. But what makes the difference is a combination of Spartan thrift, gifts from friends and well-wishers, and the student labor program."[36] With the accumulated, accelerated growth in the country's economy and the increasing government participation in higher education, contemporary thrift is not so Spartan as it once had to be when meals for a young woman cost $2.50 a week, for a young man $2.75 a week. But compared with other American colleges the Berea way of life is certainly thrifty. One finds evidence of official institutional husbandry in presidential reports and public statements. President Hutchins once said to a gathering of Homecoming alumni: "You are conscious of the fact that Berea is a strong college. It is not rich and never can be rich as long as we maintain a no-tuition, low-cost program."[37] In 1973 President Weatherford wrote in his annual report: "Once again Berea has lived within the income available and at the same time maintained a vital educational program. In order to balance expenditures with resources, we were forced to maintain our physical plant at less-than-optimum level of good repair and to budget in other areas with extreme care. However, salaries were increased more than the rise in the cost of living and, while our program was not expanded, neither was it reduced, as was necessary with so many other colleges."[38]

Through the years many "friends and well-wishers" have made the work of Berea College possible, made it possible for a no-tuition, low-cost college to provide thousands of students with quality degrees that they could not themselves afford. The D. K. Pearsons series of gifts during the early years of the twentieth century, the Hall bequest of aluminum stock, the Fay Forest from a woman who loved trees and education, the bequest of William A. Julian, valued trustee, who gave more than money to Berea College—all these helped to establish a firm foundation which has held the institution steady. Some of the best "friends and well-wishers" of the College have been its own trustees. President Hutchins and President Weatherford have consistently had strong Boards of Trustees, devoted to the College and its purposes, serving it generously with their multiple abilities. They have understood the special characteristics, the special responsibility of the institution, and they guard the College and take pride in its health and its accomplishments. Certain Berea trustee families have passed their affection and their assistance from one generation to the next. More than one generation of the Binghams, the Danforths, the Embrees, the Seaburys have worked closely as trustees with both President Francis Hutchins and President Weatherford, giving the wisdom of experience, giving counsel, funds, and personal friendship.

In 1963 the Ford Foundation, after close scrutiny of Berea College, included it in a group of selected colleges for a challenge grant of two million, on the condition that Berea raise six million in three years. Berea succeeded. Between 1970 and 1975 Berea conducted a five-year Great Commitments campaign for educational funds under the leadership of Donald Danforth, Sr., long-time friend and trustee. It sought thirty-two and a quarter million and received almost forty million. Twenty-two million of that went into endowment. For Berea, endowment is vital because it takes the place of the tuition that Berea students do not pay. It enables the College to provide education for a special group of young Americans—1,400 plus, a year—who might not be able to go to college. Berea recognizes that to do its work it must plan well ahead, must seek broad support, must always husband its funds. Its administrators and its Development Staff believe in the Berea purpose and its system of education, and they are diligent and often successful. Now Berea is in the second half of its Second Century Program, 1978–1983. It is seeking funds again to undergird the long-term vitality of the College.

Large gifts from foundations, trusts, major donors, and corporations are absolutely necessary, but so are small gifts. In the Great Commitments Campaign, there were 6,215 gifts of $10 or below, and the greatest number of all gifts to make the big total was $100 or less. Who gives? Men and women who approve the results of a work-study system of education for this country, who perhaps are giving to an American ideal; business men who have tested and know the advantage of early apprentice work under supervision; people who have children and grandchildren and think in terms of the long future; those who wish they had children and grandchildren; many school teachers across the country who know the process of developing young people into maturity; in general, those who, like Mahatma Gandhi, believe that education through productive work, mental and manual, results in "healthy, disciplined freedom." There are many reasons for investing educational money in Berea College.

Dr. Daniel K. Pearsons, early benefactor of Berea College, had two special interests. Known to be scrupulously honest, he had made a fortune for friends and for himself by investments in California and Chicago. Also, he was deeply interested in America's colleges. Before he died in his nineties, he undertook to give away most of his great fortune, five million perhaps. He was particularly interested in fifty-four colleges across the country. Berea was one of them. It received many gifts from Dr. Pearsons, including what he considered the best of all of his gifts, the $50,000 he gave to establish the Berea water works. Dr. Pearson left a message to all his colleges. He wrote: "I send this final message to the colleges I have helped. Guard your endowment funds. Use careful business methods in placing the funds of the college. But even more carefully guard your students. Keep them from harm, for the hope of the country is in the young people you are training."[39]

VIII

BEREA COLLEGE *has* guarded its students. It takes great pride in what they are, how they develop, and what they accomplish. The College knows well that there are many influences that help to shape its students long before they leave home. But a young man or a young woman who wants higher education is usually searching and willing to consider new ideas. Often students hear and heed the Berea advocacy. A veteran professor who has watched many generations of Berea students go through the College says that if the ideal is in the climate of the institution, the students will take it away with them, not always immediately but eventually. Available to Berea collegians working for a degree is more than textbook knowledge. Berea College from its 1855 beginning has been classless, interracial, coeducational, and Christian in its intention. Beyond its practicalities, the controlled work-study system can provide what Jacques Maritain called "psychological equilibrium." Often there is a life-time effect from living, studying, working for four years in such a climate.

What becomes of Berea graduates? Many go to graduate school. There are many Ph.D.'s and also other advanced degrees. In the early 1950s the Knapp–Greenbaum survey of American scholars listed Berea College as thirty-one in fifty top-ranking undergraduate institutions that started young scholars on their way to Ph.D.'s.[40] In 1964 four Berea seniors, two women and two men, won Woodrow Wilson Fellowships —in English, in history, in psychology, in sociology. In the ten years, 1969–1979, fifty-five out of eighty-eight graduating majors in chemistry have gone to either graduate school or medical school. In 1979 the Department of Psychology reported nine Ph.D.'s acquired since 1973, with four still in graduate school. In the years between 1920 and 1976, Berea graduates earned 428 Ph.D.'s; in 1967–1976 219 Ph.D.'s; in 1976, alone, seventeen Ph.D.'s.[41] The Berea total was more than that of any other private college in Kentucky. In the earlier years of this span, two-thirds of the Ph.D.'s were in science, one-third in other disciplines. In 1976 the proportion changed, and science and nonscience doctorates were nearly half and half, with nonscience Ph.D.'s increasing.

The Berea Alumni Office has addresses of approximately thirteen thousand alumni, and it supplies occupational information about the graduates—teachers, doctors, lawyers, county agents, child specialists, social workers, artists, homemakers, college presidents, pilots, preachers, missionaries, business and industry administrators and managers, deans, government workers.[42] In 1977 there were 220 doctors. Doctors, dentists, optometrists, veterinarians, nurses, and other related medical workers numbered 830; lawyers, judiciaries 121. Thirty per cent of the alumni were in teaching, all levels. Twenty-five per cent were in business and management as accountants, finance officers, company presidents, salesmen, secretaries, and office clerks. Fifteen per cent were listed in engineering, industrial technology, computer science, geology, and geography. Four per cent were in farming, farm management, USDA or FHA. Many were county agents. Those retired or unknown and housewives not employed on the public job market were perhaps fifteen per cent. It is estimated that forty-five per cent of Berea's graduates return to work in the Appalachian states. Richard Wilson, correspondent for the Louisville *Courier-Journal*, wrote in 1979: "A list of the [Appalachian] region's social workers, educators, doctors, lawyers, and civic leaders would read like a *Who's Who* of the Berea Alumni Association."[43]

Berea College is, of course, proud of its conspicuous achievers—of its fifteen graduates who have become college presidents, of its deans, its chancellors, its mayors of cities, of the foreign special student who became Secretary of State in his own country, Austria, of the young Indonesian woman who served as the Indonesian First Secretary of the Permanent Delegation to the United Nations. It is proud of its graduate who is a vice president of a New York bank, and of its former Foundation School student who was president of a national labor union. It values the young women who got started on professional careers long before the ERA movement was operative. One is a professor of pediatrics at a leading medical school in the South, one a lawyer for the TVA, one a theatre specialist in lighting plays around the world. A former Secretary of Commerce for the United States is a Berea alumna. Berea honors its V-12 doctor-missionary who took a hospital ship to innumerable sick people in the South Pacific.

But the College is equally proud of its graduate who is a county agent working in the grass roots of North Carolina, of the school teacher who trained students in both English and mathematics so that they too could climb the learning ladder. It honors the home economics teacher who for forty years taught the methods of making good homes and good food to many young and older women in her rural county. It is proud of the women graduates who have invested their major energies in building good homes, in the care of sons and daughters and husbands, in civic and church work. It is proud of the industrial arts teacher who brings skill and discipline to the high school vocational department in his own home town; of the minister and his wife who both served a small Kentucky community; of another ministerial pair working in a large Indiana church; of ten missionary couples serving in many parts of the world.

There are also six commercial air captains who have flown good planes for years with no accidents. Whatever the work, wherever it is done, if it is well done, Berea takes pride in the worker.

A graduate, an administrator in a regional Social Security office, visited the campus after many years of absence. He said to a faculty member, "Did you know that when I came to Berea College I was tall and skinny, bent over, downright stooped? This college straightened my back and taught me to think."

Berea's business is straightening backs, if they need straightening, and teaching collegians to think. But beyond the academic disciplines, beyond the work-study experience, the College offers an enlarged concept of what it means to be truly human, and it suggests ways to be human on many levels.

A SURVEY OF SOURCES

THE HISTORY of Berea College is found largely in the records accumulated during the past century, and for the purpose of this book the foremost among these sources are the official papers of the College, especially the Annual Reports.

Since 1870 it has been customary for members of the faculty, especially heads of departments, to report annually on their activities to the president of the College, who in turn transmits to the trustees his report based upon faculty reports and his own considerations. Since 1893 the president's report has been printed, but President Frost occasionally read to the faculty and trustees a longer and franker report than he had published. These faculty and presidential reports, whether printed or unprinted, are invaluable for an understanding of Berea's history.

Other official papers complement the Annual Reports. The Reports of Common School District no. 16 for 1855 and 1856 reflect Berea's beginnings. Since 1858, except during the Civil War period, 1860-1865, the Board of Trustees has kept Minutes of its proceedings. The Prudential Committee has kept Minutes since 1858, but unfortunately those for the period 1886-1908 have disappeared. The Faculty Minutes have been kept since 1866, and to these should be added the miscellaneous records of the registrar, the financial reports of the treasurer, and the surviving Minutes of the Ladies' Board of Care, which date from October 25, 1880, to May 8, 1903.

The development of the governing regulations of the College may be found in the Berea Constitution and By-Laws, 1859; *Foundations,* 1900, which includes constitutional changes to 1899; *Consti-*

tution and Statutes . . . as revised and amended, 1911; *Constitution and Statutes . . . 1855-1917,* 1917; and *Historical Documents: Constitution and By-Laws, . . . 1855-1929,* 1929.

The College early felt a need to publicize its work, and this was done by a series of historical sketches. *Origins and Principles of Berea Literary Institution* was published in 1868, and a notation in pencil adds that the first four pages were written by J. A. R. Rogers and the remainder by John G. Fee. A booklet of addresses that were delivered in 1869 before a Berea meeting at Cooper Institute, New York, contained an introduction of twenty-two pages entitled "Historical Sketches of Berea College," by J. A. R. Rogers. President E. Henry Fairchild was the author of a small book entitled *Berea College, Ky. An Interesting History,* which was approved by the Prudential Committee, published in Cincinnati, 1875, and reprinted in a revised form in 1883.

College activities may be seen in the *Catalog,* published yearly since 1867, and in the *Bulletin,* which began in 1902. Greater detail about the college people of past years is included in *Historical Register of the Officers and Students of Berea College from the Beginning to June, 1904,* 1904; *Historical Register . . . from the Beginning to June, 1916,* 1916; and *Alumni Catalogue, 1870-1929,* 1930. Among other official publications on Berea's work are *Berea General Hospital,* 1899; *Manual of the County Achievement Contest for Eastern Kentucky,* 1922; *The Berea Way. Information on Admission,* 1940 to present; and *Glimpses of Berea College,* 1953.

II

BEREA COLLEGE in its first century has abounded in publicists. Officers and faculty have given addresses, written articles, composed letters, and made memoranda which, though expressing their own viewpoints, have nevertheless reflected also the principles and life of the institution. These papers are generally less sensational and more sympathetic with Berea's complete educational program than are the writings of professional journalists. Of the hundreds of letters used in preparing this book, only the most important collections and the more unusual pieces of individual correspondence are included.

The surviving papers of John G. Fee are particularly abundant and valuable. Between June 3, 1845, and July 22, 1846, he published a series of fifteen articles in Cassius M. Clay's *True American* on the sinfulness of slavery. Two years later Fee rewrote this material and published it in an enlarged form as a book, *An Antislavery Manual*, which the American Missionary Association republished in a shorter form, 1851. This *Antislavery Manual* was the book which Clay distributed widely in Madison County shortly before Fee moved to the Berea Ridge. Between 1846 and 1881 one hundred twenty-six articles and letters written by Fee were published in the *American Missionary*. Fee's activities in the Berea region are discussed in fifty-four letters written by Fee to A.M.A. secretaries, 1855-1869, and now preserved in Fisk University, and in twenty-one letters written by Fee to Gerrit Smith, 1855-1874, now in the G. S. Miller Collection in Syracuse University. Fee's "Discourse" (ms.) delivered on November 13, 1859, in Plymouth Church, Brooklyn, N. Y., is of special interest because it was the immediate cause of the Berea "exile" in December, 1859. In 1876 he wrote a Fourth of July address entitled "Historic Sketch of Berea, Ky." Between January, 1885, and June, 1886, he published in the *Berea Evangelist* a series of articles entitled "Berea: Its History and Work." In 1891 he published his *Autobiography*, the work of his old age, and in 1896 he wrote a further autobiographical article (ms.) "for a biographical encyclopedia."

Through Clay's written list the names of those who were exiled from Berea in 1859 and 1860 have become a matter of record. A fortnight after the exiles left the Ridge late in 1859, Clay in a political speech from the Capitol steps in Frankfort, January 10, 1860, made considerable reference to the recent exodus and to his high respect for the service of Fee to education. This speech is printed in full in *Cincinnati Gazette Pamphlet, no. 1,* 1860. In Clay's *Writings*, New York, 1848, and in his *Memoirs*, Cincinnati, 1886, frequent comments are made about his relation to Fee's Berea work.

Four articles by J. A. R. Rogers in the New York *Independent* (September 23, October 7, November 4, and December 2, 1858) reveal the conditions of living in the Kentucky mountains when Berea College was founded. Twenty-three letters and articles written by J. A. R. Rogers between 1858 and 1873 were published in the *American Missionary*. Although Rogers left Berea in 1878 because of ill health, he served as a trustee for many years and never lost his deep concern in the Berea work. In 1903 he published an interesting little book entitled *Birth of Berea College. A Story of Providence.* While writing this book he carried on an active correspondence with President Frost about Berea's history, and sixty-three of his letters to Frost on this subject remain. In 1904 while Frost was writing a short history of Berea, J. A. R. Rogers wrote eighteen more letters to Frost about the early days in Berea. There also exists an undated manuscript of twenty pages written by Rogers under the title "The Exodus."

Both Mrs. Fee and Mrs. Rogers wrote interesting stories about Berea life before the war, and some of these were published in the *American Missionary;* but Mrs. Rogers' best historical writing was a personal history of life in Berea before the war, narrated in sixty-nine typed pages about 1910.

The trustees who were alumni of Berea College often spoke of Berea history. One of the speakers at John G. Fee's funeral was James Bond, a trustee who had graduated in the class of 1892. His beautiful address is printed in the *Berea Quarterly* for February, 1901. William E. Barton, of the class of 1885, performed many helpful services for Berea College when he was a trustee, one of which was to help in securing donations from Dr. D. K. Pearsons. While the waterworks which he had been instrumental in securing were under construction, Barton addressed the student body in a historical "oration" entitled *Dr. Pearsons' Birthday.* Another loyal trustee who performed many services for Berea was J. R. Rogers, eldest son of J. A. R. Rogers. In 1915 he wrote a short "Life of J. A. R. Rogers," and in 1931 the *Alumnus,* I, 6-10, published his article on "Pioneering in Berea."

Among historical material coming from trustees who were not Berea alumni should be mentioned a scholarly paper on "A History of the Day Law, 1904-1910," written by the Reverend A. E. Thomson, who became the first principal of Lincoln Institute. An excellent historical address was given by Trustee Seth Low Pierrepont upon the occasion of the retirement of W. J. Hutchins as president. This address, "Berea Then and Now," was later published among *Significant Addresses,* Berea, 1939.

The addresses and papers of Berea's presidents are of unusual value as sources because they originate in the presidential office. The inaugural addresses of Berea's five presidents are available for use today—President Fairchild's in a pamphlet, *Inauguration of Rev. E. H. Fairchild*, Cincinnati, 1870; President Stewart's in a separate pamphlet, *The Work and Claims of the Christian College*, Cincinnati, 1890; President Frost's in a pamphlet containing several of his talks, *Spent Arrows*, Cincinnati, 1893; President W. J. Hutchins' address on "Berea's Changeless Task in Times of Change," in the Berea *Citizen*, October 28, 1920; and the address of F. S. Hutchins on "Berea's Foundation Stones," published in the *Berea Alumnus*, X (1939), 79-82.

Usually the president gives the sermon or address to graduates, and these baccalaureate addresses are particularly important as sources, among them being baccalaureate addresses of 1878 and 1881 on Negro and mountain students' peculiar problems (Cincinnati, 1878, 1881); President Frost's address to graduates in 1917, "God's Dealings through Twenty-five Years" (Berea *Citizen*, June 6, 1917); President W. J. Hutchins' addresses in 1924, "I Never Lose Heart" (Berea *Citizen*, June 12, 1924), and in 1929, "The Good Cause" (Berea *Citizen*, June 6, 1929); and President F. S. Hutchins' baccalaureate address in 1949 on "Trumpet Calls" (*Berea Alumnus*, XIX (1949), 260-67), and his address in 1954 on "Berea's Pattern of Education in a Confused World" (*Berea Alumnus*, XXIV (1954), 132-33). Among other presidential material useful as sources should be mentioned Frost's "Historical Sketch of the Life of John G. Fee," in *Berea Quarterly*, V (February, 1901), *Historical Sketch of Berea College*, Berea, 1904, and his autobiographical *For the Mountains*, New York, 1937, written shortly before his death; W. J. Hutchins' article on "Programs of Rural Improvement in Appalachia" (*Rural America*, XVII (April, 1939)); and F. S. Hutchins' article on "1939 to 1949" in the *Berea Alumnus*, XX (1949), 69-71, 73.

Among the faculty whose service is concerned mainly with administration, mention should be made of M. E. Vaughn, who while secretary of the College and superintendent of extension work wrote "County Achievement Contest in Kentucky" for *Mountain Life and Work*, I (April, 1925). In *Mountain Life and Work*, July, 1931, Dr. A. G. Weidler, the dean of labor, had an excellent article on "Berea's

Student Labor Program," and his Labor Day Address on "Labor, Learning, and Leisure" was later printed as a pamphlet, Berea, 1938. H. Clyde Jones, superintendent of the bakery since 1931, gave an address on Labor Day, 1942, on "Evaluation of Student Labor" (ms.). The present dean of labor, Dr. Wilson A. Evans, is the author of a study, "Increasing the Educational Values of the Berea College Work Program," which was approved in partial fulfillment of the requirements for the degree of Doctor of Education, Teachers' College, Columbia University, 1954. The author of a valuable article in the 1948 *Alumnus*, "The New Guidance Program at Berea College," C. N. Shutt, has been the director of guidance and testing in the College since 1947. Louis Smith, author of an article in the spring number of *Mountain Life and Work* for 1950, "Negro Students to Be Enrolled at Berea," is dean of the College Department. Miss A. Gundlach, author of an article in the 1950 *Alumnus* on "What of Tomorrow?" has been registrar of Berea College since 1923.

The long list of teachers whose writings furnish good material for Berea history includes the two earliest teachers of the Berea District School, William E. Lincoln and Otis B. Waters, whose reminiscences are in the college library. "Impressions of Early Berea" was written in 1926 by Clara (Saxton) Rogers, who in her youth taught music in Berea College in 1878. A long letter written by Instructor E. G. Dodge to President Frost in 1925 contains important material bearing on the social relations of Negro and white students in the early 1890's. Among Berea's treasures is a typescript of one hundred eighty-seven pages on "The College Forest Reserve" by Professor S. C. Mason, the man who persuaded President Frost to buy the fragments of land that in time constituted Fay Forest.

For Berea's relations with the mountain people no material is more valuable than three manuscripts written by Eleanor (Marsh) Frost after her return from a 500-mile journey through the mountains in the summer of 1914: "Mountain Trip, 1914," "Religion in the Mountains, 1914," and "Report, 1914," as well her diaries from 1893 to 1946 and several hundred letters loaned to the College by Mrs. Frost's daughter, Edith (Frost) Colbert. Mrs. Frost was for many years a teacher of art history and appreciation, but outside of the classroom she was long President Frost's best helper in raising money and in binding mountain parents in loyalty to the College.

Berea teachers of this generation have written many articles on present-day movements in Berea College. For example, Frank H. Smith, Berea's instructor in recreational leadership, wrote an article for *Mountain Life and Work* in 1938 on the subject "A Year of Recreation." In 1940 Professor Rector R. Hardin presented a paper to the faculty on "The Historical Traditions of Berea College concerning Labor and Educational Emphasis." In 1952 the *Alumnus* contained an article by Professor J. W. Hughes on "Westervelt Shop." Three articles on recent educational projects should be mentioned here, all of them written by members of the Department of Education in Berea College: "Education Comes to McCreary County," by L. M. Ambrose, in the 1940 *Alumnus*, "Rural One-Room Schools can be Good Schools," also by Professor Ambrose, in the 1954 *Alumnus*, and in 1953 an article in the *Alumnus* by the staff of the Department of Education, Dr. Ambrose, Dr. C. C. Graham, and Pat W. Wear, on "How We Train Elementary Teachers."

Among the many alumni contributions to the source materials of the College only a few can be mentioned here. A biography of John G. Fee, undated, was written by Angus A. Burleigh, a Negro graduate in the class of 1875. This booklet, *John G. Fee, Founder of Berea College,* Berea, n.d., contains many interesting references to the details of college life in the early days. Bertha (Fairchild) Lauder, a granddaughter of President Fairchild, in her later years wrote "A Child Remembers Berea in the 1870's" (ms.). John H. Jackson, a Negro alumnus of the class of 1874, who later became president of the Kentucky Normal and Industrial Institute, a state school for Negroes, wrote a *History of Education from the Greeks to the Present Time* (Denver, 1905). This book gains a particular interest from the fact that the three pages on Berea College were written in the year following the passage of the Day law. E. F. White, a distinguished lawyer who graduated in the class of 1881, delivered an address in 1927 to a Berea alumni meeting in Louisville, and his words were still full of the flavor of his college days (*Pinnacle,* May 4, 1927). Edwin Rogers Embree, a grandson of John G. Fee, in his *Brown America,* New York, 1931, wrote a delightful section about his grandfather under the heading "A Kentucky Crusader." Two alumni who were very successful alumni secretaries wrote material which is helpful in understanding Berea's history.

Charles T. Morgan wrote *The Fruit of This Tree,* Berea, 1946, a book which emphasizes Berea's contribution to the education of a changing world. Charles C. Carrington in the *Alumnus* of February, 1955, had an article entitled ". . . the heart of the world to me," in which he tells the story of a Berea alumnus and his wife who returned to work in the mountains in an unusually rewarding way.

Student material is also an important source for the understanding of Berea history. One of the choicest student sources is the Minutes of the men's Phi Delta Literary Society. The motto of this society was "We love discussion," and the minutes bear out this assertion. All its books of minutes are filed in the college library, a series complete from 1868 to 1942, and they show both the variety of subjects chosen for discussion and the democratic nature of their parliamentary procedure. Doubtless the other literary societies would bear witness to the same things, but Phi Delta is the only society whose records are available for any considerable period of time.

In June, 1913, the senior class of the College indulged in the luxury of a published "Senior Book." While it contained some class and group pictures, it had a much larger percentage of descriptive material than do yearbooks of today. It also contained a historical sketch fourteen pages in length. Each year from 1925 to 1929 the *Pinnacle,* the student paper of that day, made its last number a booklet in honor of the senior class. In 1930 the College seniors published a yearbook, the *Chimes,* which was to be a reminder not only of the friendly faces of their college years, but also of those experiences which had been dearest to them. Each issue of the *Chimes* which has followed that first publication is a source book, though more can be learned about Berea from its pictures than from its paragraphs. Among the best parts are the six pages on the inauguration of President Francis S. Hutchins in the *Chimes* of 1940, and a delightful (unnumbered) page entitled "We Contemplate . . ." in the 1953 *Chimes.*

The file of thirteen annual numbers of "The Echo," mimeographed, written by the Opportunity School students between 1938 and 1950 is a unique set of documents. It is almost incredible that so much of the zest and wonder of this brief extension school could be expressed by adults so little trained in use of the written word.

Certain works written by friends of Berea should be mentioned here, for example, two books by secretaries of the A.M.A.—A. F. Beard's *Crusade of Brotherhood, a History of the American Missionary Association,* Boston, 1909, and F. L. Brownlee's *New Day Ascending,* Boston, 1946. Mention should also be made of a Founders' Day address by Dr. H. R. Muelder of Knox College, Illinois, on "The Academic Ancestry of Berea" (ms.), 1938.

In 1910 Dr. D. K. Pearsons wrote an "Address" (ms.) for the celebration of his own ninetieth birthday. E. F. Williams in his *Life of Dr. D. K. Pearsons,* Boston, 1911, has a chapter on "Aid for Berea College."

Two histories of education in Kentucky should receive mention here: A. F. Lewis's *History of Higher Education in Kentucky,* published in 1899 under the imprint of the Bureau of Education, Washington; and F. L. McVey's *The Gates Open Slowly. A History of Education in Kentucky,* Lexington, 1949, in which Dr. McVey in his chapter on "The Color Line in Education" put Berea's struggle over segregation in its larger setting.

Two articles by Miss Adele Brandeis of the Louisville *Courier Journal* staff were so full of understanding that both of them were reprinted in the *Berea Alumnus:* "Toward a Better Life," (XX (1949), 2, 4), which gives a glimpse of Berea's extension work as seen by Miss Brandeis herself; the other, "Happy Ending," an article on the recent gift of a manuscript to Berea (XXV (1955), 75, 79).

In 1919-1920 Mrs. Annie Fellows Johnston wrote a beautiful story, "Mountain Mailbag," in which two of the principal characters were students from the mountains who attended Berea College at a critical time in their young lives. This unfinished manuscript of almost two hundred pages and the correspondence that accompanied its writing were a centennial gift of Mrs. Johnston's heirs, especially Miss Mary G. Johnston of Pewee Valley, to Berea College. This manuscript is more than a story. It is an excellent source because it was written by a sensitive and perceptive woman who saw much more than a casual visitor could have seen.

Another centennial gift to Berea is a collection of Kentucky mountain ballads as written down, words and music, by a trained scholar, Mrs. Katherine Jackson French, who visited in many mountain homes in the first two decades of the twentieth century.

This collection also includes a delightful essay on "A Fortnight of Balladry" by Mrs. French.

Each reader of this bibliography will ask why the author did not mention this or that source. The best apology the author can make is that for every source mentioned, there are at least two others almost as good in the files.

III

THE FIRST PAPER published in Berea was the *Berea Evangelist*, a semimonthly publication which appeared from May, 1884, to December, 1887. Its leading spirit was John G. Fee, who was assisted by H. H. Hinman and G. F. Browne. In the first column of the first number the purpose of the *Evangelist* was summed up in these words: "The advocacy of all known good and opposition to all known wrong." Although it was a private and not a college publication, it usually contained a column of "Berea Brevities," which included both town and college news. It was printed on John G. Fee's private press. Its most important service to history was the publication of Fee's "Berea: Its History and Work" in twenty-three issues. The *Evangelist* ceased publication because the cost was not met by a sufficient subscription list.

The *Berea College Reporter* was a college publication which ran from Summer, 1885, until June 12, 1899. Its first editorial committee consisted of two professors and the college treasurer, and the first article on the first page of the first number was a "History of Berea College," by John G. Fee. The most important subject of interest on the campus was evidently the recent commencement exercises, at which Roswell Smith, George W. Cable, Judge W. M. Beckner, and General Cassius M. Clay were afternoon speakers. This number was illustrated by pictures of Ladies' Hall and Howard Hall.

A second number appeared in 1886, none in the next two years, and two in 1889. In 1890 the *Reporter* was issued in four numbers, and by 1891 it had become a bimonthly with six issues a year. In November, 1893, it became a monthly publication during the school year, and with the issue of November 1, 1897, it became a biweekly paper. By that time, however, it was no longer a faculty publication. Beginning with the issue of February, 1892, it had contained a "student column," and with the issue of November, 1895, it appeared entirely under student management. When the *Reporter* became a monthly publication, its price was raised to fifty cents a year, and there the price remained until its last issue on June 12, 1899, when it succumbed to financial difficulties. From first to last whether under faculty or student management, it was a high grade college paper which reported college life with dignity and interest.

The Berea *Citizen* began publication on June 21, 1899, little more than a week after the *Reporter* issued its final number. At first this weekly newspaper was published by the College directly, but since 1904 it has been published by the Berea Publishing Company, which is closely connected with the College in spirit, though an independent corporation. Significant college addresses are likely to be published in this paper, as well as college, town, and country news.

The *Berea News*, published from February 9, 1906, to March 5, 1908, was a noncollege local weekly newspaper which failed to make a place for itself beside the *Citizen*.

The *Berea Quarterly* differed both in purpose and in content from the papers already mentioned. It was a magazine published by Berea College quarterly from May, 1895, to October, 1916, for the purpose of cultivating friends and donors through acquaintance with the work and the problems of the College. Its real editor was President Frost himself. Its pages were enlivened by many illustrations, and it seemed perfectly natural that an address delivered by President Woodrow Wilson should appear on beautifully printed pages of the dignified *Berea Quarterly*. This magazine ceased to be published when President Frost's health no longer permitted him to prepare the *Quarterly* as well as to raise money for endowment.

The student voice, apparently silent as a source of current campus news after the collapse of the *Reporter*, was occasionally heard in the *Citizen*, which during the year 1906-1907 made room for a "Students' Journal" with editors from various student organizations. Again in 1918-1919 the *Citizen* gave up two columns to "School News from Various Departments." With the growth of the College Department the student demand for a paper of their own became more insistent, and in May, 1922, a student paper called *The Pinnacle* was established. It was published semimonthly, usually consisted of four pages, and contained a few local advertisements inconspicuously placed. It had on its board a faculty advisor, who was likely to be a member of the College English Department. Its articles were thoughtful and well written, its humor was on a high level, and its criticisms were mild and fair. In 1929 the *Pinnacle*, like the *Reporter*, ran against financial rocks. A year later the editor of the *Citizen* arranged that it be published on two pages of the *Citizen* but under the masthead of *The Pinnacle* and with its own student editors. After this arrangement had run for six years, the *Pinnacle* in combination with the "Academy Lion," a mimeographed sheet, was published as a separate publication. Again in 1938 the *Pinnacle* had to suspend publication because of its debt.

The growing College Department missed the *Pinnacle*, even though they had not supported it well enough to keep it out of debt. In 1940 a handful of eager College students set up *The Wallpaper*. This consisted of several typed columns about two feet long, tacked biweekly on the College bulletin boards. The slight cost for typewriter ribbons, erasers, and a little paper was met by the student government board. The typing was done by students on their own rickety typewriters. Late in 1943 the *Wallpaper* appeared on mimeographed sheets which were distributed in the dormitories. After six years of such effort the *Wallpaper* in 1946 appeared as a printed paper of four pages, the weekly publication of the Berea College Student Association. The paper has usually been troubled near the end of the year over its finances, but it has shown indomitable will to exist. In September, 1954, it changed its name to *The Berea Pinnacle*, with the new line at its masthead, "Custodian of the Students' Right to Know."

The tone of the *Wallpaper* was affected by the fact that it went through its early struggle for existence in wartime, and that it was struggling for its life at a time when a V-12 unit of several hundred sailors in preofficers' training was living on the campus. The *Wallpaper* from its beginning was a paper of criticism as well as a newssheet, and after the war it remained more or less a paper of struggle in contrast to the earlier *Pinnacle* and to the *Chimes*.

The *Berea Alumnus*, which began publication in April, 1931, is a monthly magazine (except in the summer months) edited by the secretary of the Alumni Association. It keeps alumni in touch with recent developments in the College, and since its contributors include administrative officers and teachers on the campus as well as alumni who are doing things out in the world, it forms an excellent source of information on current life in the College as a whole.

Mountain Life and Work, a quarterly periodical which since 1940 has been the organ of the Council (formerly Conference) of Southern Mountain Workers, was first published by Berea College. On the cover of its first number, April, 1925, the following words were printed, words which still express the purpose of the magazine: "In the interest of fellowship between the Appalachian mountains and the rest of the nation." President W. J. Hutchins in his introduction on the first page of this number wrote: "The mountains need constant re-interpretation to themselves and to the world. Again, every mountain worker needs, longs for, intellectual comradeship with others." For the three years from 1942 to 1945 it was published in Nashville, Tenn., but since 1945 its publication has been resumed in Berea under the editorship of the Office of the Council of Southern Mountain Workers.

The *American Missionary,* organ of the A.M.A., was not strictly speaking in any way a college publication; but probably no publication originating on the campus was as essential to the very existence of Berea College as was this monthly magazine published in New York, 1846-1934. Before Fee came to the Berea Ridge, he had been a contributor to the magazine's pages, and after his coming to Berea it was largely through the letters and articles of Fee, Rogers, and Fairchild in the *American Missionary* that Berea's first generation of donors in the East and North was secured and held. In the late 1870's the articles by Berea men became fewer in number, and in the 1880's Berea's name seldom appeared on its pages.

Most of the reference materials used for Chapter 9 in *Berea's First 125 Years* are in the Hutchins Library of Berea College, often in the Berea College Archives. Information on official decisions and actions of the College is filed in the Office of the President, the Office of the Academic Dean, the Registrar's Office, the Accounting Office, or the Office of the Business Vice President. Material concerning the Labor Program, including a summary of labor assignments and a survey of alumni attitudes about the effectiveness of the Labor Program, is in the Labor Office. Much information about alumni is available in the Alumni Office. Berea catalogs are in the Registrar's Office.

Printed speeches on Berea College matters, baccalaureates and speeches for special occasions are in the Hutchins Library. Reports of the two presidents and the 1951 Minutes of the Board of Trustees are in the Berea College Archives. The Minutes of the Board of Trustees for 1969 are in the President's Office.

From time to time Berea College has conducted self-studies, to apply to a foundation for supporting educational funds or to examine in detail a curriculum. The self-studies, Report to the Ford Foundation, "Profile of Berea College, 1952-1972" and the *Berea College Self-Study Report, 1972-1973* are in the Archives. Surveys that rank Berea College or Berea College graduates in relation to other colleges or to graduates of other colleges are in the Hutchins Library or in the Office of Institutional Research, Lincoln Hall. In the Hutchins Library there is a file of the magazine, *Mountain Life and Work* and of the *Berea Alumnus*, which continues good communication between the College and its graduates and among the graduates themselves.

REFERENCES

1: Early Founders

1 Fee, *Autobiography*, 14.
2 Clay, *Memoirs*, 570-71.
3 Fee, *Antislavery Manual*, p. xi.
4 Fee, *Autobiography*, 94.
5 Clay, *Memoirs*, 572-73.
6 Clay, *Writings*, 176-79, 188-92, 204-205.
7 *Am. Miss.*, VIII (1854), 61.
8 W. E. Lincoln to W. G. Frost, Oct. 18, 1909; Clay, *Memoirs*, 561n.
9 Fee, *Autobiography*, 102-105.
10 Clay, *Memoirs*, 235.
11 Fee, *Autobiography*, 121.
12 *Am. Miss.*, s2 II (1858), 40, 88.
13 Lincoln to Frost, Oct. 18, 1909.
14 *Am. Miss.*, X (1856), 14.
15 Fee to G. Smith, Jan. 4, 1856.
16 Rogers to Frost, Oct. 21, 1901.
17 *Am. Miss.*, s2 I (1857), 21.
18 Lincoln to Frost, Oct. 18, 1909.
19 Mrs. J. A. R. Rogers, "Personal History of Berea College," ch. 4.
20 The same, ch. 6.
21 The same, ch. 10.
22 Rogers to Frost, Sept. 24, 1895; *Am. Miss.*, s2 III (1859), 277.
23 Mrs. Rogers, "Pers. Hist. of Berea College," ch. 12.
24 The same.
25 The same.
26 Cincinnati *Commercial*, Dec. 31, 1859.
27 Mrs. Rogers, "Pers. Hist. of Berea College," ch. 12.
28 *Cincinnati Gazette Pamphlet*, no. 1, pp. 2-4.
29 Berea College, *Foundations*, 6.
30 T. J. Renfro to Fee, Apr. 20, 1860.
31 *Am. Miss.*, s2 VI (1862), 186.
32 The same, 278.
33 *Berea Evangelist*, II (Jan. 25, 1886).
34 Fee, *Autobiography*, 168-71; Frost, "Life Sketch of Mrs. Fee," 9.
35 *Berea Evangelist*, II (Jan. 25, 1886).
36 *Am. Miss.*, s2 VI (1862), 278.
37 *Am. Miss.*, s2 VIII (1864), 94.
38 *Berea Evangelist*, II (Mar. 15, 1886).
39 Prud. Comm., Min., Apr. 24, 1865.

2: Founders during Reconstruction

1 Berea College, *Grounds for Encouragement*, 5.
2 A.M.A., *Ann. Report*, XXIII (1869), 38.
3 Rogers, Ann. Report, June 18, 1882.
4 Sec. M. E. Strieby (A.M.A.) to Berea College, Oct. 22, 1896.
5 *Am. Miss.*, s2 XIII (1869), 103.
6 *Advance*, XLI (1901), 121.
7 Sec. G. Whipple (A.M.A.) to Fee, May 11, 1868.
8 *Advance*, XLI (1901), 121.
9 E. H. Fairchild, *Berea College, Ky.*, 1875 ed., 52.
10 J. H. Fairchild, *Oberlin: The Colony and the College, 1833-83*, 75.
11 W. G. Frost, *For the Mountains*, 66.
12 Prud. Comm., Min., Mar. 9, 1870.
13 *Am. Miss.*, s2 XVII (1873), 253.
14 *Am. Miss.*, s2 XVIII (1874), 196.
15 Bd. Trust., Min., Jan. 26, 1879.
16 G. W. Cable, *A Memory of Roswell Smith* (1892), 59.
17 *Am. Miss.*, XXXIX (1885), 251.
18 Prud. Comm., Min., May 25, 1872.
19 Bd. Trust., Min., June 22, 1883.
20 Fairchild, *Berea College, Ky.*, 1875 ed., 94-95; 1883 ed., 74-75.
21 Fac., Min., May 12, 1875.
22 *Berea College Reporter*, I (Oct., 1889).

3: A Century of Interrace Education

1 Fee to G. Smith, Mar. 10, 1859.
2 Prud. Comm., Min., Jan. 22, 1866.
3 W. W. Wheeler, Report, Mar. 31, 1866.
4 Mrs. W. W. Wheeler to W. G. Frost, Mar. 26, 1912.
5 A. A. Burleigh, *John G. Fee*, 9-12.
6 Berea College Const., 1859 (ms.), By-law 1.
7 *Am. Miss.*, X (1856), 14.
8 *Am. Miss.*, s2 III (1859), 114.
9 E. H. Fairchild to Mr. Bingham, Apr. 26, 1878.
10 E. H. Fairchild, Notes on Conf. at Fisk Univ., Dec., 1881.
11 Fairchild, *Bacc. Sermon*, 1881, pp. 6-8.
12 *Berea College Reporter*, I (Summer, 1885).
13 Phi Delta Lit. Soc., Min., June 9, 1882.
14 E. G. Dodge to W. G. Frost, Apr. 11, 1925.
15 Ladies' Bd. of Care, Min., July 11, 1878.
16 Bd. Trust., Min., July 2, 1872.
17 Alumni Res. to Bd. Trust., June 20, 1889.
18 Bd. Trust., Min., June 21, 1889.
19 Dodge to Frost, Apr. 11, 1925.
20 C. G. Fairchild to W. G. Frost, 1920.
21 *Berea College Reporter*, IV (June, 1892).
22 Frost, Ann. Report, 1893 (ms.), 7.
23 Frost, *Ann. Report*, 1894, p. 7.
24 Frost, *Ann. Report*, 1895, p. 6.
25 Frost, Ann. Report, 1902 (ms.), 6b.
26 Ky. Const., sec. 187.
27 Frost to N. D. H., Oct. 12, 1901.
28 Corr. W. G. Frost and W. E. B., Sept. 23, 25, Nov. 14, 1901.

References 269

29 *Berea Quart.*, IX (Oct., 1904), 17-18.
30 W. G. Frost to H. C. D., Oct. 28, 1916.
31 K.R.S. 158.020, 2-5; 158.990, 1-3.
32 *Berea Quart.*, VIII (Apr., 1904), 24.
33 Berea *Citizen*, Mar. 24, 1904.
34 *Berea Quart.*, X (Oct., 1906), 27.
35 Supreme Court of U. S., Oct. term, Nov. 9, 1908.
36 Berea *Citizen*, June 8, 1905.
37 Bd. Trust., Min., Nov. 7, 1906.
38 A. E. Thomson, "Hist. of the Day Law Situation, 1904-1910."
39 Berea *Citizen*, July 1, 1909.
40 Berea *Citizen*, Mar. 26, 1908.
41 Thomson, "Hist. of the Day Law Situation, 1904-1910."
42 *Berea Alumnus*, XV (1945), 240.
43 J. W. Hatcher, Presentation of J. W. Bate; *Berea Alumnus*, XV (1945), 239-40.
44 Berea *Citizen*, Dec. 8, 1927.
45 K.R.S. 158.021; *Ed. Record*, XXXV (1954), 169.
46 Bd. Trust., Min., Apr. 14, 1950.
47 Berea *Citizen*, Dec. 9, 1954.

4: The Mountain Field

1 Clay, *Memoirs*, 571.
2 *Independent*, X (Oct. 7, 1858).
3 *Independent*, X (Sept. 23, 1858).
4 *Independent*, X (Dec. 2, 1858).
5 Rogers, "Hist. Sketch of Berea College," Cooper Inst. Addresses, 1869, pp. 17-18.
6 *Am. Miss.*, s2 XVII (1873), 59.
7 E. H. Fairchild, *Berea College, Ky.*, 1875 ed., 85-91.
8 *Am. Miss.*, XXXVI (1883), 392.
9 Frost to "Brethren in Berea," July 16, 1892.
10 Frost, Mem. to W. J. H., Mar. 30, 1921.
11 W. E. Barton to W. G. Frost, Oct. 4, 1893.
12 Frost, Report, Feb. 3, 1894 (ms.), 5-8.
13 Frost, *Ann. Report*, 1894, p. 7.
14 Frost to Ohio Teachers Assoc., Cincinnati, 1895.
15 *Berea College Reporter*, VI (July, 1895).
16 Frost, Ann. Report, 1902 (ms.), 5.
17 Berea *Citizen*, Aug. 13, 1914.
18 Mrs. W. G. Frost, Report, 1914, pp. 12-13.
19 The same, 40.
20 Mrs. Frost, "Religion in the Mountains," 1914.
21 Mrs. Frost, Diary, July 26, 1914.
22 *Berea Quart.*, VII (May, 1902), 21.
23 Frost, Ann. Report, 1902 (ms.), 1.
24 Prud. Comm., Min., Oct. 4, 1915.

5: Changing Patterns of Education

1 Fee to G. Smith, Jan. 4, 1856.
2 *Am. Miss.*, s2 II (1858), 233.
3 *Berea Evangelist*, I (Aug. 1, 1885); Fee, *Autobiography*, 95.
4 A. A. Burleigh, *John G. Fee*, 14.
5 W. E. C. Wright, Ann. Report, 1883.
6 E. H. Fairchild, Ann. Report, 1878.
7 Fac. to Bd. Trust., Petition of June 19, 1884.

8 Frost to "Brethren at Berea," July 16, 1892.

9 Bd. Trust., Min., Sept. 7, 1892.

10 Frost, *Spent Arrows*, 33-34.

11 Frost, Ann. Report, 1893 (ms.), 8; *Ann. Report*, 1893, p. 12.

12 H. H. P. to H. A. Wilder, Sept. 30, 1919.

13 Frost, *Ann. Report*, 1894, p. 17.

14 Dinsmore, *Teaching a District School*, 3-4.

15 Agreement with Signatures, 1916-1917; C. B. Anderson, Ann. Report, 1918.

16 Frost, Ann. Report, 1902 (ms.), 16.

17 Frost, Report, Feb. 3, 1894 (ms.), 10-11.

18 Berea College, *Cat.*, Aug., 1920, p. 30.

19 Frost, "Farewell Report on Berea College, 1892-1920," 30-32.

20 Frost, "Mem. on Berea's Conditions," 1918, p. 5c.

21 Fac., Min., Jan. 7, 1921.

22 Berea College, *Cat.*, Aug., 1920, p. 30.

23 W. J. Hutchins, *Ann. Report*, 1924, p. 16.

24 Hutchins, *Ann. Report*, 1925, p. 21.

25 Hutchins, *Ann. Report*, 1924, p. 17.

26 J. C. Campbell, "Future of the Church and Indep. Schools" (1917), 7.

27 M. E. Marsh to Bd. Trust., May 31, 1932.

28 J. H. Kirkland to G. A. Hubbell, Jan. 8, 1906.

29 Hutchins to Dean Campbell, Apr. 19, 1924.

30 H. M. Jones, Ann. Report, 1901.

31 Bd. Trust., Min., Oct. 29, 1910.

32 F. E. Matheny, Ann. Report, 1921.

33 Hutchins, *Ann. Report*, 1924, p. 11.

34 O. H. Gunkler, Ann. Report, 1940.

35 Knapp and Greenbaum, *The Younger Am. Scholar*, 16.

36 The same, 103-106.

6: Labor for Education

1 T. D. Weld, *Report of Man. Labor of Lit. Inst.*, 1833.

2 C. A. Bennett, *Hist. of Man. and Ind. Ed. up to 1870*, 183-92.

3 *Am. Miss.*, s2 I (1857), 21.

4 Rogers, "Hist. of Berea College," Cooper Inst. Addresses, 1869, p. 8.

5 Fairchild, *Inaug. Address*, 1869, p. 6.

6 Fairchild, *Bacc. Sermon*, 1881, p. 14.

7 E. F. White, Mem. on E. H. Fairchild, 1927; Frost, *Hist. Sketch*, 1904, p. 29.

8 Fairchild, Conf. Notes at Fisk Univ., 1881.

9 Burleigh, *John G. Fee*, 14.

10 *Berea Evangelist*, II (Mar. 15, 1886).

11 *Berea College Reporter*, II (Apr., 1890).

12 Frost to "Brethren at Berea," July 16, 1892.

13 Bd. Trust., Min., Sept. 8, 1892.

14 Frost, Ann. Report, 1893 (ms.), 24.

15 Berea *Citizen*, Sept. 25, 1930; *Berea Quart.*, VIII (Apr., 1904), 5-7.

16 Berea *Citizen*, May 29, 1902; *Berea Quart.*, IV (Feb., 1900), 7-9.

17 J. L. Hill, Ann. Report, 1909.

18 S. L. Clark, Ann. Report, 1905.

19 *Berea Quart.*, XI (Jan., 1908), 15.

20 E. K. Corwin, Ann. Report, 1907; Berea Alumnus, XI (1941), 167.
21 J. L. Hill, Ann. Report, 1904.
22 M. E. Marsh, Ann. Report, 1910.
23 Marsh to Frost, July 24, 1915.
24 F. E. Matheny, Ann. Report, 1918.
25 Berea College, Cat., Aug., 1921, p. 48.
26 Frost, Report, Feb. 3, 1894 (ms.), 14.
27 Berea College, Where the Time Card Goes through College, 1953.
28 Berea College, How Some Students Earned a College Education, 1912, p. 15.
29 Berea Alumnus, V (1935), 101.
30 Berea Alumnus, VIII (1938), 240-43.
31 R. I., Theme, 1954.
32 A. G. Weidler, Labor, Learning, and Leisure, 8.
33 E. W. Lockin, Ann. Report, 1938.

7: Financing a Private College

1 Fee, Subscription Book, July 11, 1866.
2 Bd. Trust., Min., July 23, 1866.
3 Prud. Comm., Min., Dec. 6, 1869; July 13, 1871.
4 Berea College, Cat., 1877, p. 27; 1878, p. 26.
5 Am. Miss., XLV (1891), 438.
6 Petition, "To the Friends of Berea College," Nov. 14, 1891; Feb. 10, 1892.
7 Prud. Comm., "Statement from Berea College," Dec. 26, 1891.
8 Berea College Reporter, IV (June, 1892).
9 Frost, Address, Sept. 23, 1907.
10 Frost, Address, Apr. 14, 1915.
11 Berea Citizen, June 23, 1938; Berea College Reporter, VI (July, 1895).
12 W. G. Frost to Mrs. W. G. Frost, Mar. 15, 1897.
13 D. K. Pearsons to Bd. Trust., Sept. 13, 1907.
14 Frost, "Mem. on Duties of a College President," 1896.
15 Frost to Mrs. Frost, Jan. 26, 1911.
16 Berea Quart., XVIII (1915), 27.
17 S. C. Mason, "The College Forest Reserve," 5.
18 Miss S. B. Fay to W. G. Frost, Sept. 17, 1903.
19 Miss Fay to Frost, Oct. 9, 1903.
20 Miss Fay to Frost, Aug., 1911.
21 A. Ballard to W. G. Frost and Mrs. Frost, June 10, 1902.
22 Ballard to Frost, Nov. 30, 1903.
23 Ballard to Frost, Sept. 4, 1903.
24 W. E. Barton, "Mem. on Berea College Water Works," June 22, 1904.
25 Pearsons to Bd. Trust., June 2, 1904.
26 Berea Citizen, June 15, 1905.
27 Barton to Frost, Nov. 14, 1907.
28 C. M. Hall to Frost, Dec. 26, 1910.
29 Hall to Frost, Oct. 30, 1912.
30 Hall to Frost, Aug. 12, 1914.
31 Frost in Treas. Fin. Report, 1920, 4.
32 Frost, Report, May 18, 1920, p. 6.
33 T. J. Osborne to Frost, Jan. 24, 1920.
34 W. J. Hutchins to H. A. W., Sept. 7, 1920.
35 C. G. Fairchild to Frost, 1920.
36 B. Barton to Mr. H., Nov. 27, 1925.
37 W. J. Hutchins to Bd. Trust., Dec. 17, 1929.

8: A Century of Sharing

1 Fairchild, *Berea College, Ky.*, 1875 ed., 87.
2 *Am. Miss.*, XXXIV (1880), 147.
3 E. K. Corwin, Ann. Report, 1933.
4 A. Kirk, Ann. Report, 1938.
5 Corwin, Ann. Report, 1929.
6 Frost, *Ann. Report*, 1897, p. 12.
7 The same, 18.
8 *Berea Quart.*, VI (1901), 6-12.
9 W. E. B. to Frost, Dec. 24, 1900.
10 C. R. Raymond, Ann. Report, 1901.
11 Frost, Ann. Report, 1902 (ms.), 17b.
12 J. P. Faulkner, Ann. Report, 1910; *Berea Quart.*, XIV (1910), 14.
13 H. R., Concurrent Res., no. 206, sec. 7, May 17, 1954; C. Ferguson to F. S. Hutchins, May 20, 1954.
14 F. Montgomery, Ann. Report, 1913.
15 Berea College, *Ann. Reports, 1914*, 49-50.
16 Berea *Citizen*, Sept. 2, 1954.
17 R. F. Spence, Ann. Report, 1919.
18 Berea *Citizen*, Feb. 7, 1918.
19 Berea *Citizen*, Apr. 5, 1917; Feb. 21, Mar. 21, 1918; Feb. 13, 1919.
20 W. J. Hutchins, *Ann. Report*, 1922, p. 16.
21 Berea College, *Man. of County Ach. Contest for E. Ky.*, 5-31; Berea *Citizen*, Aug. 28, 1924.
22 W. J. Hutchins, *Ann. Report*, 1923, p. 32; 1924, pp. 33-34; 1925, p. 51; Berea *Citizen*, Aug. 28, Sept. 4, Dec. 27, 1924.
23 H. B. Monier, Ann. Report, 1936.
24 Monier, Creamery Files, 1953-1954.
25 W. J. Hutchins, *Ann. Report*, 1936, p. 32.
26 Opp. School, "Echo," 1940, p. 5.
27 Opp. School, "Echo," 1945, p. 21.
28 Somerset *Journal*, Sept. 19, Oct. 10, Nov. 7, 1946; Louisville *Courier Journal*, Aug. 4, 1946; Sept. 4, 1949; F. S. Hutchins, *Ann. Report*, 1949, p. 8.
29 Mem. of talks between F. S. Hutchins, Berea College, and R. C., Harlan Co., Ky., Apr. 4, 1949.
30 F. S. Hutchins, *Ann. Report*, 1949-1954, pp. 22-23; L. M. Ambrose, Ann. Report on Rural School Impr. Project for Sel. Counties in E. Ky., Dec., 1953; Louisville *Courier Journal*, Apr. 25, 1954.

9: Into a New Century

1 *Berea College: The Telescope and the Spade* (New York: The Newcomen Society, 1963), title page.
2 E. S. Peck, *Nurses in Time, 1898-1963* (Berea, 1963), p. 46.
3 John Kessler, Executive Officer, Navy V-12 unit, personal letter, Feb. 12, 1979.
4 F. S. Hutchins, *President's Report* [1943-1948], p. 7.
5 W. E. Arnett, "The Veterans Speak," *Berea Alumnus* 16 (Dec. 1945): 71.
6 F. S. Hutchins, President's Report [June 1962], unpaged.
7 Louis Smith, former Dean of Berea College, personal interview, Spring, 1979.
8 Louis Smith, "Berea College Will Enroll Negro Students from the

Southern Mountain Region," *Mountain Life and Work* 26 (Spring 1950): 23.

9 T. M. Kreider, chairman, *Berea College Self-Study Report*, 1972–1973, p. 302.

10 *Profile of Berea College, 1952 to 1972*, Part II B (1a), pp. 1-3 (mimeographed).

11 Ibid., p. 4.

12 Berea Community School Merger Agreement, Nov. 28, 1966 (typescript).

13 *Berea College Catalog, 1977–1979*, pp. 41-45.

14 Kreider, *Report*, p. 118.

15 Ibid., p. 114.

16 J. A. R. Rogers, *Birth of Berea College: A Story of Providence* (Philadelphia, 1903), p. 73.

17 Ibid., p. 141.

18 A. G. Weidler, "Berea's Student Program," *Mountain Life and Work* 7 (July 1931): 19.

19 Berea College Board of Trustees, Minutes of Meeting, New York City, Nov. 16, 1951.

20 Berea College Student Labor Program, Summary of Labor Assignments, Fall 1978.

21 Weidler, "Student Labor Program," p. 25.

22 Berea's Student Labor Program: A Survey of Alumni Attitudes, p. 14.

23 F. S. Hutchins, "Inaugural Address," *Berea Alumnus* 10 (Dec. 1939): 79.

24 R. T. Jordan, "Library Characteristics of Colleges Ranking High," *College and Research Libraries* 24 (Sept. 1963): 376.

25 F. S. Hutchins, Baccalaureate Address, Berea College, May 30, 1965 (typescript).

26 F. S. Hutchins, "Focus on Purpose and Mission," *Berea Alumnus* 34 (June 1964): 9.

27 F. S. Hutchins, "Baccalaureate," *Berea Alumnus* 18 (June 1948): 268.

28 W. D. Weatherford, *Report of the President* [1970–1971], p. 6.

29 W. D. Weatherford, *Report of the President* [1973–1974], p. 3.

30 Ibid., p. 2.

31 W. D. Weatherford, *Report of the President 1969–1970*, p. 5.

32 W. D. Weatherford, *Report of the President 75–76*, p. 2.

33 Ibid., p. 5.

34 Berea College Board of Trustees, Minutes of Meeting, Berea, Oct. 24, 1969.

35 R. V. Buckland, ed., *Rural School Improvement Project: Report, 1953–1957*.

36 Harry Hamilton, "An Idea at Large," *Minutes: Magazine of Nationwide Insurance*, June 1957, p. 5.

37 F. S. Hutchins, "Our Basic Commitments," *Berea Alumnus* 17 (Dec. 1946): 76.

38 W. D. Weatherford, *Report of the President 72–73*.

39 D. D. Pearsons, *Daniel K. Pearsons: His Life and Works* (Elgin, Ill., 1912), p. 396.

40 R. H. Knapp and J. J. Greenbaum, *The Younger American Scholar: His Collegiate Origins* (Chicago, 1953), p. 16.

41 National Research Council Commission on Human Resources, *A Survey on Doctorates by Baccalaureates in 31 Doctoral Fields* (Washington, D.C., 1976).

42 Berea College Alumni Association, Occupational Information, Mar. 19, 1976 (mimeographed).

43 Richard Wilson, "Berea College Ponders Its Role in Changed Times," Louisville *Courier-Journal*, Apr. 10, 1979, Sec. 1, p. 1.

INDEX